ALSO BY ALEXANDER NEUBAUER

NONFICTION

Nature's Thumbprint: The New Genetics of Personality
(with Peter B. Neubauer, M.D.)

AS EDITOR

*Conversations on Writing Fiction: Interviews with Thirteen
Distinguished Teachers of Fiction Writing in America*

POETRY
in PERSON

annuncement

Nine Poets Confront Their New Poetry: Works in Progress

With Pearl London and Guests

Richard Howard (Jan. 9)   W.S. Merwin *(Jan 16)*

Erica Jong (Oct. 17)   Muriel Rukeyser (Oct. 3)

Maxine Kumin (Nov. 14)   Louis Simpson (Dec. 5)

Clarence Major (Nov. 7)   Mark Strand *(Oct 17)*

                                 Galway Kinnell (Dec 12)

Course #5785-3 Wednesdays, 10-11:45 A.M., beginning September 26. $90.

In this course nine distinguished poets will read and discuss their as yet unpublished work. The student will find himself involved in the mainstream of poetry writing today. Each poet will present a preview of his forthcoming book or latest manuscript. He will discuss essential aspects of his work and share his craft with the members of this class. Using his new work as an example, he will also attempt to define what he considers the role and responsibility of contemporary poetry.

Pearl London, M.A., NYU; B.A., Smith College; studied, Columbia University, Bennington College. Taught, Long Island University. Awards: First Prize, Academy of American Poets; honorable mention, Forum Magazine contest. Contributor to New York Times Sunday Magazine; Current Expression of Fact and Opinion, translator of Middle English poem, "The Eaten Heart," in A Treasury of Great Poems, edited by Louis Untermeyer. Member, Board of New York Quarterly.

Registration in Person: Weekdays, August 29 through September 7 noon to 3 p.m.; September 10 through September 14, noon to 8 p.m.; September 17 through October 3, 10 a.m. to 8 p.m. Saturdays, September 15, 22, 29; 9 a.m. to 1 p.m. Master Charge credit cards may be used for tuition payments at in-person registration.

NEW SCHOOL FOR SOCIAL RESEARCH

66 WEST 12TH STREET, NEW YORK, N.Y. 10011 / (212) OR 5-2700

POETRY
in PERSON

Twenty-five Years of Conversation with America's Poets

EDITED AND WITH AN INTRODUCTION BY
ALEXANDER NEUBAUER

POSTSCRIPT BY
ROBERT POLITO

ALFRED A. KNOPF · New York · 2010

THIS IS A BORZOI BOOK
Published by Alfred A. Knopf

Copyright © 2010 by Alexander Neubauer
Postscript copyright © 2010 by Robert Polito

www.aaknopf.com

Library of Congress Cataloging-in-Publication Data

    Poetry in person: 25 years of conversation with
    America's poets / edited by Alexander
    Neubauer.——1st ed.
      p. cm.
    Includes bibliographical references and index.
    ISBN 978-0-307-26967-6 (alk. paper)
    1. American poetry—21st century.
    2. Poets, American—20th century—Interviews.
    3. Poets, American—21st century—Interviews.
    4. Poetry—Authorship.   5. Poetics.
    I. Neubauer, Alexander.
PS617.P64 2010
811'.608—dc22   2009029277

Manufactured in the United States of America
First Edition

To Sam and Willa and April,

who write my favorite poems

every day

am for the art of underwear and the art of
I am for the art of ice cream cones
on concrete. I am for the majestic
of dog-turds, rising like cathedrals." —
Claes Oldenburg
began to feel strongly about finding a way
that was stable in a sense, something
wasn't constantly a record of your
a record of flux" — Frank Stella
Make The myth
thanks to

It follows that poems are not so important as the poetic process, the transforming power that spiritualizes the world, turning visibility into invisibility, the world into ourselves.

—DENIS DONOGHUE
on *The Selected Poetry of Rainer Maria Rilke*

Contents

Introduction

IN THE FALL OF 1970, at the New School in Greenwich Village, a new teacher posted a flyer on the wall. It read "Meet Poets and Poetry, with Pearl London and Guests." Few students responded. No one knew Pearl London. But the seminar's first guests turned out to be John Ashbery, Adrienne Rich, and Robert Creeley. Soon Maxine Kumin followed, then W. S. Merwin, Mark Strand, and Galway Kinnell. So London upped the ante: She began asking all poets to deliver nothing less than the manuscripts of their newest poems for discussion.

"If you can come," she wrote each of them, "I would appreciate you sending me any notes jotted down on the back of an envelope, or work sheets of any sort, even doodles. This is a course concerned essentially with the making of the poem, with the work in progress *as process*—with both the vision and the revision. In a sense, the shaping spirit of the imagination is what it is all about."

Poets accepted one after another, word spread, and for the next twenty-five years London's classroom became know simply as "Works in Progress," a coveted destination for Nobel laureates Walcott and Heaney, a string of eight U.S. poet laureates, double National Book Award winner Merrill, and eleven Pulitzer Prize winners. There were poets at the height of their careers—Rukeyser, Simic, Clampitt, and Olds for instance—and poets at the cusp of their emergence in letters, like Carson and Muldoon. They came to London's door as she requested, with fresh manuscripts and sheaves of notes and drafts in hand, under-the-hood evidence of exactly "the vision and the revision" that provoked her attention.

Maybe for the poets it seemed almost natural at the time, to finish or nearly finish a poem and share stages of the process with a small class of would-be poets and a dedicated teacher. But for us, in retrospect, the sheer accumulation of key names and important poems casts this seemingly quiet enterprise in a different light. Some of the poems they shared with London's class would later be widely anthologized; many would turn out to be central pieces in the poets' careers—for instance, the title poems to Pinsky's *The Want Bone* and Hirsch's *Wild Gratitude,* Clampitt's *Black Butter-cups,* a section of Merrill's epic *The Changing Light at Sandover,* and Hass's essential "Meditation at Lagunitas."

What did the poets get in return? They got examined, dissected, valued, and exposed. And nearly everyone came back for more—some two or three times, Plumly a record five. Within four walls for an hour and a half every other week, London quietly brought a generation to light, the best poets and poetry of the last quarter of the twentieth century.

THIS STORY might have been lost or little known following London's death in 2003—as classroom magic always fades, except briefly in memory—if not for the discovery of a hundred tapes hidden in boxes in a closet at her home in Manhattan, near Washington Square Park. The tapes represent most of the sessions recorded through 1998, when she retired. That the trove existed, secreted away for so long, stunned most everyone who knew about this seminar. It made sense that a few recordings would survive and resurface, since an old-fashioned cassette player sat on a desk during class, manned by one student or another. No one paid particular attention to it, however. No one ever expected to see the tapes together again, certainly not a complete catalog of them side by side. Yet there they were, along with file upon file stuffed with copies of the manuscripts and drafts the poets brought along on the days they visited.

. . .

I KNEW about Pearl London's class, though not about the tapes or files. For five years in the mid-1990s I taught fiction writing at the New School, and if there was an empty chair and my schedule allowed, I dropped in to listen. Forché, Pinsky, Kunitz, Plumly, Hirsch—these were like no interviews I'd ever heard. It's a mistake to call them interviews at all, of course. With London in charge, as first-time guests learned soon enough, the interview model just broke down. These were conversations: passionate, human, sometimes formal or funny, tilting now and then toward improvisational theater. How did their new work reflect each poet's central concerns? Were they after form or meaning, rhythm or rhyme, lyric or narrative, protest or confession? London kept looking for the heart, the essential metaphor of their work, and often enough she found it.

OF THE HUNDRED or so newly discovered recordings, I had to winnow down to the following twenty-three for this book. They appear for the first time. Some tapes, such as Creeley's and Ashbery's, had gone missing entirely. For others, the choice was extremely difficult. How, say, to leave out W. S. Merwin? It came down to finding a particular array of poems and an array of particular voices, as I hope readers will see. In the end the poets speak for themselves. I've included brief chapter introductions to situate their visits in time: who they were when they arrived at London's doorstep, what they had written, what was later to come. But I also need to say a word more about how London set these conversations in motion and teased so much original material from so many poets for so many years. It may help to see what they saw on their way to her class.

FIRST THING: Works in Progress was held in an unusual room. You reached it through the 66 West Twelfth Street entrance of the New School, with its 1930s International-style façade, then went straight to the fifth floor. Auden, Frost, Lowell, O'Hara, and Kunitz had taught there, in a writing program founded in 1931, and Pearl London's room—best of the best— held the sprawling, nine-panel murals of Thomas Hart Benton. They surrounded the class, regionalist images of America at work and play, until they were tragically sold off just before Derek Walcott's 1982 visit. As students filtered in, Pearl London would already be sitting at a desk in the front, going over countless notes and passing sheaves of copied manuscripts among the early arrivals. She also positioned the poet's previously published books in front of her, annotated to the hilt in her signature heavy ink; with check marks beside the poems she liked, double checks beside the stanzas, underlining and marginalia flooding the page. In addition she brought her own sheets of notes for the day and a few starting quotations ready to go on the blackboard. It was preparation taken to a new level. And then there was London herself.

"When I recall her I always see her 'in color,' " Philip Levine wrote to me. "She dressed colorfully, and her speech and gestures—her whole presentation of herself—was dramatic. For that and for her beauty I assumed she had experience acting." She favored cloaks, bright red lipstick, and large necklaces, a 1950s-style of high fashion she never changed, and she doused her visitors with a hospitality bordering on devotion. Levine also recalled a woman "of some years" who "still has the presence of someone who clearly knows she is attractive but makes nothing of it." She certainly could be charming, by turns almost girlish in her excitement over new poetry and new poets and then astute, strong-minded, and clear. "*Magnificent* poem," she would repeat—and mean it.

For poets coming from afar, she played host; there would often be coffee or drinks at her row house a few blocks away on Washington Mews, gatherings for students, friends, and admirers of poetry. She served in a quiet way as literary doyenne, if doyenne is still a role possible in this world: a Natalie Barney or Mabel Dodge. She was the daughter of M. Lincoln Schuster, cofounder of publishing house Simon & Schuster, and the wife of Ephraim London, a lawyer who famously defended artists' rights of free expression. Maybe that explains part of it.

At age twenty-two London had written the official poem of the 1939 New York World's Fair. Orson Welles had read it over the radio. Louis Untermeyer had anthologized a translation she made in his canonical

Treasury of Great Poems. She earned a master's in English at NYU, and, as Robert Polito notes in his postscript here, there was some talk of late poems, but it's sure that nothing she did creatively gave her as much pleasure as those decades she devoted to teaching poetry, choosing and inviting the poets, and preparing weeks in advance for their visits. If not consciously a mission, the class anyway became her life's work.

At the start of each session, she was always gracious, formal in an old-school way, characteristically addressing her guests by both first and last names: "Derek Walcott, I'm thrilled you are here, it's really very good of you to come, we're going to start right in." And start she did, with a query about a particular line of his that bothered her. Questions were meant to be provocative and intricate, but rarely, as I came to hear them, merely literary. Again, she pushed to engage the core of the poetry. When June Jordan came a second time, London started with a quotation from her favorite instigator, W. H. Auden: "Poets who want to change the world tend to be unreadable." London knew the reaction she'd get. She invited many poet-activists to her class, from Rukeyser to a young Clampitt to C. K. Williams, and one can tell she sympathized with them. Jordan found Auden's sentiment appalling and elitist, and it provoked a rather brilliant run of thoughts. The poets understood what London was doing. Hirsch joked that he felt exposed and wanted to put on his jacket. Grennan said that if London probed any further he'd have to take off his shirt. She'd openly suggest line and word alternatives—to Peacock, to Jordan—while Kumin was brave enough to admit she actually came to class looking for help on a poem.

Far from being put off, poets rose to the occasion. They were sitting beside someone who had read every word of both their poetry and essays, recent and old, and who even remembered answers from previous visits—see Stanley Plumly's surprise at her recall. He later wrote her a thank you note: "I enjoyed especially visiting with your classes because they are *your* classes—well-prepared and caring." Where else could they find that level of preparation, that kind of complete immersion in their poetry?

And, I imagine, the instinct to prepare and immerse has a complementary instinct, which is to save and record, if only for oneself. London was so devoted to these poets she couldn't throw out any record of their visits, not a note, not a book, not a letter, not a copy of their work sheets—not a flimsy cassette tape thirty years old.

WHICH BRINGS A LAST WORD: Each of these ninety-minute tapes, transcribed, ran to some forty to fifty pages of text, so it also wasn't obvious what parts to leave behind. Some stretches of each conversation were serious and meticulous in detail, others just freewheeling and irreverent—and the balance swayed from poet to poet depending on their mood that day or that week or even that year. My primary goal was to capture the poets' voices and habits of thought as faithfully as possible, whether they spoke in complete paragraphs, like Walcott and Matthews, or sounded like telegrams. In short, poets not only spoke for themselves, they were also allowed to sound like themselves. Since cuts had to be made, much more of Pearl London's voice was lost in favor of space for the poets.

Which is as it should be, of course. London would never have stepped in front of her guests. Nevertheless, if a book like this somehow retrieves lost slices of time in art, it may also catch in its net, by luck, a voice no one would otherwise come to know. During the course of his 1993 appearance, Edward Hirsch repeats a line from Robert Frost to the effect that if a book of poetry holds twenty-nine poems, the book itself becomes the thirtieth poem. Nearing the end of her career at the time of Hirsch's visit, Pearl London loved that thought, and I think I know why. There was a narrative drive behind the rhythm of her questions, energized by a deep love of poetry—and poets. Her classroom became the thirtieth poem and, one hopes, that energy and love will be present in this book.

ALEXANDER NEUBAUER
OCTOBER 5, 2009
CORNWALL, CONNECTICUT

POETRY
in PERSON

Maxine Kumin

MAXINE KUMIN wrote Pearl London apologetically in 1985 about a potential third visit to her class: "I am reluctant to think of April because we have a foal due the third week and I want to be here . . . yet, your kind of class is so valuable that I hate to turn you down." London was luckier in 1973, when the first of Kumin's visits was recorded. It appears in the pages that follow.

Kumin was born to Reform Jewish parents in the Germantown section of Philadelphia, in 1925, the youngest of four children. At Radcliffe she studied history and literature, received her bachelor's and master's degrees, and met and married her husband. As a young mother she began publishing light verse, but it was not until 1957 that she looked seriously to poetry, taking a workshop in Boston. One of her classmates turned out to be Anne Sexton, who became a close friend and collaborator. Both women had young children, and Kumin has described how they would speak on the phone "for hours at a stretch, interrupting poem-talk to stir the spaghetti sauce, switch the laundry, or try out a new image on the typewriter." Kumin's first book of poems, *Halfway*, was published in 1961, and there have since been fourteen more books of poems, as well as novels, essays, and children's books. In 1981 she served in a role that would later be named U.S. poet laureate.

On this first visit to London's class, Kumin discussed her iconic "For My Son on the Highways of His Mind" and a newly written poem called "Sperm." That same year, 1973, Kumin's fourth book, *Up Country: Poems of New England,* won the Pulitzer Prize. It shares the direct style and keen eye of her earlier work, inflected by nature both harsh and lush, and with the rhythms of life always present. She and her husband of fifty-nine years live on an old farm in rural New Hampshire, where they have raised three children, ten foals, sheep, dogs, cats, and vegetables. "She continues to use as material the active days, the varied dreams of her life," May Swenson has said. "Experience is directly poured and cast into art."

————

"For My Son on the Highways of His Mind"
"Sperm"

PEARL LONDON: We talked about Galway Kinnell's statement that "the real nature poem will not exclude Man and deal only with animals and plants and stones. It will be a poem in which we re-feel ourselves, our own animal and plant and stone life. Our own deep connections with all other beings." Is that part of it for you?

MAXINE KUMIN: Essential. The only reason for writing so-called nature poems or pastoral or antipastoral poems is because you are looking constantly to find out the human's place in this order of things. Anything that invites reflection becomes a point of departure. That's what the nature poems do over and over.

LONDON: Auden in his essay on Frost speaks of the fact that Frost's favorite image was always the image of the abandoned house. Auden took the trouble to count the number of houses and barns in Frost's *Collected Poems* and found there were something like twenty-seven winter barns, and twenty-one of them were empty. And I've forgotten what it was, nineteen of them were at night. But that sense of desolation and really isolation just doesn't seem to be there in your poetry. It's not that kind of—your houses aren't abandoned. You're taking up quarters in one house, and it's filled with love; and in another house they're marvelously "back to back in bed." You talk about being a hermit—but you're not.

KUMIN: Well, you've caught me out. Sometimes I'm a hermit, but most of the time I'm a very sociable, often ambivalent human being. I like to be with people—particularly my family and people I love. There are not very many abandoned houses in my poetry. There are a few I could point to— "Cross-Country by County Map." But my view is not as dark as Frost's, obviously. Perhaps I just haven't lived long enough to become quite that cynical; it may happen to me, too, I just don't know.

LONDON: We talked a lot last week about your poem called "For My Son on the Highways of His Mind." William Empson somewhere says that every poet is at once a representative of his society and at the same time its critic. In a certain sense this poem—which deals with a boy who travels light with guitar, whose mother considers the various menacing situations that might happen to her child—this poem really deals very much with material that is of our time but is made more lyrical and lovely because of the way in which you've done it.

KUMIN: Well, it's in that section of *The Nightmare Factory* [1970] called "Tribal Poems." They are poems—as well as I can fix on it—that want to examine relationships between and among the generations. This poem, "For My Son on the Highways of His Mind," came directly out of experience, as most [of my] poems *do not*. It's an actual incident, and it insisted on being written. I had wanted to write it all in very short lines of the refrain because many years ago I wrote a poem in my first book, *Halfway*, which I think is just called "Poem for My Son." It was a poem for this boy when he was an infant, written in very short, mostly trimeter lines and in a fairly difficult rhyme scheme.

When I started to write this [new] poem, that's what I thought I would be able to do. But it turned out that I had so much exposition—if you will, narration—that I had to find some other way, so I hit on the two-stanza refrain, alternating it, and then telling the story in that other stanzaic pattern. Which as you see is again a little bit of a problem, because it sets up a rhyme scheme that is loose enough to move around in, but hard enough to hang on to. Every time I have something hard to tell or difficult to write I invariably find myself setting up the most elaborate stanzaic patterns to do it. As if that gives me permission to tell the truth and to say the hard things.

LONDON: That's an interesting thing. Perhaps the structure somewhat stabilizes the material. And yet about two weeks ago, Clarence Major was here telling us that in order to deal with the material of his very, very bitter urban experience he had to write in fragmented lines.

KUMIN: Just the opposite for me. The more chaos, the more insistent I am on finding a form to hammer it into. Free verse is just too scary. And I don't know . . . I suppose a good psychiatrist would have an answer why this is . . . but I suspect it has something to do with that paradox of feeling freed by conforming to the exigencies of a pattern and a rhyme scheme. That gives me all the latitude in the world with words and images and metaphors and similes to say whatever I need to say.

LONDON: A kind of scaffold.

KUMIN: I guess I am old-fashioned enough, and enough of a formalist, to believe that the metrical systems of poetry can enhance what you have to say if you handle them well enough. I don't believe that rhyme should be obtrusive—I don't like rhymes that come booming in at all—but some sort of an underbeat, a scaffolding if you want, really gives me that shiver, that response that lifts you half out of the chair when you read a poem that works.

But I will read this to you. And I'll explain the ruptured duck and the golden toilet seat. The "ruptured duck" was the little pin that signified, at the end of World War II, that you had enough points and you had mustered out of the service. Even though you were still wearing a uniform, because there were no civilian clothes around, it meant you were really out of uniform. And the "golden toilet seat" was an award of merit, according to my husband, just a wreath that was sewn onto your sleeve that you got for keeping the latrines clean. OK.

[READS]

For My Son on the Highways of His Mind
for Dan

Today the jailbird maple in the yard
sends down a thousand red hands in the rain.
Trussed at the upstairs window I
watch the great drenched leaves flap by
knowing that on the comely boulevard
incessant in your head you stand again
at the cloverleaf, thumb crooked outward.

Dreaming you travel light
guitar pick and guitar
bedroll sausage tight
they take you as you are.

They take you as you are
there's nothing left behind
guitar pick and guitar
on the highways of your mind.

Instead you come home with two cops, your bike
lashed to the back of the cruiser because
an old lady, afraid of blacks and boys
with hair like yours, is simon-sure you took
her purse. They search you and of course you're clean.
Later we make it into a family joke,
a poor sort of catharsis. It wasn't the scene

they made—that part you rather enjoyed—
and not the old woman whose money turned up next day
in its usual lunatic place under a platter
but the principle of the thing, to be toyed
with cat and mouse, be one mouse who got away
somehow under the baseboard or radiator
and expects to be caught again sooner or later.

Dreaming you travel light
guitar pick and guitar
bedroll sausage tight
they take you as you are.

Collar up, your discontent goes wrapped
at all times in the flannel army shirt
your father mustered out in, wars ago,
the ruptured duck still pinned to the pocket flap
and the golden toilet seat—the award his unit
won for making the bomb that killed the Japs—
now rubbed to its earliest threads, an old trousseau.

Meanwhile the posters on your bedroom wall
give up their glue. The corners start to fray.
Belmondo, Brando, Uncle Ho and Che,
last year's giants, hang lop-eared but hang on.

The merit badges, the model airplanes, all
the paraphernalia of a simpler day
gather dust on the shelf. That boy is gone.

They take you as you are
there's nothing left behind
guitar pick and guitar
on the highways of your mind.

How it will be tomorrow is anyone's guess.
The *Rand McNally* opens at a nudge
to forty-eight contiguous states, easy
as a compliant girl. In Minneapolis
I see you drinking wine under a bridge.
I see you turning on in Washington, D.C.,
panhandling in New Orleans, friendless

in Kansas City in an all-night beanery
and mugged on the beach in Venice outside L.A.
They take your watch and wallet and crack your head
as carelessly as an egg. The yolk runs red.
All this I see, or say it's what I see
in leaf fall, in rain, from the top of the stairs today
while your maps, those sweet pastels, lie flat and ready.

Dreaming you travel light
guitar pick and guitar
bedroll sausage tight
they take you as you are.

They take you as you are
there's nothing left behind

guitar pick and guitar
on the highways of your mind.

STUDENT: Is there a way that you determine the structure, or does it come of itself . . . ?

KUMIN: It comes. It doesn't come of itself, but it begins to take shape. Now, while I was writing this poem I was commuting. If I'm working in a form like this I tend to work a lot in my head. Because a poem is marvelously portable. You can carry a problem around with you from the kitchen sink to the automobile to wherever. I pulled off the road a lot and wrote things down. I did write much of this poem in the car, oddly enough, pretty much through traffic. The refrain came first. The work sheets for this poem are unbelievably bad. I often start off very, very badly, and the only consoling thing about keeping work sheets is that you can look back afterward and see what a mess you were and how you improved. I spent an awful long time getting that refrain to a point where it seemed to me to work.

And then the rest of the poem . . . that pattern . . . you find it somewhere in the first or second stanza. There is a definite turning point somewhere in the second expository stanza, where it begins to find its rhythm and establish the pattern. Then you know what you're going to work on from that, you can go back and correct the first stanza and begin to see a shape. [The reason] I write on the typewriter is that I have an atrocious handwriting which I can't read afterward.

LONDON: Is the poetry becoming more internalized? In "For My Son on the Highways of His Mind" there's this whole chunk of narration; the narrative externalizes the material, and yet the refrain acts as an enormous glimpse of the interior. Somehow, one feels that you're probably going to go one way or the other. But what is happening now in the newest poems? It's been said over and over again that to read Robert Frost as a poet of the pastoral is absolutely not to read Frost. Well, in that sense, I think that to read you as a pastoral poet would be close to not reading you.

KUMIN: When you say someone is a pastoral poet, it's almost pejorative, isn't it?

LONDON: Right. Of course it is.

KUMIN: I mean, it's saying, this is somebody who writes about God, nature, butterflies, and little brownies who come and drink the milk you put out for them.

And then I have a rather intricate poem called "Sperm" [eventually appearing in *House, Bridge, Fountain, Gate*, 1975]. I think I'd really rather read this one to you, because this is the poem I'm most uncertain about. You realize, the reason poets like to come to a class like this is that they love to try out their new stuff. It's really true. "Sperm" has seventeen cousins in it, and I don't know if a poem can hold up seventeen cousins. That's my problem. It's sort of a long narrative poem that's written in—you'll hear, rather bouncy rhythms. Parts of it I hope are funny.

[READS "SPERM"—STANZAS 1, 2, AND 5 ONLY]

[Stanza 1]
You have to admire the workmanship of cousins.
There is a look in our eyes.
Once we were all seventeen of us naked as almonds.
We were all suckled except for Richard
who had to be raised on a glue of bananas.
Now he is bald and breathes through the nose
like an air conditioner but he too
said goodnight, Grandfather, when
we were all sheep in the nursery.
All of those kisses like polka dots

touched to the old man's wrinkles
while his face jittered under our little wet mouths
and he floated to the top of his palsy
sorting out Jacob from Esau.

[Stanza 2]
O Grandfather, look what your seed has done!
Look what has come of those winter night gallops.
You tucking the little wife up
under the comforter that always leaked feathers.
You coming perhaps just as the trolley
derailed taking the corner at 15th Street
in a shower of blue sparks, and Grandmother's
corset spread out like a filleted fish
to air meanwhile on the windowsill.
Each time a secret flourished under those laces
she eased the bones from their moorings
and swelled like the Sunday choir.
Seven sons, all with a certain
shy hood to the eye. I call it the Hummel effect.

[Stanza 5]
Such darlings, those wicked good boys
all but one come to their manhood:
Bo palming poker chips in the frat house,
Joseph gone broody with bourbon,
Michael following the horses
while nursing an early heart murmur,
Alan surprised at the Bide-A-Wee
with an upstate minister's daughter
and diffident James in the closet
trying on Sukey's garter belt,
pulling on Sukey's stockings.

Now I really would appreciate some comment if you can take all that in. It's a long narrative poem, and I wanted to put everybody in, and then I found that I wasn't sure there was room.

STUDENT: What are your fears about it?

KUMIN: That it gets . . . boring.

STUDENT: The names and the quick conjuring of one after another in a certain section of the poem I found very exciting. I wanted to know more names and more tiny biographies, if you will.

KUMIN: I hope that some sense of the degeneracy of the whole family comes through, too. The southerners who come with their racism . . .

LONDON: One of the things that keeps the poem very exciting for the reader hearing it for the first time is the imagery. "Naked as almonds" or "Grandmother's corset spread out like a filleted fish." They're marvelous, vivid kinds of images. Don't you think that's a good part of it? That great, precise eye, the concrete thing that happens.

KUMIN: But do you find that you want to read long poems when you find them on the page, or do you find that you shy away from poems that go two or three pages?

STUDENT: The children . . . they grow up and they're people.

KUMIN: And corrupt.

STUDENT: The children have lost their special quality, and here they are maybe trying on clothes and becoming gay in a closet. I mean, that's what happens to children. It's such a clear picture of individual people, calling them by name.

STUDENT: I do think that the naming of names becomes a little bit like "begat" in the Bible. I felt myself skipping the names.

KUMIN: Yeah. I debated printing each of their names as they come up in full caps, you know, like Milton in *Paradise Lost*. I don't know how that would look. But I was playing with it.

STUDENT: The idea was sperm, yet you left that rather quickly. Perhaps if in the middle of the poem or in a refrain where in some way you come back to the sperm we might get the idea of the corruption more easily placed and also some kind of continuity. The sperm of one generation coming from the sperm of the next.

KUMIN: Except that practically everything that's going on involving the cousins also involves sperm. There are all these little games that are going on in the closet, behind the coal bin. . . .

STUDENT: It seems to me in running through this and four or five of your other poems, a degeneracy happens, these things we're not guilty of, it's simply the way it is, almost a resignation that I find very uncomfortable.

KUMIN: I think you're right. I really do. It's not something I've been acutely conscious of. But I find myself nodding in agreement. That there is this very strong sense of fatalism running through these poems. That every time man gets his grimies on something that is functioning in nature he despoils it.

[At the same time] I don't know. For me, the thing that I am consciously aware of when I am writing is a little inner admonition not to permit myself abstractions. I loathe and detest abstractions in poetry.

LONDON: Please take note.

KUMIN: There's a really lovely book by Louis Simpson called *North of Jamaica,* which is a partial autobiography; I read it and loved it and found a quote that meant so much to me that I typed it up and stuck it over my desk, which I do from time to time. He says, I'm paraphrasing, "Maybe the function of the poet is simply, as another poet has said, the naming of things. Maybe we are only here to say house, bridge, fountain, gate." And that, of course, is a reference to Rilke. I think it's in the ninth of the *Duino Elegies* when Rilke says exactly that. And I decided that I would really like to call a new book *House, Bridge, Fountain, Gate.*

Because, you see, this is what I conceive the function of the poet to be. Not to moralize, not to polemicize, not to grieve, not to praise, and not to damn. But to name, to tell, to authenticate, to be specific, to report what he sees and what he feels. I suppose if I have a credo, that would be the credo that I have.

Robert Hass

WHEN ROBERT HASS visited Pearl London's class in December 1977 he was thirty-six years old and had published a single book of poetry, the celebrated *Field Guide* (1973). It won the Yale Series of Younger Poets Award and the praise of Stanley Kunitz: "These poems are as much an expression of an organic principle as the activities of which they are an extension—walking, eating, sleeping, lovemaking—and they are equally pleasurable, equally real. *Field Guide* is an event as much as it is literature." With that one book underpinning their conversation, Hass discusses with London his new effort to give the short lines of the early poems a more relaxed breath. One of the drafts he brought to class that day was "Meditation at Lagunitas"—"the famous and beautiful 'Meditation at Lagunitas,'" as Peter Davison would later write, "with its majestic opening." It would become one of Hass's most anthologized poems. He says to London, "I can read [that poem] in a way I act and talk. It doesn't push me beyond my normal breath, as some of the poems I've written." The poem would appear in *Praise* (1979), a book that would win the William Carlos Williams Award.

Hass, who teaches at Berkeley, was born in San Francisco in 1941 and grew up in Marin County, California. In the late 1950s, when the Bay Area poetry scene was in full swing, he became friends with Gary Snyder, Allen Ginsberg, and Kenneth Rexroth, early influences. He graduated in 1963 from St. Mary's College, of California, then received his doctorate in English in 1971 from Stanford. Hass's poetry has become known for its close attention to the natural world and meditative sensibility. In 1984 he won the National Book Critics Circle Award for criticism for *Twentieth Century Pleasures,* the same award for poetry in 1996 for *Sun Under Wood,* and, most recently, the 2007 National Book Award for *Time and Materials.* "Since Frost's death, in 1963, the strongest currents in American poetry may well have pushed westward," writes Davison. "No practicing poet has more talent than Robert Hass."

Between 1995 and 1997 Hass served two terms as U.S. poet laureate, transforming the position with readings and events across the nation.

DECEMBER 14, 1977

"Meditation at Lagunitas"

PEARL LONDON: In what way does the new work that we're going to be looking at depart from "In Weather" [the eight-poem section of *Field Guide*]? Is it because they are going to be longer poems—or is it because Galway Kinnell said that the nature poem has to include the city?

ROBERT HASS: Part of the departure comes from talking to Galway Kinnell about the modern nature poem. After I published *Field Guide* I got a lot of invitations to write for conservation journals, which I accepted. I'm very interested in those issues, and I've taught courses on bird watching and got interested in natural science. I got letters from people saying, "You must live a wonderful life." But as I read the poems in urban situations—because poetry was invented in cities, and it continues to be invented in cities—I suddenly realized that the poems I was writing, and that Gary Snyder and Wendell Berry were writing, on the whole have the effect of making people feel guilty and filling them with longing for the country.

I was reading Jane Jacobs at just about that time and talking to Galway, and so writing and thinking about city life seemed to me suddenly very important. I started in a very conscious way to write about it. Of course, setting out consciously to write about anything, I'm sure you all know, does absolutely no good. But the other thing that simply happened to me was that the forms in which I was writing started to make me uneasy. The literal breath of the forms in which I was writing—

LONDON: What does that mean?

HASS: I can give you an example. I was trying to learn my craft, so I was writing in very short lines. I was trying to learn how to make poems. And the poems in *Field Guide* are very deliberate on the whole. See what you have in front of you.

LONDON: We spent a long time reading "Songs to Survive the Summer" [eventually appearing in *Praise*, 1979].

HASS: OK, "Songs to Survive the Summer" really finished me off. Let me just read a few lines for you to hear what I'm saying. It came simply out of the experience of my daughter suddenly getting panicky about death—to which I responded maturely by developing an overwhelming fear of death. And I tried to think about it, to feel my way through. [READS EXCERPT] "These are the dog days, / unvaried / except by accident, / mist rising from soaked lawns, / gone world, everything / rises and dissolves in air, / whatever it is would / clear the air / dissolves in air and the knot / of days unties / invisibly like a shoelace. / The gray-eyed child /who said to my child: 'Let's play / in my yard. It's OK, / my mother's dead.' "

Aside from the subject, what's happening in this poem—it's a long poem—is the slowness of the breath. The spirit, literally the breath of poetry, is in the vowel sounds. It was Allen Ginsberg who [told me], and when I said to him, "You always say that, what exactly do you mean?" he sat me down in his lovely, generous way and pulled off the shelf Shelley's "Ode to the West Wind" and [Ginsberg's translation of] *The Diamond Sutra*. And he analyzed the first parts of "The Diamond Sutra," looking at the pattern of vowel sounds, and showed me they were exactly the pattern of sounds in the beginning of "Ode to the West Wind." The patterning of vowel sounds, the patterning of breath, is the way a poet actually reaches into and takes over your body while you're reading and experiencing his poem.

The terrific simple example of this is that wonderful old poem of Keats, "La Belle Dame sans Merci," a thing I read in high school. I think I swooned when I read it because of this mysterious witch woman. He writes,

> She looks at me and she did love
> And made sweet moan.

I've always had that in my head, and I started to analyze "And made sweet moan." Feel what happens to the vowel sounds. "Aa-ay-ee-oh." It forces you to start here, comes a little higher up the throat, comes to the middle of the mouth, and then it spills the breath. It is like yogic breathing. Gets all the poison out of you. Deep breathing gives you a shot of blood and a shot of oxygen to the brain. Allen said about my smoking, "A poem can do that for you. You don't have to smoke if you read it correctly."

So what's happening to my breathing when I read "Songs to Survive the Summer," and what happens to your breathing when you read it, is that short breathing in this poem takes us both over. It's literally the spirit of the poem. Do you see what I mean?

[READS]

> These are the dog days
> unvaried
> except by accident,
> mist rising from soaked lawns

You see it doesn't give you time to *breathe.*

LONDON: Did you set out to do that?

HASS: It is totally unconscious.

LONDON: What did you do in the *new* poem to change . . . ?

HASS: What I tried to do was write in longer lines. To have a longer breath. And as soon as I did that I used more words and as soon as I used more words I lost control completely. And I saw that I was involved in this terrific battle with control. When I was writing [the older] poems I was serving. As soon as I started writing in longer lines I was only volleying. The emotions got larger and unmanageable and I was just happy to get the damn ball across the net by whatever means available.

So I was thinking about the nature poem and the city and trying to write in longer lines—and the other thing I wanted to do is deal with ideas in poetry. I felt my poems were so specific that I could not in any straight-forward way *think* in a poem. I could think in images, but I couldn't use ordinary discourse. The rules of modernism laid down in 1919 were to focus on the object, avoid abstraction. I didn't see why you had to do that. I thought you ought to be able to get abstract language into a poem as much as you get concrete language into one, and that there must be a right way to do it. I was working on these concerns. Shall we look at "Meditation at Lagunitas"?

LONDON: Very much so. The dictum for so long has been Pound's, "Go in fear of the abstract." Then we come to you and we come to [poet A. R.] Ammons, and we know we must deal with the abstract and consider how to do it and make it alive.

HASS: Well, I thought, The only way the abstract is ever alive to me is when it comes up in my own life. At a party people use room chatter. But ideas really matter. I have a friend who says, "The abstract is God-like." But the whole idea of the abstract bothered me. This poem, "Meditation at

Lagunitas"—unfortunately I mistakenly gave you only the first [draft] page, though there are only three lines to the second page, and I'll tell you them—is a poem which tries to use abstract language and talk directly about ideas and use a long line and deal with what I was feeling and still have a poem. And this poem makes me nervous.

About the content, what I had in mind, what I had been talking to my friends about, was French philosophy, linguistic philosophy, which in effect says man uses words as a substitute; he can't have the thing so he has words. The words arise from a distance here and there. The first time we use a word, the first time the sound becomes a word, is when the baby goes, "Ahhh." Every word, in short, is for the absent mother, our longing for her and our need for her.

I hate that idea. It is probably true. I hate it. And I think that something happens to words in art that's different.

[READS FROM DRAFT PAGE OF "MEDITATION AT LAGUNITAS"]

```
MEDITATION AT LAGUNITAS


All the new thinking is about loss.
In this it resembles all the old thinking.
The idea, for example, that each particular erases
the luminous clarity of a general idea. That the clown-
faced woodpecker probing the dead sculpted trunk
of that black birch is, by his presence,
some tragic falling off from a first world
of undivided light. Or the other notion that,
because there is in this world no one thing
to which the bramble of blackberry corresponds,
a word is elegy to what it signifies.
We talked about it late last night and in the voice
```

of my friend, there was a thin wire of grief, a tone
almost querulous. After a while I understood that,
talking this way, everything dissolves: justice,
<u>pine</u>, <u>hair</u>, <u>woman</u>, <u>you</u> and <u>I</u>. There was a woman
I made love to and I remembered how, holding
her small shoulders in my hands sometimes,
I ~~could have slashed her throat and sucked the blood~~ *felt a violent wonder at her presence*
like a ~~from~~ thirst for salt, for my childhood river
with its island willows, silly music from the pleasure boat,
muddy places where we caught the little orange-silver fish
called <u>pumpkinseed</u>. It hardly had to do with her.
Longing, we say, because desire is full
of endless distances. I must have been the same to her.
But I remember so much, the way her hands dismantled bread,
the thing her father said that hurt her, what
she dreamed. There are moments when the body is as numinous

I'm sorry you don't have the second page but it's short:

> . . . as numinous
> as words, days that are the good flesh continuing.
> Such tenderness, those afternoons and evenings,
> saying *blackberry, blackberry, blackberry.*

I'll make one comment on this poem, which is: I can read it in a way I act and talk. I'm not breathless and tight in that way, it doesn't push me beyond my normal breath, as some of the poems I've written. This one has me breathing normally.

LONDON: Do you find that in the longer line there is less writing?

HASS: No, about the same, maybe more. Two interesting things happen. The prejudice I grew up with was to distrust consciousness and trust the unconscious. I think that's a mistake. The place to begin to learn a craft is to learn to trust your consciousness so you will behave without robotlike instructions. But at some point, then, the long line is a more dreamlike line, and you also have to use more words to fill it up. So what happens is that I have to go back and look at the words. And the hard thing about revising is that I don't want to: it's always hard to know whether the impulse of the revision is true.

LONDON: Coming back to the question of abstraction, when you use words like "beauty," "death," "god," and "imagination" in a new poem like "Sunrise" [in *Praise*], are you conscious of the fact that these are abstract words?

HASS: They are very hard to use. It makes me uneasy. "This is fear and syllables / and the beginnings of beauty." I don't know if you can use a word like "beauty." I rhymed it without much thinking about it, "We have walked the city," which mutes it in some way. I think you have to be very wily.

LONDON: When one is beginning [to write poetry], the problem is to arrive at definitions of one's own. You say "beauty" [but] I don't think we have the right to throw it around as easily in the beginning until we know exactly what we mean. Also, I'm sure Robert Hass will agree with this, that one of the ways to get to the mind's eye is going to be through the eye. And the training in dealing with what the eye perceives is . . . is . . .

HASS: Yes. It's crucial. It's the whole thing.

Muriel Rukeyser

MURIEL RUKEYSER'S VISIT to the New School in February 1978 was, according to her son, William, "one of her last sessions with students." Just months after London's class, she saw the publication of her five-hundred-plus-page *Collected Poems* (1978), but she died in 1980 at the age of sixty-six, "a major and prolific American poet and writer," as Adrienne Rich writes in her introduction to the Library of America's 2004 *Muriel Rukeyser: Selected Poems*. The poem she read that day in class, "Dream Drumming," had appeared in her thirteenth and last book of new poems published in her lifetime, called *The Gates* (1976).

Born to a well-off family in New York in 1913, Rukeyser started writing poetry at Vassar, which she attended for two years. Before she was out of her teens, national events sparked an activism that would famously find its way into her poems. At seventeen she traveled to Scottsboro, Alabama, to report on a landmark racial trial—she was jailed. "Breathe-in experience, breathe-out poetry," she writes in the opening line of her first collection, *Theory of Flight* (1935). In West Virginia she witnessed the industrial poisoning of tunnel workers, which led directly to her acclaimed "The Book of the Dead" in *U.S. 1* (1938). She went to Barcelona, where anti-Fascist forces were gathering at the outbreak of the Spanish Civil War; to Hanoi to protest the Vietnam War; and later to Seoul on behalf of a jailed Korean poet sentenced to death. Her essays collected in *The Life of Poetry* (1949) take as their subject the use of poetry in a democratic society at a time of crisis.

Yet it was also the breath and music of her line that inflected Rukeyser's poetry. "The movement of meaning," she said to London's students that day, "is surely the music of poetry." Pearl London formed a long friendship with Rukeyser, who was a single parent struggling at times to make a living. London wrote to her in September 1973, "Dear Muriel, You will be the first of the poets reading to us in the new course, and nothing could be as good as that, or as right (even if it is in the morning)."

"Dream Drumming"

PEARL LONDON: An awfully long time ago and a very short time ago, in one of the early books, Muriel wrote that "poems flowered from the bone." I always think of that line because it somehow seems to be both a prophecy and a summing up of all the work that has taken place in the books that came later. I'm going to let Muriel talk to you largely about the genesis of just one or two of the new poems, the processes of the imagination, the processes of craft.

MURIEL RUKEYSER: I've been very superstitious about not talking about work in process. It's been very bad luck for me; the work is not formed until after that moment, and I haven't even talked to the people I've loved the best, I haven't shown poems as they were being made, most of all I haven't liked to talk about, as people say, what they're "about." A poem is not *about* anything, as you who have been working in poems surely know. It is informed by certain things. It's very hard to talk about the rewriting that goes into them because the major rewriting is likely to be in the matter of *sound,* the sound that is deep in the structure, almost a crystalline structure of sound in the poem.

I have been asked very often, "Don't you care about rhyme?" I do and I don't. That is, I care about the recurrence of sound deeply, deeply, and rhyme has never been enough for me. Rhyme, the European way, is a return of sound once in a poem. I have, in my greed, wanted more than that, wanted modulation of sound changing, climbing as I think of it. On the page it's going down the page, but somehow as one hears the poem, it's climbing up and up and up until one reaches a kind of tonic sound, which is the last word in the poem for me. In rewriting, I have tried always to strengthen the sound structure and to make a dense fabric, of sound, of fact, of reality, and truth.

For instance, long ago I wrote a group of poems called "Ajanta." They're the cave paintings in India. The first line of those poems is "Came in my full youth to the midnight cave" and that, I hope, has the tensile strength of an arch. "Came" and "cave" are the feet of the arch. "In my" and "midnight" go together. "Full youth" and "to the" come together as the arch, and it is that sound structure that makes it stick, I believe. The other main sounds of the poem are picked up all the way through, and they come back and modulate. And those things do play not only on the memory but on the imagination.

We are in the midst of a huge reaction against the formalism of rhyme in poetry so that a lot of our contemporary poems are way off on the other side and are, I hesitate to say this, really kind of notebook jottings. *Brilliant,* full of perception, but without the sound structure in which a deep strength fuses with the literal meanings. The movement of meaning is surely the music of poetry. There isn't any music as we mean music, but there is that movement in the body and the soul, if you like. And one longs for it; it is a deep pleasure and a deep life to us, and there is this union of a physical life and a mental life that comes to us in poetry, and the physical life is bound up with sound in that way.

The movement of our breathing is why we take pleasure in hearing poets read, even though most poets are *abominable* readers, as you know.

Mumble and gasp and stifle the words—at the same time one longs to hear them breathing and doing these things and walking up and down. There's a whole movement that comes into it, a movement of, as I say, heartbeat, breathing, all the muscles voluntary and involuntary playing and syncopated against the breathing and the heartbeat—and that makes the rhythms of poetry.

And it seems to me that the invitation of poetry is to bring your *whole life* to this moment, this moment is real, this moment is what we have, this moment in which we face each other, and if a poem is any damn good at all, it invites you to bring your whole life to that moment, and we are good poets inasmuch as we bring that invitation to you, and you are good readers inasmuch as you bring your *whole life* to the reading of the poem. And that process is the same for both of us. In that way, we are exactly alike. We are different in what we do—the writing of the poem is of course different. But it involves the same process; it's just coming at it from the other side of the mirror.

That's a rather pompous introduction to what I'm going to read. But I'd like to read a couple of the poems that *you* have been reading, and I will welcome questions. I generally dread them and dodge them, and do all the slippery things, but I'm at a very curious point in my life in poetry—a point where they've asked me to do my collected poems and I've done them. I'll read a poem from *The Gates*—this is "Dream Drumming."

[READS]

Dream Drumming

I braced the drum to my arm, a flat drum, and began to play.
He heard me and she heard me. I had never seen this drum before.
As I played, weakness went through me; weakness left me.
    I held my arms high, the drum and the soft-headed long stick
I drummed past my tiredness vibrating weakness, past it into music,
As in ragas past exhaustion into the country of all music.

Held my arms high, became that vibration, drummed the sacrifice
    of my belly.
He heard me, she heard me,
I turned into the infinity figure, reaching down into the earth of music
    with my legs at last,
Reaching up from the two circles, my pelvic sea, mountains and air
    of breast, with my arms up into music
At last turned into music, drumming on that possessed vibration,
    Drumming my dream.

"Dream Drumming" is in the form of an actual dream—the man and the woman in the dream are a real man and woman in my life—and the ensuing jealousy that I was feeling. And the dream seemed to be a translation of that jealousy into what it might be, past jealousy and past all the feelings that go with it. I've had a lot of trouble with jealousy in my life, and I've had a vision of perfect love that is connected with jealousy and the feeling that the perfect love is the love of those two people for each other and that I might not be connected with perfect love, but I can imagine it in terms of the people I was jealous of. All of that is in here and it translates, which is in the dream.

Anybody want to talk? I myself have never talked after hearing poems. I've been silent. And I know that in schools and colleges, criticism and showing-off talk is considered a very high form of response to poetry. I have thought making a *poem* is a higher response to poetry, making *love* is a higher response to poetry, *silence* is a higher response. Criticism may be way down the line, maybe number 17. But I'm inviting questions of criticism or anything you like, and this is all out of character for me. I'll keep quiet now.

LONDON: Muriel, I'm going to ask a question. Somewhere in a discussion of craft, you have said that anything that doesn't belong in a poem must be, in your own words, "gotten rid of." It would seem to me that in terms of your feeling about recurrence, about rhythm as expectation, that there really is nothing in "Dream Drumming" that could have been thrown away. Was there much that was gotten rid of? In the writing of this poem?

RUKEYSER: Well, in this one, no. This was really written down after waking up from that dream, and I thought in the beginning, this is a note on the dream. It may be that I'm now o-l-d enough that something is coherent in my spirit. Maybe I'm getting to that point. Things are coming more and more coherently, and I think you will find that in yourselves, if you work steadily all your lives, that there is something that goes on in yourself so that you begin working that way and you know it. This one was extremely fortunate. I have the manuscript in my notebook and it's a manuscript almost the way the poem is.

LONDON: This brings us to a question that I think all of us in this class have really asked over and over again, but if you could say what the *glue* is, what is it, what gives an underlying cohesiveness to your writing? Could you—do you think you *could* say that it was—let me tell you, June Jordan, early on in the year when we asked her this, she said, "Anger," and then she modified it and she said, "Well, let me say this, I move from a hostile anger to a positive anger." That was her answer. Louis Simpson's answer was essentially "compassion." If you could find an answer—is there an answer, is there a glue?

RUKEYSER: Some of the things I said about sound, because that is the coherence of the spirit, that in a curious way lets things come back and modulate. They don't come back identically as rhyme does. They modulate through sound, they climb so it's one kind of coherence.

Anger I would like to talk about, too. All my life I have protested in anger against what was happening, in rebellion, about wanting to make a new society and change the world, but I know underneath that I am a person who makes things much more than a person who protests. And I finally came to the point of saying, "I will protest all my life but every time I protest, I will make a poem, or I will plant, or I will feed children, or I will try to help a building, I will make something." We are people who make something—I take it that all of us are poets to a certain extent. I think all people are. We are people who make things deeper than we are people who protest. And we will protest, we *have* anger—we can't *stand* the world as it is. But underneath that, we want to make whatever it is we want to make—more than we want to protest. At least that's true for me. The anger is there as deep as it ever was, but there is something that is deeper and that is another kind of coherence.

STUDENT: Do you have pet poems that have never been published?

RUKEYSER: The things I'm working on now. I'm in the middle of a group of poems and one poem that I have not brought with me; I can talk about the plot of the poem, just a dramatic structure.

I have recently been hearing on TV a grandniece of Emily Post talking about etiquette, not in the old Emily Post terms, but in contemporary terms of what we do in courtesy to people and what we do in dealing with people's feelings. She was talking about women's lib and what could be done about the courtesy of women for men, something that I had never thought about openly—holding doors open for men who are carrying packages, being decent to men, giving flowers to men—all the things that we can now do in honesty and feeling. Something else that I saw on TV, a geographic movie called *The Great Whales*. A marvelous thing that started with the old *Moby-Dick* concept of the hunting of the whale and went on further to what the whale was and how to preserve the whale—it's the anti–*Moby-Dick* thing in which the whale was not hunted. Marvelous young men of the Greenpeace movement who interposed their little boats between the great Soviet hunter ships and the whales, and finally the Russians had stopped shooting the harpoon and the Americans had gone up and called, "Thank you." Then the lagoon in Mexico, which is a place of whales, where they come up and examine the people for the first time, instead of the people inspecting the whales. And a woman putting her hand out and touching this huge whale (at their biggest they're sixty feet)—and it's not a thick rubbery thing the way we think of these whales, it's a live creature—and she said she was amazed at the feeling when she touched it, him. And when she touched him, he quivered—the whole length of him responded to that touch. And I think that's the end of my poem, a lesbian place in the village. I think it's about the touch of women and what can be done. These things worked out, the courtesy and the touch. I think that's the part of the poem I'm working on now. Again, it's not the sound, it's not the music of the poem, it's not what I hope to do with it, it's the plot of it. Now I may have bitched up the poem forever—"bitch" is one of the added women words. I may have messed it up and interfered by talking about it—that's why I'm superstitious about not doing these things. So I'd be grateful if you'd talk to me now and break the curse.

LONDON: Muriel, someone, I don't remember whether it was Bloom, says that a poet is judged in part by the influences he resists. Would you say there were influences you resisted in the early years? Surely Pope.

RUKEYSER: Yes, I guess Pope. I guess the wit writers, early. But I felt I didn't like them particularly, I didn't like Restoration playwrights—I would laugh, but I didn't really love them the way I wanted to love. I was working all day yesterday on my own papers [for *Collected Poems*, 1978] in the New York Public Library's Berg Collection. They've asked me to identify things. And I saw that I took a course in sonnet poems from my adored English teacher Henry Simon, took it because he gave it, not because I had any ambition. And very early he marked my poems "reminiscent of" and they were, they were all the voices; any poet I was reading would show up in what I was doing. I struggled to get to my own voice. It was a long time, when I was thirteen to about when I was twenty, when the poems in my first book were written.

LONDON: When your first book, *Theory of Flight,* was published, you were twenty-one, and Stephen Vincent Benét in the preface to that book could only remark on the extraordinary strength of a voice for a person that young, and so her own—

RUKEYSER: He was flattering, but he was wrong. He said, "Some poets are born with their craft in their hand. . . ." And I said, I wasn't born with anything in my hand. I worked at it, I put myself through all sorts of paces. I found the exercises yesterday that I had done in baby school. All kinds of exercises, all kinds of imitations, rotten translations into French of Keats, of Swinburne, and in rotten French. Latin exercises in which I got three right out of ten—all kinds of awfulness of growing up. Painful being in love and awfulness, painful writing poems and awfulness, all of it, day after day after day.

LONDON: "Every discovery makes its own chaos."

RUKEYSER: That's how the first book was done. That prefigured a great deal of what my life has been like. Always a no the first time and then after a long, long time, a yes. And I say that to you, I say to people who ask me whether they should write poems, I always say no. Because I figure that anybody writing poems has to get not only that first no, but a great many other nos of all kinds in her life. The world says no to these things. You have to get past that—it's the first thing you get past. That's the hurdle. Nobody's going to say yes to writing poems, not in this culture.

LONDON: But how good to know that there's a yes.

RUKEYSER: There's a yes at the end if you have luck and favorable winds.

Philip Levine

PHILIP LEVINE WAS fifty years old when he first visited Pearl London's class in March 1978, something of a tipping point. "At the time [of my visit] I believe I was writing at my very best," he says in a letter, "although it would be the books to come that would win me the prizes." He'd published key early books of poetry including *They Feed They Lion* (1972), *1933* (1974), and *The Names of the Lost* (1976), which contain some of his most identifiable poems about industrial, working-class Detroit, the city of his birth. He worked in an automobile manufacturing plant, got his undergraduate and master's degrees from Wayne State University, and began to write poetry.

While the Detroit poems would become his signature, two long stays in Spain in the 1960s evoked the anti-Fascist poems about the Spanish Civil War that would find their way into much of his work, including *7 Years from Somewhere* (1979). Socially alert, often elegiac, they at times reflect the budding anarchism he's since renounced. London, writing in the margin of one of his books, notes that the impetus for his poetry isn't anger, "it is a capacity for feeling, loving that is seeking a credible form and shape."

The prizes that followed—the National Book Award for *What Work Is* (1991), the Pulitzer Prize for *The Simple Truth* (1995)—dovetail with a shift in Levine's line, which became longer, more melodic, "moving," as the *New York Times* says, "from image to image, from the beginning of an idea to its end, with the inevitability and liquid clarity of a solo by Lester Young."

Levine has chaired the Literature Panel of the National Endowment for the Arts, and he was elected a chancellor of the Academy of American Poets in 2000. For years he taught at California State University at Fresno and still teaches at New York University. He now divides his time between Fresno and Brooklyn.

"You Can Have It"

PEARL LONDON: Philip Levine, you must start with how you got to this point, this point of the incredible poems in *The Names of the Lost*.

PHILIP LEVINE: A lot of people are puzzled and surprised by my recent work, as they have been by other books of mine. I remember when I published my first book [*On the Edge,* 1963], which no one saw, a reviewer in the *Saturday Review of Literature* said I sounded like an English poet. He might just as well have said Canadian or Australian. And another reviewer said I was difficult to categorize.

I was neither delighted nor dejected by these remarks. I know my second book [*Not This Pig,* 1968] was very different, and it was popular, and the publishers of that book were appalled by the next book I wrote, *They Feed They Lion,* and they asked me to drop the title poem. And I refused and they refused to publish the book, which went unpublished for about five years, rejected by a dozen publishers. My next book, *1933,* got very bad reviews, because it isn't like the previous books. It's a book of personal remembrance and tenderness, and some people think I'm much better when I'm in my work clothes breaking roads or other things of that nature. They don't like to see me, for example, in the synagogue mourning my father or crying or yearning for lost love.

After all, wasn't I a kind of fierce guy in my other books? Pissed off, angry at America because of its variety of ugly careers that our nation has embarked on? Yeah, I was the same guy, but I have also been a *child*, as I imagine most of you have been. And I remembered my childhood with great clarity, and it troubled me. Because I'd never come to terms with a great many things that had taken place. And the book, *1933*, was an attempt, a way to go back. I had never been able to write about my childhood before. I was something like forty-three or forty-four the first time I was able to write about it.

So we come to *The Names of the Lost*, which has been well received with the exception of the *New York Times*. I guess people have stopped expecting my previous book from me. And the next one [*7 Years from Somewhere*] will be, I think, the strongest departure of any of my books—the most autobiographical, revealing book I've written. A good deal of it is about dying. Being reborn. Which is an experience that I've had.

LONDON: In what sense?

LEVINE: I'm not the person I used to be. I also came very close to literally dying and found myself quite indifferent to the whole thing. There is a line in a poem by Weldon Kees, in which a famous sleuth is trying to solve an impossible crime. He finds the note from the victim that says, "To die this way is quite all right with me." That drives him up the wall. He doesn't know what to do with that. And I found myself at the point of really thinking, Well, I've had a pretty long life and I've had children. I've known love. I'm sixteen years older than my father when he died. It's not so bad. I was glad, however, to find that I returned to health and felt good and started writing again.

But I went through some changes in my forty-eighth and forty-ninth years. I ended certain relationships that were punishing and giving me nothing and I started up new ones with people no matter where they were. It was at the time that my children grew up; my youngest child left the house. This was a period that I feared through all the years of raising my children, when my kids would leave home, and my wife and I would be cast upon the waters of ourselves. But lo and behold, it was an extraordinarily beautiful moment. And it lasts to the present.

At any rate, my recent poetry *is* very different. My last book and present book are informed by religious faith that has seized me in my forties and fifties, which I've lived most of my life without. I've lived as an atheist. Grew up in a family of disbelievers who had come to the United States from Poland and Russia for political freedom. Some were leftists and weren't treated very well. Some of them became Republicans here to make sure they were treated better. And lo and behold they were treated better.

But I recalled the glorious past that had driven them from the shores of Europe. The religion which I believe in may not strike you as a religion. It's called anarchism. And its faith is that each human being is a portion of God and that acts against people are acts against God. And that all order that's meaningful arises out of us naturally and that we have rarely lived in a society which would allow us to flourish. In *The Names of the Lost,* the poem "Gift for a Believer" is a poem to the anarchist painter Flavio Costantini. "For the Fallen" is a poem about the death of some of the great Spanish anarchists of the civil war. There are other poems that will appear in the next two books about similar people who proclaim their faith.

LONDON: Back in 1972 you said in an article, talking about Spain, "By the end of the year the landscape seemed to me like a projection of my own inner being. I felt that when I looked at the Spanish landscape I was looking at part of myself."

LEVINE: I went to Spain in 1965 after too many years of dull living in California. I had three children and not much money but a job. It was the best I could do unless I wanted to take some extravagant chance. So I said, "I will quit my teaching job and go out into the world and become the greatest shoe salesman ever." I didn't know what you know. I was never geared to do much very well. I have trouble getting jobs. I even refused to serve my government in the Korean War.

There will be a poem in the *New Yorker* about that. It's called "Dawn, 1952." The *New Yorker* called up and said, "We'd like to change the title to make it clearer, we'd like to change it to "C.O. [conscientious objector], Dawn, 1952." I said, "No, you can't do that. I wasn't a C.O. You'll have to change it to 'Draft Dodger.' That's what I was, I'm not ashamed of it. I come from a long line of draft dodgers and I'm proud to say my oldest son continued the tradition in the Vietnam War. So none of us ever fought in a war." As Dylan Thomas says in a letter, "I have this one little precious body and I'm not giving it to my government. And what are you doing with yours?" Wonderful. And if you ever saw Dylan Thomas . . . *terrible* body. [*Laughter*] He should have been quite eager to give it to anybody.

Anyway, I saved up enough money and wanted to see another world. I went over to Spain but didn't speak the language. The only language I spoke was English, though I had known some Yiddish as a child. And what you were quoting, Pearl, was at the end of a discussion in which I first said I couldn't write because everything felt foreign to me. But pretty soon people began to come up to me in the street and speak to me in Catalan, because I looked like a Catalan. You know, they're all hidden Jews over there anyway. In 1492 Ferdinand and Isabella issued the decree that Jews would have three terrific choices. They could leave, convert, or die. Yeah. Now *that* is called freedom of choice. And some of them went as far as China, but a lot of them stayed and converted.

So Spain became very familiar to me, and I got along well there and felt more at home in Barcelona, which is an industrial city—and is, say, the Detroit of Spain—than I really had in Fresno, California, which is a rural town in the center of great rural activities. And that is really what I was saying. I became comfortable there and once becoming comfortable I found I could write. I had always written twelve or fifteen poems a year. And that was the first year, 1965, when I began to write thirty or forty poems a year, which is about what I write now.

LONDON: One of the poems we've been reading all week is "Angel Butcher" [from *They Feed They Lion*].

LEVINE: Curiously enough, "Angel Butcher" is a poem spawned by the riots of 1967 or whatever you want to call them. The insurrection of 1967.

LONDON: In Detroit?

LEVINE: In Detroit, yes. I went back to Detroit shortly after the event to see what it looked like and discovered that—well, it looked terrible. A little worse than usual. But what I discovered was something about myself. That although in California I could feel very bountifully about the fact that a great many people were naming the nature of their existence as prisoners, and could act out their anger against their prison and their wardens, when I got back to Detroit I realized that I sure looked like one of the wardens and not the prisoners. It's an observation. One of the things I think the poem is trying to say is that, of course, the angels and the butcher are the same person. That one is obliged to kill one's angel in order to survive the world. To go on living, one kills a certain portion of the self.

I gravitated to all the other six people in Detroit who wanted to write poetry in the early, middle, late forties. There weren't many of us; it wasn't the fashion. And I don't really know how we all found it and found each other. But we did. Now there are only four of us left of the seven. The other three are dead. I'm the second oldest and the toughest. And I say that because two are alcoholics and they probably won't live much longer, either. In other words, my observation was, and it's also in my poem "Letters for the Dead," that if you don't kill a certain aspect of yourself you don't go on living. And I think what's happened in my recent poems is that aspect of the self, lo and behold, was there all the time, and he has come back to claim me.

Philip Levine

YOU CAN HAVE IT

My brother comes home from work
and climbs the stairs to our room.
I can hear the bed groan and his shoes drop
one by one. You can have it, he says.

The moonlight streams in the window
and his unshaven face is whitened
like the face of the moon. He will sleep
long after noon and waken to find me gone.

Thirty years will pass before I remember
that moment when suddenly I knew each man
has one brother who dies when he sleeps
and sleeps when he rises to face this life,

and that together they are only one man
sharing a heart that always labors, hands
yellowed and cracked, a mouth that gasps
for breath and asks, Am I gonna make it?

All night at the ice plant he had fed
the chute its silvery blocks, and then I
stacked cases of orange soda for the children
of Kentucky, one gray box-car at a time

with always two more waiting. We were twenty
for such a short time and always in
the wrong clothes, crusted with dirt
and sweat. I think now we were never twenty.

In 1948 in the city of Detroit, founded
by de la Mothe Cadillac for the distant purposes
of Henry Ford, no one wakened or died,
no one walked the streets or stoked a furnace,

for there was no such year, and now
that year has fallen off all the old newspapers,
calenders, doctors' appointments, bonds,
wedding certificates, drivers licenses.

The city slept. The snow turned to ice.
The ice to standing pools or rivers
racing in the gutters. Then bright grass rose
between the thousands of cracked squares,

and that grass died. I give you back 1948.
I give you all the years from then
to the coming one. Give me back the moon
with its frail light falling across a face.

Give me back my young brother, hard
and furious, with wide shoulders and a curse
for God and burning eyes that look upon
all creation and say, You can have it.

FINAL TYPESCRIPT OF PHILIP LEVINE'S "YOU CAN HAVE IT"

LONDON: It's also in "You Can Have It."

LEVINE: I'll tell you something about that poem that you don't know, and it will change your attitude slightly toward it. That's not a very old poem, that poem. November. When I first read it to an audience someone asked, "How can you and your brother be twenty at the same time?" The answer is, we're identical twins, that's how we did it. And I think the theme of identical twins runs throughout my poetry. "The Midgets," "Angel Butcher." These conversations between men, this extraordinary intimacy in one man trying to realize himself or regain some portion of himself though his communion with a brother.

Part of my optimism of the recent years is due to the rediscovery of my brother and how rewarding, stimulating, a relationship like that can be, if it works.

LONDON: Who was it that said, "To be human is to be a conversation"?

LEVINE: I don't know, but I'll say it.

STUDENT: We've noticed a lot of the same words coming out in your poems. "Roses" . . .

LEVINE: Oh, yes.

STUDENT: . . . and I was wondering how aware you were of it—it seems like you have your own tool chest of words—and if you made a conscious effort to use them or avoid them.

LEVINE: Yes, I have become conscious of it in the last four or five years, and I try not to use them so often. I don't consider it a strength, their presence. And when I can, I get them out. I have myself promising to take flowers to someone in a poem in my next book. They'll be carnations.

[*Laughter*] Yeah, I'm aware of it, and, again, I don't think it's a strength, and I would like to expand my vocabulary and not be so dependent.

LONDON: One of the things that we spent a good deal of time talking about last week is that, in Philip Levine's works, it is not so much vocabulary that's critical as it is the use of syntax, that jammed grammar. As in the title "They Feed They Lion." So tremendously indicative of the need to impart the muscular quality of the work.

LEVINE: Oh, well, *that* I like.

LONDON: Yes, you must like it.

LEVINE: Oh, yeah. Of course until earlier this year the Library of Congress listed the title of the book as "They Feed the Lion." Thus making me an English poet. Obviously I think the phrase is derived from black grammar, and it is a poem that grew out of the racial distress of the late sixties. It is a poem in which a great many natural elements from the natural world are brought to the city of factories, and they are transformed sometimes with disastrous effects.

I mean a factory's a place where you take the earth—its iron ore, which is earth—you dig it up, you bring it in, and you apply techniques of heat and pressure and you transform it into bumpers and fenders. But you also bring people in there and you apply other kinds of pressures to them and you transform them. The factory eats the natural world. It eats the rubber and wood and sand to make glass. I had especially in mind the River Rouge Plant, downriver from Detroit, which is measured in square miles in total size, the largest industrial complex in the world, built by Henry Ford in the late twenties. Every portion of an automobile is manufactured there from raw products. So that the rubber, now synthetic, is manufactured to make the tires. The glass is made. The steel is made for the cars. Everything is made. I had in mind that place which takes everything and transforms it.

But most importantly, since I don't give a damn for the feelings of cars, I was aware of the enormous wounding of people who went through this process and how this process remanufactured them.

LONDON: In "Detroit, 1948," the last line of it is "We burn this city every day." Way back in 1972 again you said, "I have a Detroit that vanished about 1952 for all I know when I left. I live it. It is in my head. And it's got nothing to do with what's back there now. It's the life I lived and the lives it included and that's what I'm trying to transform into poetry."

I think it is that whole nightmare landscape of the self that we really have to understand in the Detroit poem, don't you?

LEVINE: No.

LONDON: No? All right, good. Please contradict me.

LEVINE: I don't see a nightmare. In reviewing *1933*, Richard Howard talks about the fact that I've gone down to the lowest depths to accept a world that is almost unacceptable. Richard Howard can say that because he grew up in a very expensive suburb of Cleveland. But I don't find Detroit's people ugly. I find them precious and gorgeous. They were the people that gave me my life, my values, that nurtured me. And it's an act of great pleasure to be able to have developed enough distance, emotional distance and poetic technique, to go back and memorialize those people. I mean, Richard would find my apartment appalling. Richard would find my wardrobe unthinkable. He just lives a different life.

Detroit is not a nightmare landscape to me. The nightmare is the lives that many people have to live because they have no other choice. And it is a very wounding experience to go back and to discover that men of my own age are old. I mean really old. And I look at them and they look at me across an extraordinary chasm of wonderment. "What happened to you?" "What happened to *you?*"

The past is not nightmarish to me. As much as it once was. I couldn't write about it before, but "One for the Rose" comes out of going back to Detroit in January of this year. I turned fifty in January, and my twin brother turned fifty on the same day. [*Laughter*] So we had a party. And I flew my kids all the way from California. It was wonderful. In the airport they met some friends who said, "Where are you going?" "Detroit," they said. "*Detroit?* What *for?*" "For a party," they said. That just seemed terrific.

Louise Glück

IN FEBRUARY 1979, when Louise Glück was thirty-five years old, she visited Pearl London's class with two new poems. They would eventually become part of her third book, *Descending Figure* (1980), and her conversation that day captures a moment when her early style was in transition. She had received recognition for *Firstborn* (1968) and *The House on Marshland* (1975), the first two books. But as she explains here, she was about to break free from their tighter, more punctuated lyricism. "Recently the poems I've written have been much more matter of fact," she tells London. "They don't have gorgeous little moments. But that's what they have to for-swear. . . . Something can be marvelous and still need to be stopped. Otherwise you don't change. It's as simple as that. And if you don't change, then you stop writing good poems."

In the three decades since her visit, Glück has become one of the most influential American poets of her generation. For *The Triumph of Achilles* (1985), she received the National Book Critics Circle Award; for *Ararat* (1990), the Library of Congress's Bobbitt National Prize for Poetry; and for *The Wild Iris* (1992), the Pulitzer Prize. In 2001 Yale University awarded her the Bollingen Prize for Poetry. Speaking of her "characteristically spare and elegant style," Robert Hass has called her "one of the purest and most accomplished lyric poets now writing." In 2003 she succeeded Billy Collins as twelfth U.S. poet laureate.

For Glück, paradox and "the unsaid" exert more power than confession. "I would like to write poetry that was intensely personal and seemed absolutely devoid of egotism," she says here. "I believe that it's possible."

Louise Glück was born in New York City in 1943 and grew up on Long Island, attending Sarah Lawrence College and Columbia University. She has taught at Willams College and is currently writer-in-residence at Yale University.

"For My Mother"

"Autumnal"

"World Breaking Apart"

PEARL LONDON: As we go through *The House on Marshland,* the whole world is such an interior world. It is really not an external landscape at all. Nor is it intended to be.

LOUISE GLÜCK: That's true.

Recently at a Goddard residency, Bob Hass remarked that one couldn't write poetry without a knowledge of history. And immediately I started to think of all the poets who were not imbued with that knowledge who wrote quite dazzling poems. And it occurred to me that there are at least two kinds of approaches. There's the poetry that encounters phenomena and then places them in context; sees the historical reverberation of the present tense. And then there's the poetry that encounters the world as though for the first time. So that, as in Dickinson, you have the feeling that grass was never seen before, that relationships are perceived not as they play out or fail to play out earlier conceptions of what those relationships should be; they're perceived with no prior information at all.

As I thought of that as a definition, it seemed obvious to me that where my work fell was in that [second] category. And as soon as I had decided that, I decided that I had to write a completely different poetry.

LONDON: In the category of seeing the world . . .

GLÜCK: The first time.

LONDON: Waking up every morning as though it were the first morning of your life.

GLÜCK: I'm not making a value judgment. It's simply that as soon as you can place yourself—well, as soon as I can place myself and describe myself—I want immediately to do the opposite thing. And the definitions are slow in coming, fortunately, so I haven't always got to reshape my mission. But as soon as I could see that that's what I did, then I wanted to try doing something else. When I finished my first book [*Firstborn*], I knew that I wanted to write a second book called *The House on Marshland*. And I knew why I wanted to do that. I was raised on Long Island, and much of the land there is marsh. It's been filled in because it's profitable acreage . . . and all over there are horrible tract houses, house on house on house. There always seemed to me something poignant in the construction of a house—which was supposed to be the reliable protection on earth that was itself unreliable. That seemed to me very moving. And I must have started in 1966 trying to write a poem that would be called "The House on Marshland." I wrote drafts and drafts of lousy poems, each one different and each one just awful. I did start to accumulate a lot of marsh imagery, some of which was good. But I never managed to write the poem.

When I was about midway through the poems of this book, I started working on a poem called "For My Mother." The first seven lines— "Screened / through the green glass / of your eye, moonlight / filtered into my bones / as we lay / in the big bed in the dark, / waiting for my father"—these came intact and complete and quickly. And that was it. I could not think of anything else to do. That was May. And I wrote nothing all summer. You know how you sort of circle around, you try to approach it innocently, as though you'd never thought of it before? So I'd just casually type down all the lines, and I'd stop at the same place.

And then, at the end of September, suddenly it occurred to me that this might be the place where I could use that marsh imagery. The last lines— "A marsh / grows up around the house. / Schools of spores" et cetera— they must have been written in around 1968, '67. As soon as I knew where the new poem had to go, as soon as I saw that as a possible ending, I was able—I can't say rapidly, but in about a month's time—to write the middle.

LONDON: We were talking about the discontinuities in some of the new poems. The use of the fragmented line sometimes, almost collage. Somewhere along the way we felt that these were really signs of an attempt to depict an internal rather than external world. Do they seem discontinuous to you at all?

GLÜCK: Oh, yeah.

LONDON: What kind of awareness do you have of how you're going to order them if they're discontinuous? Why use discontinuities in a poem?

GLÜCK: These poems were written, of course, over a period of seven years, so I can't say that there was a single aesthetic that informed the composition of all of them—it's not true. But the attempt in the poems that are elliptical in the ways you described is an attempt to render silence; to use silence to . . . almost . . . if you can properly frame an image or a verbal gesture in white space, in silence, you can make of that whole movement something equivalent to a single word; that is, the way a word, a contained word, explodes into meaning. It's like those little Japanese stones that you drop into water. They become flowers. That's a metaphor very attractive to me—the idea that something small should ramify. Of course it has to be controlled. Also, it has to be unexpectedly beautiful. Its ramifications can't be those that would have been anticipated. So the pauses were an attempt to encircle with silence; to make silence a powerful presence in a poem.

I should say that none of this was framed as a philosophy when I was working. I would hope that that would be obvious. There was simply a sense that . . . well . . . the furthest along of those poems, I would say, is "Messengers."

If you saw it as a single stanza it would be just horrible. I've never had much problem having a sense of where a movement ended and where I wanted to break a stanza. Though what happens is, you learn to write a poem that breaks stanzas in a certain way, that takes certain kinds of linguistic, syntactic turns to stand for closure. You recognize that turn as closure, and as soon as that moment of recognition happens, then you've got to stop doing it. Because then what you're doing is simply making of everything the same poem. You look at a tree, and you turn that into a tree poem, and you look at a rock, and you turn that into a rock poem. They all have the same arc. As soon as you can recognize a consistent shaping principle, recognize that a certain kind of sentence is always a cue to you for an end, then you've got to resist the cue.

One of the ways I got out of writing the kinds of poems in *Firstborn* that evolved into, really, little bulletproof poems was to set myself a task of writing poems that were one sentence. And the earliest poems in this book [*The House on Marshland*] derive from that task. I also wanted to write poems whose endings were not summaries. Those were the two things that I had seen myself do too many times, and I could see how . . . I had stopped learning, because I could convert all I saw only into one kind of truth. And it was no longer interesting. So I wanted to see what I could do when those habitual devices were refused.

LONDON: That's awfully interesting, because several of us have been dealing with the same problems and strategies. Although I think it's an awful poem, we've been talking about Frost's "Silken Tent," the sonnet, which is one sentence long, and . . .

GLÜCK: I love it.

LONDON: Do you love it?

GLÜCK: Oh, I love it.

LONDON: It's such a contrived image, though.

GLÜCK: Oh, I love it. I love that sinuous sentence. . . . Doesn't that use, is it "bondage"—"of the slightest bondage made aware"? "Bondage," it's wonderful.

LONDON: Oh, but the image is so wrong. How can one deal with a woman who is a silken tent in this day and age? It's contrived!

GLÜCK: We can't. Of course it's contrived. It's an insane projection, but it's a wonderful poem.

LONDON: But how can we separate it from its content?

GLÜCK: Well, because it's personal. I mean, it's *his*. As a way to see women it's obviously of no use at all, and one could say it was offensive that he saw his wife that way. Or romantic in an unimaginative way. But, but, but . . . that's not my response to the poem—at all. And I don't feel that I have to think that his wife was a silken tent to think it's a complicated, profound, marvelous poem.

LONDON: When I feel twenty-eight empty barns—as Auden counted them—in his work, then I know I'm dealing with something that's out of his own . . . you know, he walks in darknesses "not of woods only." . . . But to come back to the silences—

GLÜCK: There's such venom in it, too.

LONDON: Oh, there is. It's a mean poem.

GLÜCK: But mean on both sides.

LONDON: He doesn't feel kindly about any . . . I want to come back to the business of the silences in your work. Denise Levertov says that the pause at the end of a line is worth half a comma. What I really feel in your work is such a marvelous sense of different values at the end of a line, one of the things that enrich these poems.

GLÜCK: As you can tell from the poems I brought in, I'm now very deliberately trying *not* to use that.

LONDON: Do you think perhaps you'd like to read "Autumnal" [from *Descending Figure*] to us, so we get the feeling of it?

GLÜCK: [READS ALOUD FROM HER FINAL TYPESCRIPT OF "AUTUMNAL"]

LONDON: Marvelous poem. You said before that in your work you were moving away from the depersonalized voice. That you wanted terribly to move toward not necessarily more "I" and "me" but toward a greater communication of self, as I understood it. Is that—?

GLÜCK: No, no, not communication of the self, that's not what I want. The issue of ego is a sensitive one. I think that most contemporary poetry is horrifically disfigured by it. The territoriality in most poetry that goes out to claim "my pain," "my father," "my mother," "my past." There's a

Autumnal

```
Public sorrow, the acquired
gold of the leaf, the falling off,
the prefigured burning of the yield:
which is accomplished.  At the lake's edge,
the metal pails are full vats of fire.
So waste is elevated
into beauty.  And the scattered dead
unite in one consuming vision of order.
In the end, everything is bare.
Above the cold, receptive earth,
the trees bend.  Beyond,
the lake shines, placid, giving back
the established blue of heaven.
                        The word
is bear:  you give and give, you empty yourself
into a child.  And you survive
the automatic loss.  Against inhuman landscape,
the tree remains a figure for grief; its form
is forced accommodation.  At the grave,
it is the woman, isn't it, who bends,
the spear useless beside her.
```

July 78

swagger in it that offends me greatly. I would like to write poetry that was intensely personal and seemed absolutely devoid of egotism.

Dickinson is the easiest example. I hate to mention her twice, it's as though I read no one else. Her poems are agonizingly personal, but they're not exclusive. The one—"After great pain, a formal feeling comes"—that ends "As freezing persons recollect the snow— / First—chill—then stupor—then the letting go.—" The analogy—"as freezing persons recollect the snow"—*that* includes the audience. It doesn't exclude them. It tells them "After great pain," which is clearly *her* pain. She doesn't have to detail it. She doesn't say, "And first they strapped me to the table, and then they took the knife to me." The dignity and restraint of that phrasing doesn't obscure its source in her life. But the poem assumes that other people have like experience. I would like to do a version of that. I don't mean I want to write poems that are like Dickinson's. But I would like them not to be rife with the first person. I don't think that a poem is communicative or personal to the extent to which it uses that pronoun. I think that a poem can be immensely personal and communicative and contain no "I" at all. I believe that it's possible.

LONDON: What I think Stanley Plumly said when he came here one day last spring was that bringing the disparate parts into immediate and very intimate relation was the hope he had for his poems. And I think that in a sense "Autumnal" has disparities in it, in terms of the movement of the poem, which at the very end—listening to you now—are brought into a very intimate kind of relation. This pinpoints something that I think is crucial in your work, and I wish you'd comment on it for us, and that is your use, throughout, of certain conjunctions. There is implicit a kind of logic when you use the word "so," as though one thing were the consequence of another. It's a highly unpredictable result or fruit of consequence. Expectations are forced into new channels very suddenly. It is part of the syntax of the poem.

GLÜCK: I think that the "so" is a characteristic move.

LONDON: It's a good one.

GLÜCK: Good only up to a point. Something can be marvelous and still need to be stopped. Otherwise you don't change. It's as simple as that. And if you don't change, then you stop writing good poems. Really. I believe that. So when you can identify something as a maneuver, however successful, even if you never do it badly, you should stop doing it. Every once in a while you'll have to do it again. I think the "so" in "Autumnal" is a different kind of "so." But I know the "so" that you mean. Its tone is one of a child's clarity and calm that makes assumptions that are not natural assumptions, but it's a way of introducing into the poem those unnatural assumptions in an unstrenuous way.

LONDON: Quite wonderful. Because the unpredictable happens as though it were inevitable.

STUDENT: "So waste is elevated." Would you comment on the word "elevated"?

GLÜCK: ["Elevated"] is an enlargement of the literal. The prior description is of the gathering of leaves, which are burned. The leaves on the trees acquire gold. And that gold prefigures the fire they will become. So they become gold, they fall, and in that act is the prefigured burning. Almost immediately after it, the burning is accomplished: "At the lake's edge, / the metal pails are full vats of fire." And waste, this waste that they are, this spent substance is raised to some higher importance. So "elevated" is a pun. It's not meant to be experienced as a pun. It's meant to be experienced as a verb that works two ways. The burning leaves do, literally, ascend as fire. They are, equally, dead things "elevated into beauty." I guess there's a sense of an ordering principle behind it that would say that beauty is the Platonic ideal of the leaf. I mean, it's a high form of what the leaf was. The scattered dead, again, that's the leaves.

But the poem is now making grander and grander statements about leaves. "And the scattered dead / unite in one consuming vision of order." Those leaves seem in that line to have been brought together by their own desire. Of their own accord they unite in this consuming vision, this thing that reduces them to nothing but is seen as consuming, again, in two ways. They are literally consumed, but it is a consuming vision. It is a passion. On the leaves' part. On the dead's part. And then everything's bare.

LONDON: "The word / is *bear*": We are jolted into that, to move into the next stanza. We are suddenly unsettled and unseated and moved into an entirely other kind of feeling.

GLÜCK: Again, it's got two meanings. I feel as though I'm writing in two languages, like I'm writing poems in German and English at the same time.

What the poem is about, if you could say it's about something, is forced accommodation. It's not about any kind of accommodation, it's about the kind of accommodation that is necessary, in this instance, when a child dies. So, "The word / is *bear*": You bear a child, but you also bear this grief. And one of the things that I wanted to happen after that is in the line "And you survive / the automatic loss." I wanted that to seem not only the particular loss to death, but also the loss that is the loss of the mother giving birth. "You give and give, you empty yourself / into a child." It also mimes the physiological process by which a child is formed. And you survive. You remain whole after its "automatic loss."

LONDON: Is "automatic"—you see, I don't know how all of you felt about it, but I was very stumped by the word "automatic." It concerned me, even in childbirth, to think in terms of automatic. Only because of the implication of something more mechanized than it really is . . .

GLÜCK: It's a vicious word, it's a terrible word . . .

LONDON: It's a terrible word. It really is. And . . . it's precisely what you wanted—it's saying precisely what you wanted to say.

GLÜCK: Yes.

STUDENT: But how does it then apply to the death of a child? Because that certainly isn't an expected or automatic event. A parent usually dies first in ordinary sequence; so this would not be automatic.

GLÜCK: Well, that's a good point. The state of mind of someone so stricken with grief reverses those orders, though. Or so it seemed to me. A child very close to us died recently, and this poem arose out of that event. It's almost as though loss to death at that moment seems but a further extension of the earlier loss. Of course you're going to lose them; why would you ever dare hope otherwise. I mean, it's not realistic, but it's true,

I hope, to the spirit of violation that attends that kind of grief. As though everything you love is taken from you. It attempts to render that state of mind. Love and loss are utterly bound together.

LONDON: And the image of the spear?

GLÜCK: Works in about eight ways. Or else it doesn't. That's the male principle. Weaponry is useless in that situation. The spear, the thing that would do damage to the adversary, is pointless in that situation, when one has lost to death. Death is immune to human spears; untouched by human spears. So there's that. Then there's also the rigidity . . . I mean, the woman bends, and the spear, the useless spear. I like the idea of rigid, straight, vertical—and useless. Because there's an assumption that the thing that bends is useless and hasn't contained and controlled its energies, whereas the thing that remains rigorously straight is always bound to be useful. And in this situation it's not. This is a situation unsuited to the hunter. But I think if that line works at all it works well beyond those definitions. I feel some hesitation around the idea of going any further. I would hope that it would call up many such associations.

LONDON: Let's take a look at "World Breaking Apart." This is just one of the most beautiful poems you've written.

GLÜCK: This and "Autumnal" seem to me to be of a mode. And they seem quite different from *The House on Marshland*. I found writing them that I had much greater difficulty knowing when something was good and when something wasn't good. This is always true when style changes. Because your editorial judgment has been honed to a particular method. The tools you have for recognizing errors and inventions in that method are no longer of any use. So you have to develop a whole other critical sense. And the transition is difficult, because you usually have very little sense of whether or not you're written anything—I mean, you keep thinking, This is absolute trash; this is trash. But you've got to write it.

World Breaking Apart

```
I look out over the sterile snow.
Under the white birch tree, a wheelbarrow.
The fence behind it mended.  On the picnic table,
mounded snow, like the inverted contents of a bowl
whose dome the wind shapes.  The wind
with its impulse to build.  And under my fingers,
the square white keys, each stamped
with its single character.  I believed
a mind's shattering released
the objects of its scrutiny:  trees, blue plums in a bowl,
a man reaching for his wife's hand
across a slatted table, and quietly covering it,
as though his will enclosed it in that gesture.
I saw them come apart, the glazed clay begin
dividing endlessly, dispersing incoherent particles
that went on shining forever.  I dreamed of watching that
the way we watched the stars on summer evenings,
my hand on your chest, the wine
holding the chill of the river.  There is no such light.
And pain, the free hand, changes almost nothing.
Like the winter wind, it leaves
settled forms in the snow.  Known, identifiable --
except there are no uses for them.
```

                                          December 78

LONDON: Marvelous.

GLÜCK: I can tell you how I wrote this. This is really odd.

LONDON: Oh, good.

GLÜCK: I had had a fruitful fall. Having had a terrible spring. And so I felt more fluent than I usually do. I had just finished something a while back and it seemed that I could just try pushing myself a little. So I said, "OK, I'll just write about what I see out the window." It was a task: "Sitting at your desk, Louise, what do you see? Write about those objects that you see." And I was absolutely astounded to see the rage that came out. It would have seemed to me that this would be a poem that would have arisen out of a clear sense of a state of mind, which would then attach itself to emblems that embodied it. But it began indifferently. Nothing was charged. It's a mistake to say, "Oh, I looked at those things and I saw how angry I was." I mean, yeah, I was angry, but because I had no stake in writing the poem, I was able in this particular piece, for whatever good or bad it is, to completely give over to the notion of those objects outside as a fiction. OK, what world did they imply, those things? Independent of my need to project a world upon them. The composition of it seemed very different to me.

STUDENT: It seemed to me that in this poem you have a different rhythm: a longer line, but even beyond that, a different pace.

GLÜCK: Oh, completely different. I'm trying to try different things. I mean, this is close to a book. And there are, first of all, a lot of sequences in it. So there are a lot of what seem to be longer poems. But most of those are poems that seem like *The House on Marshland* in many ways, except that the architectural principles are different. And now recently the poems I've written have been much more matter of fact, much less going for magic. I think that the best poems in this book have a magical emanation, but there's also a sense that that was wanted. That was the ambition. And that's all right, but I think that there might be something more interesting.

I sometimes feel uncomfortable, when I look at the newer poems, because I'm not sure of their surfaces the way I have learned to be sure of other surfaces. They're not gorgeous. They don't have gorgeous little moments. But that's what they have to forswear. I don't want to sound like I'm coming down on the lyric. I'm not. I like lyric poetry. I mean, we write what we love to read. I love to read lyric poetry. But the more recent things are much less lovely, just generally speaking. Unlovely.

LONDON: "I dreamed of watching that." The "that" suddenly became important. It is positioned in the line in such a way that an enormous weight falls on it. Each word is carrying its burden. And even a small word like "that," which you are so used to seeing in a particular kind of grammatical context, is changed here.

GLÜCK: It was once pointed out to me that my poems had almost no articles but the definite article. Always "the." That's the mythic again—the single example. So now I'm trying to write poems with "a." And boy, is it hard. "*A* man reaching for his wife"—I was so proud of that! *A* man. Not *the* man. *A* man. Any man!

The thing you're describing is a manifestation of the same impulse as the impulse to use the definite article. It's encapsulating an experience and making a paradigm of it. And I won't do that again.

LONDON: Oh, don't say that. I think it's what gives it excitement, and—

GLÜCK: But it's only exciting because it's not expected. If I have any message to any of you who write, it's that you cannot sit calmly repeating yourself. And the hard thing about that is, oftentimes when you change, the new poems, the adventurous poems, may be less successful than the evolved poems of another mode. So you have to be willing to set aside that degree of finish, that degree of polish, for something that might seem to you more primitive.

Now, not all such transitions work that way. Occasionally you will discover a new kind of language that will seem to you an advance. Or will make the other poems look thin. Which is I guess how you experience advance—the rug's pulled out from underneath you; it's never completely positive; if you like what you're doing, then it makes everything else that you did look crummy.

But oftentimes it won't happen that way. Oftentimes what will happen is that you will find yourself writing less accomplished poems, and you have to be willing. Because there's no other choice. You can't go on writing poems in those rehearsed ways. I remember there was a review of my first book, and the writer of the review, which was mildly favorable, said, "And I think what we can expect from Louise Glück in the future are poems even more intensely personal," and so on. I was outraged that anyone should think that it was so clear what could be expected. And that review had a great deal to do with shaping the book that followed. Because I was absolutely determined to violate that reviewer's expectation. As soon as an expectation begins to form around your work, either on your part or on the part of readers, you must do your best not to gratify it.

LONDON: "There is no such light. / And pain, the free hand, changes almost nothing." Please comment on that—not in terms of syntax anymore, just specifically.

GLÜCK: The fantasy is of a glamorous dissolution, a dissolution that's like watching fireworks—yes, things are shattering, but it's very lovely and it is a spectacle. And, like certain spectacles, produces light. The object shattering, the world shattering—all that energy must be quite a show. "I dreamed of watching that / the way we watched the stars on summer evenings"—watching the spectacle of dissolution. But "There is no such light." Dissolution produces no light. In fact, the point of the poem is that it produces no movement. It's a withdrawal of movement from the world, not an increase.

"And pain, the free hand, changes almost nothing . . ." Dissolution and pain are supposed to accomplish freedom; you may be suffering, but at least you're no longer constrained. As, presumably, the shattered bowl is not constrained to a pure bowl. In fact, according to this poem, "pain, the free hand"—it's the hand released from obligation; it's the wife's hand no longer under the husband's domination; it's pain as the thing not subject to any control—"changes almost nothing." In this spectacle, in this household, changes nothing. And then "Like the winter wind, it leaves / settled forms in the snow. Known, identifiable— / except there are no uses for them." The idea being that the object is not destroyed; it is simply deprived of any function. So that it is an artifact. And the horror is its permanence, not its dissolution.

LONDON: Helen Vendler, writing about Robert Lowell, once said that what is most marvelous about his work is that there is no line that is unshadowed. In a sense that might be said here.

GLÜCK: I would like most things in the poem to admit of multiple meanings. But there should be occasionally something so absolutely clear and simple . . . It's like an opera. You can't listen to endless song. One of the ways I used white space—silence, whatever you want to call it—is as straightforward interruption. I think there have to be simple sentences from time to time. Sentences that are clear, communicative, and unshadowed.

June Jordan

JUNE JORDAN VISITED London's class in March 1979, just as she'd published *Things That I Do in the Dark,* a volume of new and selected poems, edited by Toni Morrison. She was forty-two at the time and had been writing for more than ten years, but *Things That I Do* marked the start of a series of mature works that would continue until her death in 2002. Born in 1936 in Harlem to Jamaican-immigrant parents, raised in the Bedford-Stuyvesant section of Brooklyn, and educated at Barnard College, Jordan wrote much more than poetry: she was a journalist, a playwright, an essayist, a children's book author, and a librettist. And she was an activist. Alice Walker, who became her lasting friend when Jordan visited Mississippi on assignment for the *New York Times Magazine* in 1969, said, "She is among the bravest of us, the most outraged. She feels for all. She is the universal poet." For Morrison, Jordan's was a "tireless activism coupled with and fueled by flawless art."

Jordan wrote extensively on issues of racial inequality and civil rights for a range of magazines, and those issues coursed through her poetry. To London's class that day Jordan brought several draft pages of a poem that could serve as her signature. Begun in August 1978 for a celebration at the United Nations, "Poem for South African Women" (at the time called "Poem in Honor of South African Women") is pure lyrical drive, euphony, almost incantation. "Rising like a marvelous pollen," she writes, "irreversible as light years / traveling to the open eye. . . . We are the ones we have been waiting for." Her discussion about the forging of that poem in its successive drafts reveals how seriously she took the process of composition, how deliberate her effort was to express in language what was "commensurately singular" and to "engage the audience in a chant with me."

When London asks about a poetry that is of the self but also of the world, Jordan says, "You are *in* the world. . . . When I write poetry my purpose is to express myself, about whatever it is, to as many other people as possible."

"Poem for South African Women"

PEARL LONDON: I'd like to start with a quotation from W. H. Auden in which he says, "Poets who want to change the world tend to be unreadable."

JUNE JORDAN: When I came into the room I saw that statement by Auden on the board, and I said, "What is that?" I thought it was appalling. I think, on the contrary, that when we talk about poets who want to change the world, what we find is work that is eminently accessible. Accessibility is a preeminent characteristic of work that lasts, work that therefore has the possibility of a world-changing impact.

Whether we're talking about Shakespeare, Tolstoy, Auden, or Robert Frost, if you are a poet who has some chance of being remembered—and having that kind of impact upon the world—you have to be accessible to people on the first reading or first hearing on some level.

That statement by Auden is characteristic of an elitist set of values that prevailed for a long time in the establishment in America and England. If

you thought that Robert Frost was writing poetry that you could understand immediately on reading it, the establishment was going to tell you
that "No, he's a really important poet, which means that you missed it. You
need somebody to teach you this poetry. You can't pick up this book and
say, 'This is a wonderful poem about snow.' That's just your naïveté."
That's an example of the kind of elitism that was dominant. I happen to
think that Robert Frost can be read on any level at all. Clearly, that's why he
wrote that way. But the establishment, in order to legitimize him, had to
say, "You think you understand him, but you really don't. This man is sick.
He's despairing."

That is not to say that you cannot be taught more about Tolstoy or
Shakespeare or Robert Frost. But I don't think it's incorrect if you pick up a
poem of Robert Frost and say "This is a poem about snow. I really like
this," and you're eleven years old. I think it's a tribute to his poetry that it is
accessible to an eleven-year-old who says, "I like this poem." But there is a
real difference between poetry since 1945 or 1950 and poetry that preceded
that time. Values have now become very much more democratic. A recognition of poetry as an oral art, for instance, as much as an art of any other
sort, has become entrenched.

The idea is you should try and reach as many people as possible on a
first hearing. Then when people read your work something else can happen and when they reread it something else can happen again. But they
should be able to understand it on first hearing in some useful way.

One of the reasons for that fundamental change was the era of the 1960s,
in which you had a tremendous activity in the black arts community to create poetry that would be immediately available to people on the street, people in rallies, and so on. And you had the anti–Vietnam War movement,
when all kinds of poets who previously had never written anything political
at all suddenly began writing about the war and writing poems to be read
at rallies where you would have hundreds of thousands of people. And this
was then followed by the women's movement, which also has been able to
command huge audiences for a given artist on a given evening.

That changed the expectation of who your audience was and how you would find it. You no longer had to imagine the reader, you actually stood in front of two hundred people or two hundred thousand people. And with that change the view of poetry as an oral art, an art which should be immediately available on some meaningful level, became the dominant view for most important writers today in poetry.

LONDON: When you are writing, how much of your approach to the poem comes out of your feeling for it as an auditory experience, and how much as a visual experience? Are you thinking in images? Or would you say there's a sense of musicality right from the beginning?

JORDAN: It varies from poem to poem. You will find as much imagery as in anyone else's poetry. But the difference is that I don't think about images; they're just there. That's the way I think. That's the way I see or feel things. And when people say, "That's an interesting symbol" or "That's an interesting image," I'll say, "What image?" In a way, I don't mean it as an image. That's just the way I see it.

But I do self-consciously think about the words as far as how precise the word is: Is this really what I mean? How does this sound? Because I am so interested in the music of our language, one thing that I have to guard against is excessive euphony. If I'm writing about something which is not a happy experience I have to be careful that it doesn't sound pretty. Other-wise the sound of the poem may lull people into a kind of aural satisfaction when I'm really trying to ask them to think.

STUDENT: I wanted to ask about your decision to give this book the title *Things That I Do in the Dark*. Was it in response to that sort of elitism? It sounds to me kind of like hype, but the poetry isn't. Perhaps it brings a lot of people to poetry that wouldn't ordinarily pick up the book?

JORDAN: Well, that's a line from the opening poem in the book, which is a statement of my purpose, my view of myself as a poet. I meant that these poems are things that I do in the dark. These are things that I do, not knowing exactly what I'm doing. That I am in the dark with the rest of you.

STUDENT: You don't feel that there's a double meaning—a sexual suggestion to the title?

JORDAN: No. And I was horrified by the cover. I felt cheapened immediately. Because that was not what I intended at all. I fought against that cover and lost. *Things That I Do in the Dark* is only the third time in all of publishing history that the selected poems of a black poet in this country have been published. The other two are Langston Hughes and Gwendolyn Brooks. So this was a very important event to me and to my people about being taken seriously. I thought the title should say—as it would for any white poet who was publishing twenty years of his or her work—*Selected Poems by June Jordan 1955 to 1975.* That's all they say about Auden. That's all they say about Adrienne Rich. Why do I have to have a title and a cover with a sexy picture on it? I thought it was ridiculous, I was very offended. I thought it was racist.

STUDENT: Why can't you control the cover? It's your book. They're your poems.

JORDAN: My editor for the book was Toni Morrison, and I said, "Toni, this is cheap, this is offensive." She said to me, "Poetry doesn't sell. The publishing house feels it's doing a poet a favor to publish poetry at all. And if you're not going to cooperate with what they think is making it marketable, then we're just not going to do it."

So you do have a choice. You have control. You can say, "OK, don't publish it."

LONDON: June Jordan, there are those poets who say that the direction now is toward the unconscious. I'm thinking of poets like Merwin or Mark Strand, and the phrase "Let's tap a vast otherness." You want first a communication at another level so that people will find you accessible to them. But some of these poets say, "We can't have it both ways. If I'm going to really tell the truth about my interior landscape, then I can't deal with an exterior landscape." How do we answer that?

JORDAN: Well, the poets you mentioned, Mark Strand and Merwin, represent a completely different value system. So I certainly could not defend them in any way. And I wouldn't presume to explain them, because I don't agree with them at all. You have an either/or formulation and anytime you do I think you have something that's fake. It's phony, superficial.

I don't believe in either/or anything. It's not about *either* you are trying to be in touch with yourself, *or* you are trying to be in touch with the world outside yourself. You are *in* the world. Those boundaries are ridiculous. I don't understand how I could do anything without the participation of my unconscious. How could you function? The unconscious is part of us just the way your liver is part of you. It's not something that you turn off.

LONDON: Certainly that beautiful poem "For Christopher" is very deeply inside of you.

JORDAN: I don't see things in terms of outside and inside—of inside myself or else relating to the world. I think of myself differently. When I write a poem I sit down in as much silence and solitude as possible. I want to be sure I can hear myself whether I'm talking about a railroad strike in Illinois or about anguish over a romantic relationship. I withdraw and create an environment in which I can be as listening and as quiet as possible. So that I can hear myself. Whatever it is that I am responding to I have to be in touch with myself. And that means all of myself, obviously. I think that we can safely assume that the subconscious realm is always in gear.

I do think that what Merwin is saying reflects a very real difference. And it's a valid difference, a difference of purpose. What he's saying, I think, is that his purpose is to express himself to himself. His purpose is not to express himself to other people.

LONDON: I think that puts it very, very accurately.

JORDAN: When I write poetry my purpose is to express myself, about whatever it is, to as many other people as possible.

STUDENT: In your poetry, do you feel that the line breaks are very important? And what kind of criteria do you use?

JORDAN: I think they're critical. And in much of the work I use line breaks instead of conventional punctuation. When I teach poetry to young people, unless they are writing in a form, I don't let them use commas or colons or anything else. So you have to accomplish what you want by your choice of words and your line breaks.

My idea is that in poetry everything should be accomplished by the word. Not the period. Not the question mark. The word. The syntax, the rhythm, and, as you say, the break. Emphasis should be upon the word. This is because of the emphasis on oral. When you read a poem aloud you don't say, "The boy laying in the evening, comma." If you mean comma after "evening" you have to do something with the word so that meaning has been communicated to the reader.

LONDON: Let's get into the new poem and the revisions, because that is really very exciting. The poem in honor of South African women.

JORDAN: One of the reasons I'm always happy to come here and visit Pearl London's class is because she likes to have poets talk about drafts of their work. And as a black poet I find that very often there is an assumption—there was even an assumption, as a matter of fact, in the *New York Times* review of my work, where he talked about "unconscious virtuosity"—there's an assumption that a black poet does not really work at the poetry. Doesn't know what she or he is really doing. I welcome this opportunity, so you'll know it is very conscious—whether it is virtuosity or not—it is very conscious and is very deliberate from one step to another. It doesn't come from nowhere. It comes from something that is not alien to people who are not black.

LONDON: What was the genesis of this poem?

JORDAN: I was asked to participate in a celebration of South African Women's Day at the United Nations last summer. There were going to be representatives and ambassadors there, and I thought I should write a poem for this occasion.

It commemorates a day—August 9, 1956—when forty thousand South African women and their children protested against the extension of apartheid in Pretoria, South Africa. They made bodily protest against this and risked their lives. It was an enormous event.

When the phone call came, I happened to be reading *Letters to a Young Poet* by Rilke. He's one of my favorite poets. In the passage I was reading, Rilke was talking to a young poet who was in despair because he thought that he had lost God. And Rilke was saying, "Lost God? How could you lose God? You *are* God. You cannot lose what you are." This was Rilke's point of view—you are what you are looking for. You need nothing outside yourself.

And when I went back to the passage that I had been reading just before the phone call, I thought, This is amazing. Because this is what I was thinking about the women in South Africa. This perception of yourself as the means of your own perfection, of your own change, of your own destiny. And I thought, That's what I want to say about the women of South Africa.

LONDON: That's wonderful.

JORDAN: So I used that quote at the beginning of the poem. And then I began, as you see on the first page, with "We see our shadows disappear." What I meant was that if you recognize that you are what you are looking for, then what is shadow, what is insubstantial, what is epiphenomenal disappears. The shadow is nothing.

In the first draft I had:

> Our shadows disappear as the feet of thousands
> by the tens of thousands pound the stolen earth
> into new dust that
> rising like a marvelous and ecstatic pollen
> will be fertilized even as the first
> woman and the first man (whispering
> imagination soft among the golden apple
> trees the golden . . .

This was changed right away. I didn't want to say "fertilized" as against pollen itself being fertile. Because that was departing from the major concept I wanted to convey, which is that *you are* what is happening, not something that is having something happen to it. Therefore it wasn't about being fertilized, but that you are fertile.

When I spoke about the golden trees—first it was "golden apples on golden trees"—I was reaching for a statement about a kind of paradise. But I didn't like that because obviously that's Robert Louis Stevenson "I would like to rise and go where the golden apples grow." It's been done.

In the *second* draft "the first / woman and the first man" has been changed to "the first woman." The reason for that is I'm trying to hone this to the concept. I'm not talking about South African men *and* women; I'm talking about South African women.

LONDON: Could you read that line to us?

JORDAN: Let me read the whole section [of the second draft].

[READS]

Our own shadows disappear as the feet of thousands
by the tens of thousands pound the stolen earth
into new dust that
rising like a marvelous pollen will be
fertile
even as the first woman whispering
imagination to the trees around her
made for righteous fruit from
such deliberate defense of life
as no other still
will claim inferior to any other safety
in the world

By this time "ecstatic" has come out of the fourth line. Not "rising like a marvelous and *ecstatic* pollen," but "rising like a marvelous pollen." I felt that was more than adequate. "Ecstatic" was hyperbolic. Then with "whispering / imagination to the trees around her" I took out "golden" and everything else. I felt I wanted to have this as elementary a scene as possible. It is the woman in her own circumstance. Never mind the color of the trees or what the tree is bearing. That's not the point of the poem. The poem is the woman in the circumstance.

Then I realized from "fertile" what I wanted to say. I spoke then, in the rest of that second draft, of the woman's elementary function, which is giving birth. That is, "made for righteous fruit," which is the capacity to give life. "From / such deliberate defense of life," which is one's own body or carrying a child. "As no other still / will claim inferior to any other safety / in the world," which says there is no other safety in the world that is comparable to the safety of the embryo—being carried by a mother. That was another way of talking about the holiness of what you embody, which is the concept of the poem.

LONDON: One of the things that we talk a great deal about in this class is Roethke, "Anchor the abstraction," and Pound, "Go in fear of the abstract." And then we come to [your] "deliberate defense of life." When and where do you feel it's valid to put in a phrase that moves us into a generality like that?

JORDAN: I don't see this as vague here, because it clarifies "righteous fruit" in the previous line. It is explaining that this function of carrying life within oneself is a deliberate defense of life.

LONDON: So it's really very precise in that context.

JORDAN: I'm interpreting that phenomenon. And notice that when I said, "such deliberate defense of life" there are two kinds of alliteration going on. Obviously the *d*'s but also the *l* from "-liberate" to "life." And I did that very deliberately because when you use *l*'s in alliteration it helps you to glide through. So if it's a concept that may be a little difficult, the sound will carry you.

In the [later] line "of all peaceable and loving amplitude" the reason I use the word "amplitude" is because almost anytime you use a word that ends with a *d* sound you slow up everything. Like "dredge," "drudge." I used the word "amplitude" very deliberately because I wanted people to slow down there, I wanted to really slow down and have the sense of something colossal happening.

LONDON: It is astounding to see the amount of blood, sweat, and tears that goes into a poem that reads as though it were given.

JORDAN: We were speaking about euphony at the beginning. In the second stanza . . . third line from the bottom. There is the line, "sound a certainly unbounded heat." Now that's very deliberately euphonious. What I was talking about there was something I meant to say was positive.

Then in the next line I changed "unbounded heat" to a "baptismal smoke," so that you have this sibilance. That clustering of *s* sounds is not pleasant and suggests the changing function of the heat to the fire in the next line. That is an example of a place where I'm trying to control the use of sound so that it is echoing the sense.

LONDON: In terms of time, these seven draft pages represent what? A week? Two days and nights? Three months?

JORDAN: This was about three days and nights of constant revision. Just revising, revising. Think about it, go on walks, think about it, think about it.

I just want to bring out a couple things before I read the end of it. All the way through I kept saying "the stolen land." I realized just before I was ready to finish it that that was out of place. Since I'm saying that the South African women are fertile, what I should say about the land is not that it's stolen but that it is fallow. The fertile women on the fallow land. That was

high as the stars so far unseen
will nevertheless hurl into the ~~~~ so
a moving force ~~~~~~~~~~
~~~~~
irresistible as light years
traveling ~ the open
eye

Because these nameless
holy multitudes ~~~~ victims ~~~~
nore
And ~~~ who ~~~ will join this standing up
~~~~~~~~~~~~~~~~~~~~~~~~~~~~~~
mean the ones we have
up and ~~~~ you who stood so ~~~~
We are the ones we have been waiting for
we are the body and the glow

much more to the point. It was no longer complicated by the concept of stolen, which suggests a third party.

If you look at other lines such as "high as the stars so far and unseen" on page 6 or "because these nameless holy multitudes, these victims / nevermore" or "these nameless women and our children" and "you who had stood so patiently." All of those are eliminated because they are not precise, they are hackneyed.

The level of language is, in comparison to the rest of the poem, like journalism. "Nameless multitudes." You can read that in the *New York Times*. I'm trying to say something else. I'm trying to say something very,

Poem In Honor of South African Women

   (in particular commemoration of the 40,000
   women and their children who, August 9, 1956,
   presented themselves in bodily protest
   at the Capitol of Apartheid)

Our own shadows disappear as the feet of thousands
by the tens of thousands pound the fallow land
into new dust that
rising like a marvellous pollen will be
fertile
even as the first woman whispering
imagination to the trees around her made
for righteous fruit
from such deliberate defense of life
as no other still
will claim inferior to any other safety
in the world

The whispers too they
intimate to the inmost ear of every spirit
now aroused they
carousing in ferocious affirmation
of all peaceable and loving amplitude
sound a certainly unbounded heat
from a baptismal smoke where yes
there will be fire

And the babies cease alarm as mothers
raising arms
and heart high as the stars so far unseen
~~will~~ nevertheless hurl into the universe
a moving force
irreversible as light years
traveling to the open
eye

And who will join this standing up
and the ones who stood without sweet company
will sing and sing
back into the mountains and
if necessary
even under the sea

WE ARE THE ONES WE HAVE BEEN WAITING FOR
WE ARE THE ONES WE HAVE BEEN WAITING FOR
WE ARE THE ONES WE HAVE BEEN WAITING FOR

DRAFT TYPESCRIPT OF JUNE JORDAN'S "POEM IN HONOR OF SOUTH AFRICAN WOMEN" very precisely about a very delicate process, a very delicate phenomenon. All of those things that you see crossed out on pages 5 and 6 were eliminated for that reason. What I was talking about was something I had learned for the first time. So I should express it in language that was commensurately singular.

LONDON: One small question. Over and over again my students hear me say, "Please, no capital letters." If the word has enough meaning it will speak for itself, you don't have to rely on typography. What about three lines [in the typescript draft, at the end] in capital letters? Do we need them?

JORDAN: Well, I don't know. I'm not decided about it, as a matter of fact. On the occasion that I read it at the United Nations, I wrote it this way because I wanted to be sure to remember to try to engage the audience in a chant with me.

LONDON: Aha.

JORDAN: And that's what I did do at the United Nations. I said it and then I changed it from the rhythm of the line as it occurs at the end of the poem to the chant. And it was really beautiful to me. There were men and women in the audience so you had the full sound of people I didn't know saying, "We are the ones we have been waiting for."

LONDON: Is there a central impulse, a central concern, that seems to move and order and knit all of these poems together? Is there an impulse that binds?
     I'm going to tell you what you said when I asked you that question last time, because I've always remembered it. You said, "Well, I think it once was hostility. But my hostilities are more positive now." And I thought that was a lovely answer. Would you change it?

JORDAN: I'm amazed that I said that. My God. I don't know. Today I would guess it's about knowing something. Something I wanted to know—urgently. And I want to know it in a way that other people will know it, too.

LONDON: Arriving at truths.

JORDAN: Yeah. For me, the writing of a poem is, among other things, a process of discovery. I do always have a premise. There's something I want to say. Here, for example, I thought I knew what I wanted to say, but the poem was a discovery. I didn't know the poem. I wanted to know it. It was urgent. I was moving on a sense of urgency. There's nothing hostile in this.

LONDON: No, not at all. It's very embracing.

STUDENT: In your introductory remarks you said that the establishment doesn't take black poets seriously.

JORDAN: I think Adrienne Rich is one of the very few well-known white poets who freely acknowledges her debt to black poetry. Black poetry has had enormous impact on the art of poetry in this country. Just as jazz has had an incredible impact on mainstream culture.

What is distinctive to black poetry is the emphasis on sound, emphasis on oral tradition, emphasis on accessibility, and spoken language. And a lot of people have learned from that and have been strengthened in their own work by their interest in spoken language as a legitimate part of literature—in fact, perhaps the most legitimate language to be used in a poem.

James Merrill

SHORTLY BEFORE HIS drive down to New York from his house in Stonington, Connecticut, on May 16, 1979, James Merrill wrote to Pearl London: "I've unearthed these drafts. Perhaps they give rise to a discussion. Xerox them if you like." The annotated typescript pages belonged to *Mirabell: Books of Number,* which had just won poetry's National Book Award (his second). It came to serve as the middle installment of a trilogy published three years later as *The Changing Light at Sandover.*

Merrill, whose father, Charles, cofounded Merrill Lynch, was raised in

Manhattan and on Long Island. At just sixteen he wrote his first book, a precociously accomplished collection of poetry, prose, essays, and translations. Through the first decades of his career Merrill wrote exquisitely poised and elegant formal verse. By contrast, *The Changing Light at Sandover* is sprawling, a nearly six-hundred-page visionary epic about experiments with his companion, David Jackson, and a Ouija-board séance, with appearances (watch for them) by the late W. H. Auden, Mirabell the peacock, bats, a deceased friend, and others. "The degree to which his trilogy is open-ended, indefinite, and undetermined should not be understated," writes Robert Polito in his reader's guide to the work.

London, asking Merrill to take her through these early drafts, keeps raising the question of an autobiographical "I," the maneuvering of which has proven to be one of the distinguishing marks of his poetry. "Even the first line of 'Stopping By Woods' is phrased backwards so that it doesn't begin with the first-person pronoun," Merrill tells her. The Ouija board, "in however clumsy or absurd a way," he has said, enables him to get beyond the self. "Or if it's still yourself you're drawing on, then that self is much stronger and freer and more farseeing than the one you thought you knew."

Merrill won the Bollingen Prize for *Braving the Elements* (1972), the Pulitzer Prize for *Divine Comedies* (1976), and the National Book Critics Circle Award for *The Changing Light at Sandover* (1982). "At his best," writes August Kleinzahler, "in a handful of poems where he's most restrained and the emotional core of the work, however camouflaged or subdued, is most intense—Merrill has few peers. . . . If one were to bypass his work, one would be missing some of the finest poems written in English in the middle of last century." James Merrill died in 1995.

———

Mirabell: Books of Number

PEARL LONDON: Now we've all agreed, reading all of your poems these past weeks, that the center of gravity in your work is autobiography. But in the first books the word "I" rarely occurs. We find "we" rather than "I" as the characteristic pronoun.

JAMES MERRILL: I suppose that my sense of pronouns when I began to write, by the age of nineteen or twenty, had been shaped by reading Rilke's shorter poems. He never says "I," but in the *Duino Elegies* he seems to invite his readers into a community of shared suffering, or shared sensitivity. I couldn't wait to accept the invitation. I loved the feeling I got from those first-person plurals, as if one were being consoled and elevated at the same time.

We're all full of ourselves at the age of nineteen, but I don't think we have what you'd call a self, or what *I* would call a self from the perspective of thirty-odd years later. "I" seemed embarrassing to say. Then I think one saw the possibilities, perhaps through Elizabeth Bishop, where "I" could be used with the greatest self-deprecation, humor, a sort of rueful sense of "Well, yes, I did this, but you know what to expect of *me.*"

LONDON: David Kalstone said that James Merrill likes to use the first person "but with a veil drawn." Could you comment on that veil?

MERRILL: Well, I am so sick of seeing poems that begin "I sit down" or "I open a book." It's not the way one ever talks. You know, you say, "I *sat* down" or "I am sitting down." Anything that will shelter the glare of that strong present verb. Even the first line of "Stopping by Woods" is phrased backwards so that it doesn't begin with the first-person pronoun. "Whose woods these are I think I know." By then he's got you, because everything has been put in its proper order in that line.

LONDON: Somewhere you said that you don't really have to state what you're feeling in a poem—the landscape will rule in the house, be reflectors.

MERRILL: *That's* the subterfuge, exactly. It's the details of your setting, your actions—they shed a great deal of light and you don't really have to be present registering it all and feeling it. I think this is something we learn more swiftly from prose fiction than we do from most poetry, where there is still the sense that one must strike overt chords of feeling and resonance and show that your emotions are involved through saying so.

LONDON: Would you say that, in the later poems, you're still using the landscape as reflector, because there's so much more "I" now in "The Book of Ephraim." "I" is all over the place.

MERRILL: But there, you see, it's not the same thing as autobiography because I have an almost incredible story to tell. I mean, many readers are not going to believe in the experience of séances and transcripts and bats and all of that—and it did happen—but it must really be made to seem as if it happened on the page. So [I use] many humble details and trivial glimpses of household life to reassure you that there is a world in which these other things are going on. . . . The autobiography makes this more plausible.

LONDON: Like the bats on the wallpaper at Stonington.

MERRILL: Yes, yes.

STUDENT: I've been sort of overwhelmed by *Mirabell,* particularly that you sustained the poem for over a hundred pages. I was just wondering from the standpoint of a writer how you managed to keep so alert through the whole thing. I have trouble with a poem that runs two pages.

MERRILL: Yes, I know just what you mean. Well, of course a lot of the actual transcripts [of the séances] sustain it—nearly everything in capital letters has been, if at all, only slightly changed. Having transcripts as the core of the book, my problem was to break them up, to cut whenever possible . . . to try to bring the level of *lived* experience in the book up to the level of the transcripts. To make a kind of balance and therefore a kind of suspense. Because one is eager to know what the bat is going to say, or verifiable things like David Jackson's operation. They keep you going on the most trivial narrative level. But you may be the rare reader—others might throw the book across the room.

LONDON: We looked last week at "Lorelei" and "In Nine Sleep Valley"— the use of metaphor, particularly of the word "stones." Someone said that for James Merrill [the idea of] creativity is represented by precious gems and crystal prisms and geological rock. In "Lorelei" the marvelous use of the word "strands," as in the "stones stranding you," and the ambiguity of meaning.

MERRILL: The stones in "Lorelei" are big and opaque, but it would work for any kind of stone. I think what moves me about these things is the sense of compression and the tremendous forces that have made some-thing as small and *purged* as a crystal is. Purity and symmetry. And one sees how magical they must have been to early people. Clytemnestra comes out early explaining to Elektra, she says, "I'm hung with jewels, every stone has a power." . . . The idea that this thing would be exerting some influence upon you . . . I mean, I don't believe any of that, but I'm very *moved* by it and by thinking of it.

STUDENT: Every time I write the word "stone" I want to throw it out of the poem because I feel I don't know the particulars.

MERRILL: Exactly, [many poets] never describe the stone. You have no idea what it's like. It's just named as a sort of numinous word. I think even light should be described. It's not enough simply to invoke it. If you can't do any better, simply say it's the kind of light that van Gogh uses, some-thing you can verify when you're reading about it.

LONDON: Let's look at the texts themselves in *Mirabell: Books of Number* and the enormous changes between the final copy and the earlier drafts. And you can see what processes of thought went into the vision and revi-sion. This [page 1 of the draft, beginning "For when they landed"] of course is early in *Mirabell* where David Jackson's parents, Matt and Mary, arrive from California and they are put up in a flat and they are ill and they are old. . . .

MERRILL: I'm not usually this prodigal with the amount I write. I try to put it to use. But what I saw here—I wanted to start in on *Mirabell* and I wanted an opening that would set a human context to take up the thread of the inhuman voices [from the séances] and I had no idea what my pro-portions were going to be—or how long this opening section needed to be—and by the time I got through writing these pages I saw that it was completely out of scale. That this was not a poem about old Mr. and Mrs.

```
For when they landed in the famous Greek
Lucidity, all was confusion, your mother frozen
In her wheelchair by a jet's departing shriek,
And "Well, well, look who's here!" your father yapping
As if you had lost your mind, who never flew,
And landed in L.A. out of the blue--

Back there where the growth had, week by week,
Reached the brain, so nothing further grew.
Just more old people up and down the street,
Deaf as stones. No running feet, no laughter,
No childhood anywhere, unless on television
Or in the looking-glass their terminal one
Peered back from, lit by reason's fading beams.
Or photographs. That cracked and dogeared cherub
Was--Junior? No. Junior was...wasn't here...
Was you, was David! Eyes wild, wattles quaking,
The world an ax-flash. "That's right, Mary dear"
--Ida's voice, the mild black mountain
Who cleaned and coped and comforted by day--
Whereupon, with any luck, your mother smiled.
```

Jackson, that they must be used as a kind of springboard into my real subject. Much as I like a lot of this—liked it when I was writing it—it seemed to me that if I was going to treat them in such detail, the whole *Mirabell* book would have been eight hundred pages long.

LONDON: I found this [next] part tremendously interesting . . .

MERRILL: Yes, well, I think this probably came at the point when I saw what I wanted to emphasize.

LONDON: The [draft] section begins, "Oh, there was plenty to do. Teeth to be pulled." Ending in "A scent of panic and incontinence."

MERRILL: And that's at the bottom of page 5 in [the published] *Mirabell*.

Time for stupor, fear, incontinence
To fill the house. For such compulsory
Treats, then, as a farewell, original-cast
Restaging of the Play that, seasons past,
Inaugurated, as it had and would
Countless other Western theatres

There's a line break [in the draft], "compulsory / pleasure." Even here I've begun to see that I wanted the line break after "compulsory." And [in the

```
                    Oh there was plenty to do. Teeth to be pulled.
                    A bad skin cancer on the cheek. And iron
                    Corset fitted for the old man's back.
                    After the doctor, some compulsory/pleasure.
Pleasure, a line, in  Ice cream by the sea, your mother pleading
                    To be left in the car--which had acquired by now
                    A scent of panic and incontinence.

                    At 5 o'clock you'd go to dine with them.
                    The bread was wrong. They wanted moist white slices.
                    He spat out his first taste of moussaká.
                    We settled for purées, or a boiled egg,
                    Or sweet creamed baby corn out of a can.
                    You poured the grape juice from a wine bottle.
                    "What about me," Georgía cried, "I'll starve!"

                    Rushing forward with a café chair
                    For the tottering scarecrow all
                    Bandaged from yesterday's, from last week's fall,
                    The waiter seemed to genuinely care.

                    Or the policeman, seeing a cross crone
                    Being wheedled from your car
                    Outside the doctor's--"Kyrie, leave it here,
                    I'll watch it"--in a strict no-parking zone!

                    People, to your amazement, understood,
                    Viewed you with respect for once:
                    Worker in a universe of sons
                    Playing your small part in the common good.
```

published version] the "incontinence" fills the house, not [as in the draft] the car, transferred to simplify as much as possible. But excuse me, let me say something.

LONDON: Yes, please do.

MERRILL: You've noticed that on this [draft] page, the two stanzas [beginning "Oh there was plenty to do"] together, unrhymed, make up a fourteen-line unit. The three quatrains that follow at the end of the page [beginning "Rushing forward with a café chair"] are one of my favorite tricks, to move from the relatively amorphous level of blank verse to something relatively strict, like in music an allegro that follows a kind of toccata, a free-form improvisation.

But the reason this doesn't stay in [the book] is that it's good for me to end a poem this way—but it creates too much of a stasis in the middle of something that's going on. It can end, it can bring to a close a narrative section, just as the sonnet about Avebury brings the first book of *Mirabell* to a close. It's a matter by and large of winding up a subject [but here] in fact I've barely begun. It's inappropriate to have those lines here.

LONDON: The next page [draft] begins "How to keep them both in sight." We compare that with the final book, page 6, in *Mirabell*.

[READS]

> [. . .] Here they were,
> Old Matt and Mary, for their graybeard boy
> Still to . . . keep together? keep apart?
> Problem now scalding clear as a hot spring,
> Now ancient, blurred, a tatter of papyrus.
> Nature, still the prompter, overcomes
> (While a robust Greek nurse looks on enthralled)
> Their stage-fright: "Get your fucking hands off Mother!"

"My wife, goddamit!"—poor old eyes ablaze,
Old claws brushed from the son's shirt like crumbs.

There's this tremendously violent explosion between David Jackson and his father over his mother, that truly Oedipal kind of conflict. There are changes you've made in the final text, where here " 'God dammit, she's my wife!' / 'Well, she's my mother!' " becomes " 'Get your fucking hands off Mother!' / 'My wife, goddamit!' " A great deal more violent in its language than it was in this earlier draft.

MERRILL: I know, it's very plaintive, that "Well, she's my mother." That sounds, not . . .

LONDON: Did you feel the intensities just weren't enough in the earlier draft?

MERRILL: I suppose, I can't think what went into my head at that point, but I changed it very promptly after this. Toward the end of that draft page, the "baby boy / In his yellow sunsuit and high shoe" and "The little herm between his legs . . . Cupid on tombstone," this came out of a book Jung and somebody else wrote about the divine child and a kind of infant Dionysus figure, explaining why these children often appeared on tombstones or on steles for the dead. I can't remember it now, but clearly there was a kind of infant Apollo behind the phrase "the yellow sunsuit."

And I decided that that was a very confusing thing to put in a poem, because the child here in question is David Jackson as a child, as remembered by his dotty mother. In a poem that deals with superhuman powers, you would be very ill advised to identify, even slightly, a human figure with a god. I didn't want any of those overtones because the realm of the gods was something that we would be approaching, at least that would be the illusion. Towards the end, you can perfectly well admit that God works within us, but for telling the story the separation has to be absolute and gradually coming together.

How to keep them both in sight
Without his coming near...   Or giving her "a good poke" with his
          "Now Dad, you stay away from her"   cane.
Furious blue eyes popped from his head,
Two brown spotted claws went for your throat,
"God dammit, she's my wife!"
                    "Well, she's my mother!"

The problem was hot and fresh as a sulphur spring,   *scalding*
Old and frail as a tatter of papyrus.
The country woman who was meant to cope
Sat smiling like a sphinx, crocheting horrors.

She (Mary looked pleased to be fought over.)   *children kissing her*
    A cactus watered after years, in bloom.

The snapshots in her hand, she remembers...

And with her dies the truth borne witness to
By sepia gradations without hue:
A heavy towhead kneehigh baby boy
In his yellow sunsuit and high shoe
So soon to be outgrown and dipped in gilt.

The little herm between his legs
                    cupped in his hand, shrank back.

                                        the egg-and-dart
Cupid on tombstone, child as beginning and end

"Send them to me, I will dispose of them"

He watched the archimandrite on TV
Celebrating Easter noiselessly
—Or uttering the holy baseball scores
Dubbed from the US Forces Radio.

[And on the subject of a final change] This page corresponds to the first two pages of book 3 in *Mirabell*.

[READS PUBLISHED VERSION]

SHALL WE RESUME? WE SPOKE OF THE BLACK HOLES & MUST AGAIN
USE METAPHOR
    "Vulgar" though it is, and "negative"?
      HOW ELSE DESCRIBE (WITHOUT THE FORMULAS
EVEN WE LACK) WHAT IS TO US A RIDDLE? IMAGINE
A WORLD WITHOUT LIGHT A LEWIS CARROLL WORLD THAT KEEPS PACE
WITH OURS A WORLD WHERE WHITE IS BLACK OF STILLNESS IN THE
    PLACE
OF SUCKING WINDS MORTALITY? DESIRE? WE FIND NO TRACE
    DJ: You *find*? You sound as if you'd been there.
    JM: Where Mind is Matter, and Time Space . . .
IS IT THE ORIGINAL? ARE WE ITS CARBON COPY?
OR: ARE WE IN THE PRESENCE OF A BLACK TWIN PARADISE
    Wherein, accordingly, you would appear
    White-winged, your own cool opposites—oh dear!

    For the cup goes reeling to the Board's brink—
    AH MES ENFANTS HE FELL BACK AS IF STRUCK
    Had you been listening? NO AN EVER LOUDER
    RUSTLING OF THEIR 28 WINGS DROWNED OUT

    Wystan (as if deafened): WHAT WHAT WHAT

    Violent crosscurrents. Then: MES CHERS
    MAY I? YR OLD SLAVE Ephraim! WE WILL PAUSE
    A MOMENT POOR DJ YR GHOSTS DISTRESSED U?

The problem here to be solved was to find some way of making it easy for readers to see who was talking. It had not occurred to me clearly at the

```
SHALL WE RESUME? WE SPOKE OF THE BLACK HOLES
+ MUST AGAIN/RESORT TO METAPHOR
"Vulgar" though it be, and "negative"?
BUT NECESSARY  HOW CAN WE WITHOUT
ENDLESS FORMULAS/DESCRIBE WHAT IS
EVEN TO US A MYSTERY? IMAGINE
A LIGHTLESS LEWIS CARROLL WORLD THAT KEEPS
PACE WITH OURS  A WORLD WHERE WHITE IS BLACK
And spirit matter? WHERE WE FIND NO TRACE
OF MORTALITY  You "find"? You've been there?
STILLNESS IN THE PLACE OF SUCKING WIND
How do you know this? EDUCATED GUESSES
IMAGINE THEN THE EXISTENCE OF A TWIN
PARADISE A BLACK ONE  In which you
Would accordingly be visible,
Your own cool opposite, with great white wings

--Oh dear! (for the cup has reeled to the board's edge)
MES ENFANTS HE FELL BACK AS IF STRUCK
Had you been listening? NO  AN EVER LOUDER
RUSTLING OF THEIR WINGS DROWNED OUT
EVERYTHING[U SAID OR HE PROPOSED)
AFTER THE WORD MYSTERY[WE DID NOT]

Wystan (in amazement): WHAT WHAT WHAT

Violent crosscurrents; then. an old MES CHERS
Familiar voice: MES CHERS  Ephraim, it's you?
Who...?                        ! WE WILL PAUSE
A MOMENT  POOR DJ  YE GHOSTS DISTURBED U
```

R we iN
CARIBoN CoPY?

time when I was making this very draft to use a smaller left hand margin.
A simple glance [at the published page, unlike the draft, and] you understand that this will be Mirabell or one of the bats talking, you know you
will be looking for a fourteen-syllable line, and there's no possible way of
confusing this with Auden's voice or Maria's or of course our own narrative voices [depicted] in lowercase.

This wouldn't be the kind of problem that comes up in *everybody's*
work. But it was the greatest relief to me, I can tell you, when I thought of
this simple way. It was the margin I resisted most, moving it out—I somehow couldn't bear it, thought it was a transgression, to change the margins. And then, typing it up, I got used to it.

JAMES MERRILL   95

LONDON: In this whole part of *Mirabell,* one of the questions that comes to mind is that in the earlier poems, "An Urban Convalescence" and oh so many of them, it's as if you say, "One does not really need to state one's feelings, it is enough to feel and feel sensitively and the room will echo back the landscape," and so forth. Yet when you come to this whole part of *Mirabell* with Auden, a lot of it *is* statement, as it is indeed with Wallace Stevens. How do you reconcile this?

MERRILL: Well, the subject is the lessons we are being given. This is a dramatically dogmatic poem.

LONDON: But how did this form and shape come to a writer like yourself who says, "One doesn't need to state."

MERRILL: It probably came as punishment. [*Laughter*]

Marilyn Hacker

IN APRIL 1980, Marilyn Hacker had published only two books of poetry, *Presentation Piece* (1974), which won the National Book Award, and *Separations* (1976). Praised for reviving—and reinventing—traditional lyric forms like the sonnet and villanelle, she can be heard in this early conversation with Pearl London already disavowing credit for launching a revival. "My reason for using [old forms] is really, selfishly, pleasure; it's the same reason I like to bike downhill. Or, in another way, the same kind of challenge as doing three extra laps in the swimming pool more than I did yesterday. It is both a challenge and I think a constant reminder of the element of poetry which is craft, making something out of language." Poet Jan Heller Levi has said of Hacker that "no one has done more, particularly in the last decade of formalism, to demonstrate that form has nothing to do with formula."

Born in 1942 in the Bronx, New York, Marilyn Hacker graduated from the Bronx High School of Science and, at age fifteen, entered New York University. After working in New York and London—and working through a marriage that ultimately didn't last—she published her first book at age thirty-one. She has edited literary magazines, translated numerous works, and taught at City College and CUNY Graduate Center. Her many books of poetry include *Taking Notice* (1980), which contains the poem she brought to London's class (republished as the title poem to *The Hang-Glider's Daughter: New and Selected Poems,* 1991), and *Winter Numbers: Poems* (1995), which concerns the loss of friends to AIDS and breast cancer.

J. D. McClatchy has written that Hacker "dredges her romantic impulse with irony, and her candid, self-knowing, generous manner deals effectively with both the lesbian affairs she recounts and the pointed feminist attitude she maintains." In 2008, Marilyn Hacker was elected a chancellor of the Academy of American Poets. She divides her time between New York City and Paris.

"The Hang-Glider's Daughter"

LONDON: Marilyn Hacker's work, more than any almost, is immensely the work of communication about the human condition. You know, Matthew Arnold says that loneliness is the inescapable human condition. And I think that these poems, dealing as they do with loneliness, with separation, with loss, with absence, often appear in very complex forms because it's not always a simple feeling or situation. It seems to me that there the burden of communication is borne by this work almost more than any other.

We have been asking, since you are so able to wrench the line out of regularity, to take traditional form and deal with it so imaginatively and innovatively, why have you left it behind and gone into this entirely other voice in "The Hang-Glider's Daughter"?

MARILYN HACKER: Actually, if you notice, "The Hang-Glider's Daughter" is written in stanzas which are in fact sonnets. I certainly don't feel bound by forms or bound to them or want to write out of them; but as it happens that particular poem uses the sonnet as a stanza form instead of as a chapter or paragraph form. They're Petrarchan sonnets with two quatrains and three couplets.

LONDON: Then they're marvelously innovative sonnets. I hadn't realized. And yet, when we look at the poem, the texture is profoundly contemporary. In what way do you feel that it's necessary to use the sonnet form? Why not write it all in free verse?

HACKER: Very simply—I enjoy doing it. My reason for using them is really, selfishly, pleasure; it's the same reason I like to bike downhill. Or, in another way, the same kind of challenge as doing three extra laps in the swimming pool more than I did yesterday. It is both a challenge and I think a constant reminder of the element of poetry which is craft, making something out of language. I'm certainly not saying that cannot be done *outside* of traditional forms. I happen to enjoy the interplay that happens between form and content, if you will, when there is not only the question of expounding a particular idea or recounting a particular incident or analyzing and immersing oneself in a particular emotion, but also the question of "How am I going to do this with these words?" Isn't that the challenge in writing poetry anyway? It becomes a particular challenge when there is not only the story I want to tell but also the shape I've given myself to tell it in.

LONDON: Now, in "The Hang-Glider's Daughter"—it was just handed out this morning—I'd like very much to look at that contrast, that tension that's created between the vocabulary and the imagery and the form. Would you read it to us?

HACKER: The only thing I'd like to say about it first, which is probably obvious from the poem—well, not in intimate detail—but the speaker of the poem is a sixteen-year-old girl who is half French and half American and lives in France. This is the hang-glider's daughter speaking:

My forty-year-old father learned to fly.
Bat-winged, with a magic marble fear
keeping his toast down, he walks off a sheer
shaved cliff into the morning. On Sunday
mornings he comes for us. Liane and I
feed the baby and Mario, wash up, clear
the kitchen mess. Maman is never there;
that is the morning she and Joseph try
to tell the other pickers how the Word
can save them. Liane gets me good and mad
changing her outfit sixteen times, while I
have to change the baby. All the way
up the hill road she practices on him, flirt-
ing like she does at school. My back teeth hurt

from chewing Pepper Gum on the bad side.
She's three years younger. I'm three years behind.
Did he *mean* that? Shift the gum. Did I remind
Mario, if the baby cries, he needs
burping? I can stretch out on the back seat.
The olive terraces stacked in the sunshine
are shallow stairs a giant child could climb.
My hiking shoes look giant on my feet.
Maman says "a missed boy." What do I miss?
I wonder what the word in English is
for that. Funny, that we should have been born
somewhere we wouldn't even understand
the language now. I was already three
when we left. If someone hypnotized me

would I talk English like a three-year-old?
The bright road twists up; bumpily we shift
gears, breathe deep. In the front pouch of my sweat-
shirt, I've still got my two best marbles. Rolled
in thumb and finger, they click, points gained, told
beads. Not for Joseph's church. If I forgot
French, too, who would I be inside my head?
My hands remember better: how to hold
my penknife to strip branches, where to crack
eggs on a bowl rim, how to pile a block
tower—when I was little—high as my nose.
Could I, still? The box of blocks is Mario's
now. My knee's cramped. I wish that I could walk
to Dad's house, or that I was up front, talk-

ing to him. How does he feel, suddenly slung
from brilliant nylon, levering onto air
currents like a thinking hawk? I'd be scared.
I'd be so scared I can't think it. Maybe a long
slope on my skateboard's like that. Climbing
isn't scary: no time. The air's fizzy, you're careful what rock you hang your weight from, and where
your toes wedge. My calves ache, after, ribs sting,
but I'm good for something. What I like high
is mountains. I'll go up the hill behind
Dad's house this afternoon. I'll pick Liane
flowers. Nahh, we'll be leafing magazines
for school clothes on the sunporch after lunch.
I like those purple bell-spikes. My cleats crunch

the crumble; I stretch to the ledge and pull
out the whole rooted stalk. Sometimes there's twelve

bells, purple as—purple as nothing else
except a flower, ugly and beautiful
at once. Across my face come the two smells:
grandmother's linen-chest, spice-sweet petals
and wet dirt clinging, half metal, half metal,
all raw. Between them, I smell myself,
sweaty from climbing, but it's a woman's
sweat. I had one of the moon dreams again.
I stood on the flyover facing purple
sea, head up, while a house-huge full moon hurtled
toward me; then it was me flying, feet still
on the road. We're here, on top of the hill.

LONDON: Absolutely marvelous poem. About the underlying metaphor, to what extent should we read the hang-glider as a contemporary person who moves off a precipice and into space? The artist or the writer, or whatever you want.

HACKER: First of all, I would like the poem to be taken literally as a piece of fiction, "spoken" by a fictionally real adolescent speaking about her life, her father, her sister, and her half brothers: to take the facts from that as one would take them in a short story. I think for a poem to be coherent, like any other piece of writing, it's got to exist on that level first of all and only after that on the level of connotations in other dimensions, other ramifications.

LONDON: "Levering onto air / currents like a thinking hawk." That "thinking hawk . . ."

HACKER: Of course, that's just exactly what hang-gliders do. That is, just in the same way that hawks—or any other kind of soaring rather than flapping bird—flies by making use of air currents, being able to sense when a thermal is going up and how far it's going up and riding them.

LONDON: Or an artist. And "What I like high / is mountains" and then you move in from there—in this Petrarchan sonnet context we have this extraordinary thing of an entirely other vocabulary—"the air's fizzy." "What I like high / is mountains. I'll go up the hill behind / Dad's house" and then come to "Nahh," which is so colloquial. Was that really done as a kind of antidote to the form, or did the form provide limits?

HACKER: The form provided useful limits in creating what could also be the believable interior monologue of an adolescent. I think one of the things that the form did was assist in the compression, of not letting it ramble the way, in fact, an adolescent would.

LONDON: That business of giving it order . . . the artist imposing order . . .

HACKER: Yes. As far as the metaphorical level of the poem is concerned, I think there is a reason why the poem is called "The Hang-Glider's Daughter" and not "The Hang-Glider." When I sat down to write the poem it was the young girl and what she might be thinking [that] I imagined. It was something I wanted to write about. I don't think that symbols or metaphors can be injected into a poem like pints of fresh blood; they have to grow organically out of the subject.

LONDON: Not adornments on that Christmas tree . . .

HACKER: There's a difference between the rather untrammeled figure of the mature man, the forty-year-old father who learned to fly and who comes and collects his two daughters every Sunday afternoon, and the chores and worries and details of ordinary life that quite naturally concern the girl, from having to take care of her younger siblings, worrying about what's thought about her. A "missed boy" is a translation—the word for "tomboy" in French is *un garçon manqué*—which means, exactly, "a missed boy."

But I suppose the hang-glider's daughter and the hang-glider are, just in that limited sense, metaphors for where the woman artist must start out. Which is not jumping off the top of the mountain—or if it is jumping off the top of the mountain, [first] it's rather laboriously climbing one. With all of the paraphernalia of ordinary life as gear. But sometimes the paraphernalia of ordinary life prevent one from getting up the mountain. The hang-glider may be the artist, but the hang-glider's daughter is also the artist . . . someone looking with a comparatively unjaundiced eye at her aspirations and what stands in the way—or, rather, what she has to include in them.

LONDON: In terms of the rhythms that you use, you know Lowell says somewhere that "I'm sure that rhythm is the poet himself." But here is this sixteen-year-old child . . . you have these marvelous caesuras all over, these wonderful line breaks. Is that how you rescue her from orthodox form? Because it is *her* own rhythm.

HACKER: That's the part that is difficult to talk about—not because it's sacred but because it's something that comes out of writing a line, then saying, No, that's wrong, crossing three words out, putting in another one, and thinking, Well, no, it ought to break here. I think the rhythm is occasionally useful for when the poem has got to make a bald statement in the midst of it. For example, the lines: "Maman says 'a missed boy.' What do I miss?" or "My forty-year-old father learned to fly." In those cases the iambic pentameter line stands on its own and, I would hope, inscribed itself in memory. Lines which stand boldly in their own rhythm have made many poems memorable to me.

LONDON: I keep thinking of the metric of [T. S. Eliot's "The Love Song of J. Alfred] "Prufrock," where every time there is a conversational tone of voice you get a line with four stresses in it and every time you have a commentary on life you have an iambic blank-verse line. As a poem develops, do you begin to think, Ah, I want to keep a kind of unity here in the number of stresses to keep the momentum?

HACKER: Yes, in a word. Certainly when I've begun to write something and see more or less what the form is going to be like, that becomes a consideration, whether it's a question of shifting stresses or unifying them.

LONDON: Don't you really feel that the idea that form is imprisoning simply means that you are not really dealing with form innovatively? Frost said, "Freedom is feeling easy in your harness." You're so at ease in [these forms].

HACKER: There seems to be an increased interest in the use of form among many contemporary poets. I think of the sort of "Apollonian" poets like Richard Howard, whom I admire enormously—but also of poets of diverse horizons like Carolyn Kizer, Hayden Carruth, the early James Wright, Marie Ponsot—and, in the previous generation, Lowell, Jarrell, Berryman, and Bishop, but also Gwendolyn Brooks, Robert Hayden, and, when it interested her, Muriel Rukeyser. Both Anne Sexton and Sylvia Plath were virtuoso prosodists. For English-language poets in other countries—I'm thinking of Derek Mahon and Seamus Heaney in Ireland, for example, or George MacBeth and Geoffrey Hill in England, or British expat Thom Gunn—it is a nonissue, a choice which is not polemical. Metrical form is something that people find useful, and find delightful, at different times and for different reasons. Both in poetry and in painting, since the teens and twenties of this century, the so-called avant-garde has become as much a tradition as the tradition is. I don't think it's any more liberating at this point—any more daring, certainly—to write in free verse than it is to write in form. I think it's a question of choosing what you find appropriate. It is possible to be entirely inventive in the creation of metrical forms. John Berryman does it all the time—

LONDON: And Merrill, too.

HACKER: Oh, definitely Merrill. This has meant different things to different writers. Adrienne Rich wrote strongly that she did have to abandon form in order to find her authentic voice. Yet at the same time, her work is still very much informed by what she learned. I don't think she would be the same poet, or as fine a poet as indeed she is, if she hadn't served that apprenticeship. Someone like Berryman can go on writing in forms his whole life, make them his own, invent new ones. Rukeyser can move from open forms to her own permutations on fixed forms according to the dictates of the work. Marianne Moore can make totally idiosyncratic and individual forms which remain forms nonetheless—as does May Swenson.

I would hope that there is nothing excluding in them. People come to reading poetry for different reasons: for a love of language; because they're looking for writers who express their own concerns and can create some order, at least verbal, musical order, in those preoccupations. Art, at the very least, has the function of taking one's mind places it hasn't been before—at least that's one reason why I read.

Galway Kinnell

GALWAY KINNELL visited Pearl London's class twice, once in 1981 and again in 1991. The conversation that follows is from the earlier visit and draws as its subject a range of iconic Kinnell themes, from nature in poetry to the invention and rescue of words. Although, as he says here, he has "no aspirations to make any so-called technical advances in poetry," Kinnell's natural imagery and the music of his line, together with a spiritual concern for the physical world, have made him one of America's most revered poets. For Robert Hass, Kinnell "stands for the Wordsworthian impulse in

American poetry of the last half century . . . a poetics that seeks to take its form from—and find its inspiration and its meaning in—nature, or perhaps the nature of things." His *Selected Poems* (1983) won both the Pulitzer Prize and National Book Award; he was a National Book Award nominee again for *A New Selected Poems* (2000).

At the time of his visit Kinnell was fifty-four years old and had published six of his eleven books of poetry, beginning with *What a Kingdom It Was* (1960). Born in Providence, Rhode Island, in 1927, he graduated from Princeton University, later receiving a master's degree from the University of Rochester. In the 1950s he traveled widely and in the 1960s, back in the United States, joined CORE (Congress of Racial Equality) and became active in the civil rights and antiwar movements, out of which his book-length poem, *The Book of Nightmares,* emerged in 1971. It was his fifth collection and serves as the cornerstone of this conversation with London. "I like poems best where I hear the person in them," he says here. "I think that's the only time they live, when you hear the person speaking them—someone else with whom you are able to sympathize so much that when you speak of his life you are speaking of your own."

Kinnell has been a professor of creative writing at New York University and a chancellor of the Academy of American poets. He lives in Vermont.

———————

"Little Sleep's-Head Sprouting Hair
in the Moonlight"

PEARL LONDON: You have said that the nature poem in our society had to be revised, that the real nature poem will include the city, too, it will not *exclude* man. It's a poem in which we can refeel ourselves. Our own animal and plant life. Our own deep connection with all other beings. And then this made me think that Frost's nature was a very indifferent one. And Melville's nature was a malignant one. And Auden's nature was a very cold one. He said that there could not possibly be a Mother Nature in New England. And then we come to your nature. A dimension of the human condition, almost.

KINNELL: That sounds good; I didn't know I'd said that. [*Laughter*]

LONDON: You did.

KINNELL: That's very nice.

LONDON: I loved it. But tell us about it.

KINNELL: Well, any city, any poet, is a nature—I mean the whole. The only thing is that people have divided us earthlings into man and nature as if they were different things. And of course that was a fairly recent division. Sort of a Platonic and—at least in the West it's kind of Platonic—and then Christian division. With very bad consequences. Because once the Christians projected everything sacred, including themselves, to heaven, nature became, so to speak, a kind of inert matter. Once the notion of heaven has disappeared from the earth, nothing on earth is sacred. I think that's the source of what we call alienation. The realization that the animals are our ancestors and that the planet and the creatures that make it up are our ancestors is not very startling. Obviously they are our only ancestors. We were not set down here from heaven. We are as much nature as anything else, and it's only our special self-regard that makes us draw an absolute division between man and nature. Probably doesn't make any sense at all, does it?

LONDON: It makes a great deal of sense. But I'm not quite clear about how you revoke the malignant nature of Melville.

KINNELL: Well, I mean, the cancer exists, and I suppose you'd say that's malignant. But it's alive and it shares the earth with us. As all disease germs do. They're only malignant because they kill us; but from their point of view they're not malignant. Melville had a rather wonderful view of nature. I think the most malignant thing in *Moby-Dick* from Melville's point of view is Ahab. Remember that passage where there are these lumps in the spermaceti and they have a big tub, and half a dozen of them sit round and their job is to reach in and break up the lumps so that the whole thing will be liquid. The spermaceti from which perfume is made. So they sit there squeezing and squeezing, and through this immersion into the very liquefied flesh of the whale they begin squeezing each other's hands as if they were lumps of spermaceti, too. And they begin to wish they could squeeze each other into the very perfume of human kindness, as Melville says. Then he has a dream that night that the angels in heaven have no higher dream than to come down on earth and dip their hands in a jar of spermaceti. It's a very beautiful conception of animal life and our relationship to it.

STUDENT: T. S. Eliot talks about poetry that has been depersonalized. I know that you're not a confessional writer, yet is your voice a distant extension of what you are and your experience?

KINNELL: Even in Eliot's poetry the really lovely parts are those in which we hear his voice. What is that passage where he talks about the garden in *The Waste Land*, the flower garden? It's a little memory he has—and I don't know whether he got it from a text or whether in fact it's a memory from his own childhood. But it draws forth suddenly one of these little amazing moments of tenderness in *The Waste Land*. For me an individual's voice is something that you hear rather than something you can describe. I think the voice in his later poems is often a rather liturgical voice, where you don't have the sense of a person talking about his own inner experience. It's as if a priest were describing everybody's experience. I like poems best where I hear the person in them. I think that's the only time they live, when you hear the person speaking them—someone else with whom you are able to sympathize so much that when you speak of his life you are speaking of your own.

LONDON: That brings us to yourself and Whitman. Your poems are enormously contemporary in every deep sense of the word, and yet there are no subways, there are no fast automobiles, there's none of the technical paraphernalia of our society. Auden had said about writing in a scientific age that there is no nature out there that can be truly imitated. He said modern science has destroyed our faith in the naïve observation of the senses. On the other hand, there you are embracing a physical universe . . . loving in Whitman that which is so profoundly in touch with the physical senses.

KINNELL: Our friends still have faces. And when we talk to them we look at their faces. Those faces are expressive of physical reality. To describe such a face, if one should want to, is perhaps even more possible now than it used to be. Because in a way, we've only recently come to understand that the earth is all we have. The physical face of our friend means more because when it goes, everything goes. I think it's what Rilke was talking about in the ninth part of the *Duino Elegies* when he said don't try to tell the angels about the glory of your feelings, but rather—because you don't really know much about these glories—tell them about what you really know, which is the things, the creatures, and the persons that surround you, the things that you've dealt with all your lives. That's one reason why Neruda is so interesting. Because at a certain phase of his life he was able to turn completely to the evocation of the physical thing.

I suppose what I like most in Roethke is particularly that interest he had in real things. Including slimy things that everybody thought were too base a subject for poetry. There aren't any angels in Roethke's poems, but there are slugs and worms, and I like that about him.

LONDON: And marvelous green things come out of it.

KINNELL: Yeah. I like the struggle he had within himself to overcome his revulsion at slime. So his poems are not static crafted objects that were so characteristic of the poems of his time.

LONDON: And in *The Book of Nightmares* one isn't really as preoccupied I don't think with dream imagery, the direct reaching into the unconscious I'd like to talk with you for a few minutes about the whole question of language, if we can. And invented words. In "The Porcupine" there is that lovely word, which we all enjoyed: "spartled." The porcupine "spartled through a hundred feet of goldenrod." I have no idea what you meant, but for us it was spurt and sparkle and startle; I don't know whether we were reading into it.

KINNELL: Did you look it up?

LONDON: No! Should we have?

KINNELL: If you want to know, it's an actual word.

LONDON: Really! Now, not any of us thought you hadn't invented it. What about "droozed" [in "Under the Maud Moon"]? "The black eye / opens, the pupil / droozed."

KINNELL: Well, I made that one up.

LONDON: And then there was—what was the poem?—the unbreathable "goaf."

KINNELL: "Goaf," yes. That's in *Nightmares,* at the end there. That's an actual word, too. That's the space that's left in a coal mine where the coal has been removed. The empty space left is the goaf. Those little empty places in the earth.

LONDON: And what about "smarl"? "The smarled ashes."

KINNELL: Smarled. Well I think that's a word. I heard it. I looked it up, and I couldn't find it in the dictionary. But I did know a Welshman who said, "Well, we smarled a fire at night." Instead of "bank the fire," as we say. I couldn't find it in any dictionary, so it may just be an old Welsh localism. Those are all rescued words.

LONDON: Rescued words. And to rescue a word is really to say, *Well, all right, you're ignorant of all the associations that have gone on for centuries, but let's try to create them anew.* Can one do it?

KINNELL: Well, no. It's true that language is a thing that depends on people using the words. However, literature plays a huge role in the language, too. For example, there are many words that would certainly be obsolete today if Shakespeare hadn't used them. I'm not saying *The Book of Nightmares* is going to have a comparable effect on "smarl" and "goaf." But still, the fact that you didn't know that "spartled" was a real word and yet you could feel what it meant just by its character as a word means that the word isn't altogether dead.

LONDON: I've always been interested in a society for the rescue of words. And I have a favorite I don't think can be rescued. In the old Anglo-Saxon there was of course the word "hope." And then there was the word— maybe you know it—"wanhope," which was its opposite. It was the waning of hope. And when the French influence came in, "wanhope" went out and was taken over by "despair," which was from the French *l'espérance.* And I've often thought, Oh, it would be really nice to say I'm filled with wanhope. But I don't know that one can do it. I don't know that one can bypass those centuries.

KINNELL: Doesn't Hopkins do it periodically?

LONDON: Yes. And it works. Talking for a minute about form while we're doing this, you had said somewhere along the way that you doubted that there would be a return to form, even as an exercise.

KINNELL: Form in the strict sense of rhyme and meter. And stanzas of equal number of lines and lines of equal number of feet. Yeah. I just don't think that strictness has much of a future in poetry. Could be, but I find it difficult to imagine.

But form is a much deeper thing than whether there's a certain number of rhymes at the ends of lines. Whitman's poetry, you know, is very formal to me—as it is to you. There's a lot of rhymes in Whitman's poems. They happen inside, not at the end of, the lines. And that's much better. As I understand it, Irish was one of the two or three languages where rhyme always belonged to the poetry. The Irish brought rhyme into Europe and then European poetry became rhymed and the Europeans brought it to England. At the time that happened, English was a chaotic language. You could put things any old way, and they'd come out right. You didn't have to have a subject and a verb and the object and the predicate, the adjective before the noun, and so on. English has become very rigid, and as it has become rigid as a spoken language the forms that used to be imposed on it you can only do by wrenching around the language and making it old fashioned again and unreal, as if it didn't come out of a living mouth but was just kind of hatched in a library by the mating of Tennyson and Milton. I doubt if we can have any much rhymed poetry just for that reason.

LONDON: Well, it had a function.

KINNELL: It had a function and it also had a meaning. There was a kind of ritualistic—that is to say a devout—aspect to rhyme. Nobody who rhymes today feels any kind of devotion in the act of rhyming. It's a fillip to make the poem seem more whole, the wit more telling. The solution, of course, has been to expand what rhyme means to a point where there's just a little echoing along the end of the stanza, of sounds. But that echoing exists throughout the whole web of language. And it seems to me kind of fancy to distill it out to the ends of the lines. The whole poem ought to be rich with those repetitions and echoes. The sound of written language is so important. I don't see any virtue in getting it all only at the line breaks.

LONDON: The whole quality of coming to a climactic feeling at the end of a line no longer exists in much of what's being written. The enjambment, the forcing of the end of the line down into the next and making it over-flow, this is a very conscious thing; it is being written because people are saying, "Look, this is the way we feel writing must happen now. The other becomes too fragile and too forced." It's really what you were saying about rhyme. The line itself has almost become an artifice.

STUDENT: In "Lost Loves" [*Body Rags*, 1968] "baking" and "quaking" are complete lines.

KINNELL: You know, I couldn't say why "baking" or "quaking" come out in lines by themselves. It felt like they ought to. I notice on the facing page [of the book, in the poem "Another Night in the Ruins"] there's a line that consists of "it into." "Finds / it. Rips / it into / flames."

STUDENT: And then you have "is" down below, third line from the bottom. Which was kind of a courageous move.

KINNELL: I have to say it that way: "our one work / is / to open our-selves." I've got to have a pause *before* the "is" and *after* the "is." And that's when I break a line—when I've got to have a pause even when the syntax doesn't dictate it. I mean the whole advantage of the line is that you're not limited in the placing of the pauses, the musical units. They can go in where you want. Therefore I get to say "our one work / is / to open our-selves." On the other hand, probably somebody could take these poems of mine and change half the line endings and they'd still be all right. I have no aspirations to make any so-called technical advances in poetry. When I give a reading I am a bit uncomfortable if I see somebody there in the audience following it in the book. And I think: I've got to stick exactly to those line endings or they'll realize how arbitrary they sometimes are.

LONDON: You were talking before about Neruda. We mentioned a week or two ago William Carlos Williams's statement that the difficulty of sur-realism is that it invents without discovering. Would you hold with that?

KINNELL: That's true. I don't really think of Neruda as a surrealist. I have a French understanding of surrealism. From Breton. That's much less interesting to me than Neruda.

LONDON: Because the French don't transcend it.

KINNELL: For them it's a technique and a system. And actually a cause. It's a good thing to have happened, you know. I think it's freeing to poets who came after it and lived through it, telling them that one doesn't have to stick to rational sequences.

LONDON: And that brings us back to the whole risky thing of breaking down the barriers of the irrational. Although yours is "a book of nightmares," it isn't really dominated by dream imagery. The degree of free association is strictly not as wildly loose . . . it doesn't do the things that Ashbery's poems do. The relevance is always there.

KINNELL: While I know it's always rational, there are bound to be some passages which are influenced by or made possible by the existence of surrealism. I'm going to read a little passage. I'm going to read it clearly, you don't have to look at it.

[READS]

from "Little Sleep's-Head Sprouting Hair in the Moonlight" in The Book of Nightmares

I would blow the flame out of your silver cup,
I would suck the rot from your fingernail,
I would brush your sprouting hair of the dying light,
I would scrape the rust off your ivory bones,
I would help death escape through the little ribs of your body,

I would alchemize the ashes of your cradle back into wood,
I would let nothing of you go, ever,

until washerwomen
feel the clothes fall asleep in their hands,
and hens scratch their spell across hatchet blades,
and rats walk away from the cultures of the plague,
and iron twists weapons toward the true north
and grease refuses to slide in the machinery of progress,

And so on. I mean, I think the existence in the world of the surrealistic movement made it possible for me to write that way. And yet obviously, there's nothing very mysterious about any of those lines. They mean something that the intelligence can apprehend. So when I write all I try to do is be as clear as possible with what material, what feelings and thoughts, I have. Try to bring them into as great a clarity as I can. I try to use everything that I have. All my intelligence as well as everything else. So I like it that they're rationally intelligible; I want them to be. And I don't regard that as better or worse than freely associated dream sequence, I simply don't have the ambition or the inclination to write a freely associated dream sequence. The nightmares here, you know, are strictly metaphorical nightmares. They're the events of ordinary life. Nothing in here happens in dreams. These are the nightmares that happen in waking life. If they happened in dreams they might be rather amusing.

Derek Walcott

IN THE SPRING of 1982, at the time of his visit to Pearl London's class, Derek Walcott was fifty-two years old and ten years away from the Nobel Prize in Literature. He eventually won the award on the heels of, and in tribute to, his book-length poem *Omeros* (1990), an eight-thousand-line Homeric epic about his native St. Lucia. Long acclaimed for his use of West Indian history, myth, and vocal rhythms, as well as the formal invention of his poems, Walcott left St. Lucia when he was nineteen to study at the University of the West Indies, in Jamaica, and spent years writing and producing plays in Trinidad. But St. Lucia has been the island of his return and the substance of much of his most important work. "There is the buried language and there is the individual vocabulary, and the process of poetry is one of excavation and of self-discovery," he has written.

Walcott won early praise for his poetry, which he started publishing when he was a teenager. In his early thirties, at the time of his first widely recognized collection, called *In a Green Night* (1962), he received the support and friendship of Robert Lowell. While teaching poetry and theater at Harvard and then Boston University, he befriended Joseph Brodsky and Seamus Heaney, who said that Walcott "possesses English more deeply and sonorously than most of the English themselves."

Despite the acclaim he got for *Omeros* and later works, a number of critics focus on the middle years of Walcott's career. "[His] most fluid and achieved work lies in the books from *Sea Grapes* (1976) through *The Arkansas Testament* (1987)," writes William Logan in the *New York Times,* noting that "in *Midsummer* (1984) Walcott's poetry becomes the registration of sensibility—and in texture and sensibility he has been a master." In this conversation with Pearl London, rhyme by rhyme, line by line, Walcott unpacks the process of thinking and writing his poem in *Midsummer,* "XLVIII," two years before its publication.

"XLVIII"

PEARL LONDON: In one of your classes, you said language must be as exact as describing an ashtray. When I read that I thought about "Sunday Lemons" [*Sea Grapes,* 1976] and that wonderful line "as the afternoon vagues / into indigo," and I thought, What marvelous exactment I hear there. Is it in the music? Is it in the metaphor? Is it in the rhythm that moves as the line moves?

DEREK WALCOTT: This is going to be very detailed, what I'm going to say: I don't like that line anymore.

I think the pitch of a line is where one tests the honesty of a poet, and by "honesty" one doesn't mean a moral honesty. The strange thing about poetry that makes it survive and makes it immortal is that somehow in the language of the mind of any race—West Indian, American, Falkland Islands, anywhere language is spoken—what survives is that reality, that vibration that happens differently to millions and millions of people over generations, and that is where the validity of the thing is.

I'm not making any claim, all I'm saying is that when I heard [you repeat] the line "as the afternoon vagues / into indigo," I didn't remember that I'd written it. I looked at it outside, just as any writer or any painter is entitled to look at a passage of a painting and say, "In this little bit here, I am being a little rhetorical. I am heating up the poem or the painting to a pitch where I know I can do it, but what I'm doing is dishonest in the sense that I'm using one extra key, one extra note up, one extra pitch up that is not true to the harmony, or maybe the modesty, of what is being painted."

If you look at a passage of a painting by Degas, the difficult thing about trying to imitate Degas is how thinly he paints, right? You cannot put the surface texture of a Monet next to a Degas. Bad painters like me, what we try to do is to accommodate styles and maybe have a passage that is reminiscent of Degas, moves into an impasto that we get from Monet, and the whole passage is not right—but can be effective.

The whole point of effectiveness is where the honesty of a line of poetry lies. Somebody said of Wordsworth that he used plain words instead of the right ones. That is also true in many ways of writers like William Carlos Williams, who insists too much on a modesty of American speech, whereas poetry is not only concerned with the modesty of speech, no more than it is concerned only with the rhetorical attitude to speech.

What is wrong with that verb "vagues" to me here is, if I looked hard enough at it, this is what happens: Here we have three chunks. The blocks are "afternoon," "vagues," "indigo"—in which the last stroke, like a Degas, should be a blur, right? And should not be a reality. Because what should happen is, if it were a truth, a metaphorical syllogism, what would happen is you could reverse it: "indigo vagues afternoon." Whereas if the sentence can work in both directions, what is happening is the verb itself is calling attention to itself. The verb is magnetic and it's a little overmagnetic here, because the extra touch of saying "indigo" somehow hits a note that's a little too affected for me. It's pitched a little too high.

Now you can say, with all due respect and gratitude for liking the line, if it were only possible for the "vagues" not to have an s—and v-a-g-u-e could melt into i-n-d-i-g-o and you'd have a v-a-g-i-g-o. Then you would not have the action of the verb drawing attention to what it was doing. You want to scramble as in paint, you want to erase really. The *s* is doing something that is not visual but assonantal . . . and there is no assonantal quality in "vaguing."

I'm being tough on myself. Let me just make another point here.

Vago is the Latin, "to wonder." But at the back of my head there's a stronger word, which is a French word, *vague,* which is wind [agitation of the water]. *Vague* is a very strange word. There's another poem in which I was exultant after I got it, and I went up to a friend and I said, "Jesus, you know . . . I just got it, 'the vague sea.' " Again, the idea of blur and mist and melting. Because you have *vague,* which is the wind and sea, then you have "vague," which is a sea itself being blurred, right? And what may work for it is within the tonal quality of the two words, the two sibilants. "Vague sea." It's like one word "vaguesea," one stroke almost, a small stroke.

All I'm saying about that line is, what we do, why we make ourselves mercilessly victims of our own judgments—rightly so—is that when we develop some domination of technique, the higher you climb, the better the view looks, with the devil next to you. Technically, the more you ascend, the more the temptations are there. In Auden's poem called "In Praise of Limestone," he says, "to ruin a fine tenor voice for effects that bring down the house."

I once saw on television Pavarotti teaching at Juilliard, and I saw this terrific student singing, and I thought, This is fantastic, listening to this man sing. Then they switch to Pavarotti, who says something like, "You know, it's not bad, I mean you just have to breathe it." Which is the equivalent of Nijinsky's reply [to the question] how did he jump so high, and he said, "Well, I go up and then I stay a little bit." [*Laughter*]

How do you do it? That thing of floating, this effortlessness that comes . . . but I don't mean anything ethereal or vague or wispy. I mean something that can be equally strong as an idea. There is no rest, really, there is no rest, there is just a joyous torment all your life of doing the wrong thing. [*Laughter*]

LONDON: Yeats in *A Vision* had written about the moon as that "yellow curd of moon," and at that moment it seemed absolutely visual and right and even exact. And then he took it out and he put in "brilliant moon." Because, he said, "I cannot let it become so theatrical." In a sense, we're not talking about theatrical, but it is calling attention to itself.

WALCOTT: Can I say something?

LONDON: You can say everything.

WALCOTT: There's a poem by Larkin that I quote very often, and he says, "If I were asked to construct a religion, it would be of water." And the poem ends, "Where the many-angled light would congregate endlessly," which is lovely. A glass of water, the element encased in something, is the clearest, truest kind of simplicity, elemental in its simplicity.

A writer like Rilke, at the end of the *Duino Elegies,* saying that what a poet lives for is ultimately to arrive at the point where when he says "house, bridge, fountain, gate" it is itself. It is like the thing Blake arrived at. Blake as an old man could write as an experienced child. The simplicity in Blake that Yeats went for, and every great poet arrives at, is finally when you can use nouns, and those nouns are reborn in the experience and life of the poet's work. That when it is said, it is renamed. To take out the "yellow curd of the moon," which is Pre-Raphaelite or mid-Yeats, and simply say "the brilliant moon" is so cliché that it is stunning. You don't think he would dare say something that any guy walking out on the beach would say. "Wow, what a brilliant moon."

LONDON: When we move into your poem "North and South" in *The Fortunate Traveller* [1981], we move away from "Sainte Lucie" [in *Sea Grapes,* 1976] and that use of language. I think it's very crucial.

WALCOTT: Well, honestly, I have two kinds of experiences that run through me. One is simple, the life I lead on the islands. And of course [the other is] the metropolitan New York and Boston experiences. For each experience, there's almost a language that runs along like the sound of traffic or the meter or beat of a city or a metropolis, you know, that Hart Crane tried rhythmically to capture. But there's not only the beat, there's also the aura of that culture which in the center of a world like New York is multitongued, tonally diverse, tonally contradictory in ideas, and Apollonian in experience.

Reason is the god in cities. Time dominates logic and reason, conversation, and life. It's a polysyllabic existence that doesn't confront certain numinous experiences, such as boat, sea, tree. The reduction of the relationship of the experience is not superior in a metropolis; in fact, I think it is inferior. I think it reduces thought to a standardization of exchange. You really cannot tell the difference between the *New York Times* and the *New York Post* tonally. You cannot tell the difference between the *New York Review of Books* and the *New Yorker* tonally. There is a metropolitan tone to New York. And it may have been the same for Rome in its heyday, or Athens. All these tributaries are fed into one sound, which is the sound of New York. And I don't mean its accent.

We have to be very careful that we aren't insulted, or we don't insult ourselves, by using language defined by the metropolis to define us. In other words, when people tell me I come from a "primal," which I now use instead of "primitive," society, that's fine with me. Backwards societies of course have what is great in them, and that is the numinous, the household gods, the immediate—all these things have more presence.

To me the West Indies is a beginning society, very exhilarating with all its faults, and I do feel, as the whole world feels, that it's possible, quite possible, that Western civilization is probably suicidal in its direction, and there's no doubt that one is playing with a loaded revolver and that we live in this despair. I'm in the position where if I write a poem like "North and South," I am then entering the echo of that rhetoric in a language that I can address it to. When I am writing "Sainte Lucie" I am talking very simply to tree, sea, stone, person.

LONDON: [Critic] Denis Donoghue, when talking about *The Fortunate Traveller,* said, "Derek Walcott wants to bring back heroes. He is a mythmaker." "Mythmaker" in the very good sense, in the sense of an enlarging context, which is what I think "North and South" does, bringing in larger and more universal context.

WALCOTT: The Caribbean has been looked at since Trollope as a place that has no heroes, no background, no nothing. And the answer to this is very simple: we are taught in history that trash came to the Caribbean. White convicts—trash. People from India—trash. Niggers from Africa—trash. Sephardic Jews—trash. Chinese—trash. You gave us all our trash. This makes the best kind of trash fire; you light a trash fire, see what happens.

What is really true is, you have not the weakest people, you have the strongest kind of person, because to endure the Middle Passage, to be in the hold of a ship among the shit and the pain and the sores and survive how many weeks of this, and to land on a place in America, a new world, and survive that, that is not weakness. That is formidable, physical endurance.

Now I'm not talking about morals; I'm just talking about the lies in history that you look at and were taught as a child that it takes you all your life to wipe out. All I'm describing, and I've never spoken in such detail before about things, is that whether it's a line of a poem I began to check out for the truth, or the history of that truth, the language, all it has to do with, I think, is severity and honesty. Remorseless honesty.

LONDON: In "Sainte Lucie" you say, "I'm growing no nearer / to what secret eluded the children / under the house-shade." No nearer the secret, and yet the reason I wanted so much to talk about "North and South" is because I had a very strong feeling that Derek Walcott in *The Fortunate Traveller* is much nearer the secret. Much nearer. You really do know what you feel the secret is that eluded those children, and you are dealing with it, you're giving voice to it. In all honesty I don't think you could have written "Sainte Lucie" today as you did four or five years ago. Am I wrong?

WALCOTT: I think if you told any artist on Monday morning, "You have achieved your goal," he would say, "No thanks." And you could tell this to

Michelangelo on Monday morning in the Vatican—"You made it, Mike"—and he'd say "No, no, I didn't . . ." [*Laughter*]

There is something that is a divine discontent in the artist, which he has to control, and it's very perilous because if he doesn't realize that it's uncontrollable and he tries to dominate it by different things, like liquor or drugs or ambition, then he will be destroyed. The secret I'm talking about is obviously the same one that has been in all the legends of the poetic journey—whether it is a myth of the will-o'-the-wisps, whether it is a holy grail, whether it is the distant princess who must not be married. The day a guy gets up and he says, "Get your eggs yourself," that's the end of Dante and Beatrice. I mean, that's it.

LONDON: Or cornflakes.

WALCOTT: Or pizza. The secret that is eluding the children underneath that house is a presence that, when they move away, they leave behind. The same thing happens with a poet and the process of a poem. Innocence is reborn in the poem at the same time that knowledge, ordinary knowledge, is there.

LONDON: You think that's what Eliot had in mind when he said tradition cannot be inherited, that you have to labor for it, you have to paint it by great labor? Do you think that's what he really meant?

WALCOTT: I think for any poet of any modesty the ambition of his reading is illimitable. That's what Eliot is saying, and this is nothing that anybody did not know. There's one vessel walking around in the world and that's a poet, one poet. We don't really need more than one. Thank God we have two or three or four, but we don't ever have many. But the head of that vessel is supposed to contain the entire body of his language, really, and most poets try to know it, not because it helps their work, but because they know the responsibility of being the vessel of that language. And to arrive at that, life is one whole act of memory for the poet; he lives and acts the memory. And that memory that he has is very rarely of his own work.

Astonishing beauty in the intelligence of poets, in the best intelligence, is that they don't give a damn about their own work, but they are elated about the achievements of other poets.

Just the other day, Seamus Heaney and Joseph Brodsky were at [my] home and nobody quoted his own work; all we did was just throw back lines at each other of other poets. What keeps the thing going is that perpetuity of homage that continues in poets; that is what poets are, and that's what I think [Eliot] means by tradition that you labor at.

LONDON: You know, when Stanley Plumly was here, we talked a lot about [the] advantage of the long poem over the short lyric. Is it that you need room for the development of an idea, is it that you want to give voice to the narrative in a many-faceted way, is it all of these things? In "The Star-Apple Kingdom," the lyric is maintained from the first line to the last. So I'm not sure that hardening of the categories isn't taking place here. What do you think?

WALCOTT: Two of the great poets of the world, Homer and Milton, were blind. The function of the bard in a primal society is [as] a guy who sits by the fire and recites the epic of the race. The length of what he's saying is no different from the length of the lyric. I hate to tire you with the idea of the Greeks. It is not that they discovered anything; it is that they wrote it down. Memory absolutely is the mother of the muse. If I recite a poem to you, I'm asking you to commemorate it by remembering it. I should not ask you to hear it unless I want you to know it. The attraction of memory to the word is the act of the poem.

But what seems to be happening is that cities affect human memory, quite apart from the air. We don't remember; we jot down. Memory is not practiced in cities. There is too much pressure; books that are read are not read for commemoration's sake, they are consumed like cereal. Things are not learned by heart. Poetry is not recited; it is read. The Russians remember that the duty of the poet is to be bardic and outward, consequently Brodsky will get up and recite. A poet is like a dancer. You can dance?

Dance. You can play? Play. You can write a poem? Recite. Now confront an English or American poet with that and he says, "Oh gee, I don't even know my own work."

It's phenomenal what memory can do. The act of writing the stanza is an act of commemoration. Homer composes to a rhythm, he is in a trance, the hexameters are there and he sings, he plays, he composes with the percussion of the harp. This is the image of Homer composing. Can he remember what he sang? Well, we don't know. Quite likely. Shakespeare's plays had to be learned and performed sometimes within a span of a couple of weeks. Now we have actors who come in at eleven o'clock, look for their motivations for four hours, say one small line, and then go back home, and three and a half weeks later they're still reading the book. The whole idea of the bulk, resonance, and memory of the epic declines with the metropolis, it definitely does.

LONDON: Derek Walcott, if you could point to a saying, an underlying metaphor in your work . . .

WALCOTT: I would stop. [*Laughter*]

Somebody said you can take two words by certain poets and that's the gist of what we're saying. And for Lowell, I forget what it was . . . for Wordsworth "dark" and "light," for me "beach" and "speech." That's very disconcerting. Somebody says, "Yeah, we get it, we get it, OK, OK, beach, speech, right." And the next time you [write about a beach], they go "Yeah, beach, you know. . . ." They see it coming.

I am going crazy right now because I just have to get back to what I know and where I am completely myself. So if I am walking on a beach early in the morning, and it's going to be a clear day, and there's nobody on the beach and nice coral water, that's not just touristy, it is as much me as a farmer from the Midwest who may feel "I can live in New York all my life, but until I get up in the morning and smell the stables or the farm I am not living." For Brodsky, it is what I am horrified at, dirt and mud, snow and cold . . . he hates summer.

LONDON: I grew up in a house at the edge of the water and I'm waiting to get back. Of course it's all sold and I'm not going back.

WALCOTT: Where?

LONDON: Up in Long Island.

WALCOTT: I spoke to a Greek girl the other day, I was reading some poems and I could see it in her face, she was saying, "You were talking about the islands and the water, and I'm from Greece." It may be something atavistic, or it may be just that we may need salt if we are used to salt. Of course, that makes a lot of bad poetry: beating waves, Gulf Stream, all that sort of stuff. But so does any pastoral poetry, really, if you're not careful.

LONDON: We would like to keep you a few more minutes, if you have that time [to discuss "XLVIII," in *Midsummer*], but I agreed to let you go to other commitments.

WALCOTT: If you want me to stay, I will. When I was asked to do this, about this succession of drafts, I thought, Really, I don't want to show how I proceed through a poem. And then I thought, Really, honestly, it might be interesting. I've never done this before. Please do me a favor, when you leave this room, don't tell anybody, OK? [*Laughter*] It's not meant as an example of how to write, or how you get a poem. I'm just trying to go into an operation; it's open-heart surgery and you're all looking. I am not saying that this is of any use to anyone.

OK, I'll tell you the background [of "XLVIII"]

I just got married again recently—don't applaud. [*Laughter*] For the third time. But in a sense, I'm fifty-two, and I thought, Well, wait a minute, life may be divided into thirds, let's say one marriage, second marriage, third marriage: act 1, act 2, act 3 . . .

And somehow I thought of the start [of the poem]. It may have been the light from somewhere. I keep trying to write poems that would be transparent, in which the light would be there. But you see, you have to name the light, right? The light I was talking about was an afternoon light, and when I thought of light I thought of panes of light, I thought of shapes of light. I thought maybe of corners of Renaissance paintings where on the side you see a light that is on a cliff.

Now this light, moved and brought center, is not chiaroscuro. I'm talking about light itself, no black, no dark, just the light. That kind of light is a last light, it's not sunset, it is like a late-afternoon light that is not harsh and may make a lot of shadows but has a particular clarity, like in the tropics maybe about four-thirty, five o'clock. And I thought, That's what Sophocles and *The Tempest* have: these masterpieces have a light that is very calm and is the end of a day, end of a time, an end of the world.

This is very close to me as an image because you see this all the time in the tropics; you see it everywhere when I'm in my own place, in the late-afternoon light, when the bugs collect, and the sanderling, which is a sandpiper turned white in winter and come from a long, long distance.

And so I thought I saw this light and I thought, somehow, if this is a third of my life, let me see, let me very frightenedly put down what's beginning: and the first line is written.

"In life's last third, the tempest." And now I'm beginning to build it. I don't know if it's the end or the beginning, but it's there at the beginning. Then you've got, "As the orange light . . ." then "Washes the precipices sways the gold-berried kelp." Take out the "gold." And then for some reason the next line I have is: "Inferno, Purgatorio, Paradiso." Then it falls apart. I stop. And I say, I'm not writing this thing. This is getting to be one of those built-up, predictable associative things that some critic is going to say, "Yes, what Walcott is doing here is . . ." and that's giving somebody work that I don't want them to do.

So what we have [so far] is:

[READS ALOUD FROM FIRST DRAFT]

> In life's last third, the tempest, as the orange light
> washes the precipices, sways gold-berried kelp,
> Inferno, Purgatorio, Paradiso.

The one, two, three. And when I wrote that down, I thought, Well, maybe what I'm saying is, you can reverse life the other way, too, right? Paradiso, Purgatorio, Inferno. But no, my marriages were not *that,* nor has my life been *that,* because any way you turn it, the middle is Purgatorio, and that's stuck on my second wife. [*Laughter*] So that's not what I meant.

But there's some weight in that "one, two, three," some idea of acts, some idea of the theater, some idea of Prospero leaving, and some idea of the light. So one line that's there, and this may be a little later: "Holds up his lightning rod. Farewell, farewell"—in brackets. "Farewell farewell," my God, this is very Shakespearean. And then I have: "The gaunt master" in another place—terrible—"hurls down his lightning rod and watches the scepter roll in the sucked wave and the pebbled shell."

OK, this is *not* going well. [*Laughter*]

So another day, big deal, I get up and I say, "I have it"—and what is it? Light. It's all I have, light. It's like Dylan Thomas saying that he gets up in the morning, and he sits down and he writes a very large O. Because most poems begin with "O." [*Laughter*]

So I go back to light, and then I have, "Dry ocher cliffs in the slanted afternoon." The whole line comes, "Dry ocher cliffs"—ocher is the yellow ocher—I begin to see where I am now, the cliffs are dry and the slant of light across the face of the cliff. "Dry somnolent shallows where the exhausted"—I was feeling exhausted—"surf," but no, "abandoned scepter." "Abandoned scepter" is Prospero's rod.

Now this is a habit that I think all poets have. As soon as you put down a word that's challenging, you say, "I'm going to get a rhyme for this mother"—excuse me—"for this *thing.*" "Scepter." OK, "scepter" 's over here—"kept her," "leapt her"? You know, you're doing this thing, and you've got to get back to "scepter."

Why? Why bother? Well, a rhyme is harmony. A couplet to me encloses the word. It is the truth. And, you know, it is that concluding circle that makes rhyme reality, right? The necessity of rhyme is a philosophical, organic necessity. When Milton can dismiss rhyme, it's [only] after he wrote "Lycidas." He said, "I don't need this stuff anymore." It's like Charlie

Parker not playing "Melancholy Baby," or Ornette Coleman—you don't ask him to play "When the Saints Go Marching In."

So: "Dry ocher cliffs in the slanting afternoon." I've got a problem now. "Dry ocher cliffs in the slanted afternoon." The afternoon is tilting and the light is . . . I have a big problem here. This is a past participle in the present—"in the slanting afternoon." [But] if I say "slanted afternoon," I'm in torment either way because the present participle can be affected, can be "glowing dust," something; and the present participle is "dust." The past participle is even more affective—so you've got two show-offs you've got to pick from. And one of them, the pluperfect, is so presumptuous that you have to chuck it out, slap it down. The present participle is so pathetic you feel like kicking it, you know what I mean? So something has to happen preceding that. And then you go back.

[READS ALOUD FROM SECOND DRAFT]

> Dry ocher cliffs in the slanting afternoon,
> And somnolent shallows where the dead scepter spins.

So now I've faked it, now I have "spins" at the end of the line, but I want "scepter." And then, "Elevation into print," I don't know what happened, suddenly I've thought of Auden's face: "Elevation into crinkled waterless rock like a sage's face."

Then I have the "sanderlings." Now I realize immediately I'm preceded by Shakespeare's line, "chase the ebbing Neptune and defy him when he comes back." I can't compete with that. There's Bishop's terrific poem about sandpipers also. But I can't help it. I saw the birds so I'm going to put them in.

So I have: "The sanderlings"—next line—"Spitted down to ground and picked . . ." Well, this is good writing because up there I had "and stick." [*Laughter*] I don't know why I'm exposing myself like this anyway. And then—can I still continue?—"Like a flame lowered, the sail goes out on the horizon." Now I have an idea: somehow the light on the cliff is a reflection of a smaller light of a ship going out or a sail caught in the light that somehow is connected to the light on the cliff's edge. I have: "The sanderlings skitter after with surf and pick with quick white stabs of shellfish between the shale."

Now up top I have "sail" and later "shale"—all right—"with quick white stabs." I thought, Well, maybe that's OK because I'm trying to get the action of the sanderlings picking between the pebbles, right? And they're white and I don't know if it's "quick white" or "white quick stabs," the jab of the big bird's beak at the shellfish. But then, you have to watch for the sibilants, because [if] you go with "quick white stabs of shellfish between the shale," you flub the audition. Now I've got to think. Now I've got something shaped like a stanza.

"Like a flame, the sail goes out on the horizon"—I'm in trouble, because I've got "horizon" and I've got to rhyme "horizon"—"eyes on," "goes on . . ."

"The island darkens to . . ."—something—"to a cinder," but it all "goes on."

So I'm trying for "horizon" with "the sanderlings skittering after the surf to pick." The imitation of the line is almost as fast as the birds moving, because I'm writing fast. By taking lines from all over and fitting them in. And this is beyond the reality of a poem. People have said that rhyme dominates reason, but it's deeper than that. It refutes reason.

This is now a kind of a poem of stained glass, which has been corrected. The rhyme for "scepter" now came quite naturally, because "In life's last third, its movements, we accept the / measurements." "Accept the"—not a hard rhyme—with "scepter." So that "in life's last third" we learn "to accept her," I thought it was the Sybil, "accept her measurement of our acts from one to three" and so forth.

So this is the last [so far] . . . worth all this:

[READS ALOUD FROM THE THIRD DRAFT]

Dry ocher sea cliffs in the slanting afternoon,
at the rocky end of Balandra and the beach's end,

Stop. I have "the rocky end of Balandra," but then I thought, Why did I? The end of that particular beach does not have high cliffs. Somebody would never check it out, but it's not true so I'm going to take that out.

[READS]

> White sanderlings race the withdrawing surf to pick,
> with wink-quick stabs shellfish between the pebbles,
> ignoring the horizon where a sail goes out
> like the light of Prospero from his island kingdom.
> Come light, make weightless the burden of our thoughts,
> let our misfortune have no need for magic,
> be untranslatable in verse or prose.
> Make us like stones that have never frowned or known
> the need for medicine or art, for Prospero's
> snake-knotted staff, or sea-bewildering stick;
> make useless the ciphers of birds' prints on sand.
> Proportion benedict us, as in fables,
> so that in life's last third, we may accept the
> measurements of our acts from one to three,
> and boarding this craft, sail with the last bright wind
> that rolls this pen on a desktop, a scepter
> swayed by the surf, the scansion of the sea.

Well, that's what [the draft] wound up as. But it needs—well, I would say it's a little heightened and now it has to be . . . not watered down, but diffused and leveled out in some way. The pitch of it is a little too high.

LONDON: I can't think of anything that could have been more of a privilege for us. Here we come to the meaning of the shaping spirit of the imagination. This is it.

[Published version, "XLVIII" from *Midsummer*]

Raw ocher sea cliffs in the slanting afternoon,
at the bursting end of Balandra, the dry beach's end,
that a shadow's dial wipes out of sight and mind.
White sanderlings race the withdrawing surf to pick,
with wink-quick stabs, shellfish between the pebbles
ignoring the horizon where a sail goes out
like the love of Prospero for his island kingdom.
A grape leaf shields the sun with veined, orange hand,
but its wick blows out, and the sanderlings are gone.
Go, light, make weightless the burden of our thought,
let our misfortune have no need for magic,
be untranslatable in verse or prose.
Let us darken like stones that have never frowned or known
the need for art or medicine, for Prospero's
snake-knotted staff, or sea-bewildering stick;
erase these ciphers of birds' prints on sand.
Proportion benedict us, as in fables,
that in life's last third, its movements, we accept the
measurements of our acts from one to three,
and boarding this craft, pull till a dark wind
rolls this pen on a desktop, a broken oar, a scepter
swayed by the surf, the scansion of the sea.

Amy Clampitt

AT THE TIME of Amy Clampitt's first visit to Pearl London's class, February 22, 1983, she was ten days from receiving what Mary Jo Salter called "one of the warmest receptions for a first book of poems by any American in this century." The book was *The Kingfisher,* and Clampitt was sixty-three years old. In her memorable March 3, 1983, review, Helen Vendler wrote that in a hundred years *The Kingfisher* would "take on the documentary value of what, in the twentieth century, made up the stuff of culture. And later yet, when (if man still exists) its cultural terminology is obsolescent, its social patterns extinct, it will, I think, still be read for its triumph over the resistance of language, the reason why poetry lasts." Clampitt had just twelve more years to live and would publish only four more collections: *What the Light Was Like* (1985), *Archaic Figure* (1987), *Westward* (1990), and *A Silence Opens* (1994).

Her 1983 visit with London, seen in retrospect, suggests the forces that would win over so many readers: the sensual pleasures of sound and smell, that lush use of language, the dueling pull of home and exile, "the love of being carried, the fear of being dropped," as she says here. Three years later she returned to London's class and in her discussion of "What the Light Was Like," she pointed again to that awareness "of the doubleness of everything. That we're all a little bit manic-depressive. You respond to what's exhilarating; and you are cast down by its opposite."

Born in 1920 in the Quaker village of New Providence, Iowa, and raised on farms there, Amy Clampitt graduated from Grinnell College and then moved east for good. In New York City she wrote novels that remain unpublished and found a succession of jobs—as a secretary at the Oxford University Press, as a reference librarian for the Audubon Society, as an editor at E. P. Dutton. She traveled, took a poetry class at the New School, spent stretches of time in Maine, and then, in the late 1970s, the *New Yorker* started taking her poems. It led five years later to her overwhelming success with *The Kingfisher.* Amy Clampitt became a visiting professor at William and Mary, Amherst, Smith, and elsewhere. She died in September 1994.

———

"Black Buttercups"

PEARL LONDON: Let me say that, first, I'm so delighted, because we've all been wondering who Amy Clampitt is and what she looks like, and now we have you with us. Tell us about the metaphor of "Black Buttercups" [eventually to appear in *What the Light Was Like*]. Are there really "black buttercups that never see daylight"?

AMY CLAMPITT: No. [*Laughter*] I'm very happy to talk about this poem because I think perhaps this poem has been longer in the making than almost anything I've ever finished. In various forms I was trying to write about what for strange reasons was for me a very traumatic experience—it sounds simple enough, moving from one house to another. But in the process of thinking about that experience, I suppose I began going back into something that went deeper. I'm not being psychoanalytical, but the metaphor of the black buttercups has to do with unfulfilled possibilities. I suppose we all know about such things in our own background and among our own families, among friends: about the experience of being moved from one place to another—"uprooted," as it were—at the age of not quite ten.

I can't explain except that when you have something you've been thinking about for a long time, and you have tried to deal with a set of experiences that have obviously affected the way you see things, then you're going to run into problems. One problem I ran into in writing this poem— I was going to describe an idyllic place I was forced to leave, but the fact is, although it was an idyllic place in my memory, there's also a place where I discovered a lot of nonidyllic things. So have you got a poem there anymore? I don't know. That's one reason why it took me a long time to write this, because it turns out that when I started thinking about the years I spent in that house, which was the earliest house I remembered, I had to acknowledge that there were many things that were anything but idyllic. So I suppose that's kind of the central core of the poem—there are these contradictions and there is this sense of things that went wrong that were never acknowledged. So that's the black buttercups really.

LONDON: In "Black Buttercups" you ask, "When / . . . did the rumor / of unhappiness arrive?" And then we know that there's that whole sense of menace and there is no safety—menace in the water, menace where the bull is in the pasture, and menace walking in that graveyard, I think it was. But that one understands in childhood. What was difficult to grasp for us were some of the particulars. Let me read you these lines and see if you can comment for us: "The look of exile / foreseen, however massive or inconsequential, / hurts the same; it's the remembered / particulars that differ."

[READS]

> How is one to measure
> the loss of two blue spruces, a waterfall
> of bridal wreath below the porch, the bluebells
> and Dutchman's-breeches my grandmother

had brought in from the timber
to bloom in the same plot with peonies
and lilies of the valley? Or out past
the pasture where the bull, perennially
resentful, stood for the menace of authority
(no leering, no snickering in class),
an orchard—or a grove of willows
at the far edge of the wet meadow
marking the verge, the western barrier
of everything experience had verified?

CLAMPITT: That whole catalog is really things that—I could go on forever. Part of the difficulty of writing that poem was to narrow down all of the things that I remembered, and they're mostly growing things. My earliest memories were flowers, and it seems as though the pleasure I found in being a child had to do with spring arriving and finding things in bloom, and when you're a child, of course, it seems like a thousand years since the last spring; you don't believe it'll ever arrive again. So they tended to gather around things that bloom; that's what I meant. The whole idea of exile—it seems hard to explain why moving three miles down the road should be so traumatic. And you feel, *Look at these people who were moved from one continent to another, look at the Indian tribes who were uprooted and put on reservations.* What is this that I'm so upset about it?

LONDON: But of course we have that abandonment a little later on in some of the other poems, too.

CLAMPITT: I think that is really quite universal. I have heard that there are two fears that are instinctive in babies; one of them is loud noises, and the other is being dropped. I partly feel that myself, and I have also heard, and it seemed kind of natural, that being carried is a great sensation. Everybody wants to go back and be a baby and be carried, and it must be that the other side of that is the fear of being dropped, and abandoned psychologically, of course. It simply travels into that new mode, but it's the same thing. I'm not really a Freudian; I just feel there's something in those ideas.

LONDON: Tell us more about the background of "Black Buttercups"—was this a farm in Iowa? And did you just move to a place next door?

CLAMPITT: Well, three miles away. It was a location that lacked the charm and comfort about the house where I lived for almost ten years, the first place I could remember. Physically it had certain aspects that were hard to get used to: it was on a hill, and it was not protected, it was exposed. And this is one reason I think I was reluctant to move into it; I didn't like it when I saw it the first time. I was familiar with it because it was in the neighborhood, and we had been traveling around looking at farms in various parts of the state—much farther away than at that point—and I remember: the child sitting on the windowsill in the summer crying dates to a Sunday afternoon when we had either gone or were going to go look at a possible farm to move to, and I sort of remember that one we saw was very attractive, but it didn't console me.

LONDON: In the poem, you say, "In what shape / was it we first perceive it—the unstanched / hereditary thing, working its way / along the hollows of the marrow . . . nothing but sick headaches / passed down like an heirloom?" What was the "hereditary thing"? Was that part of a nightmare, was there a specific thing? Why did you say that in the poem?

CLAMPITT: It's somewhat generalized. The fact is, at the time I was beginning to write this poem, my second brother was very ill—he's since died of leukemia—and so I was thinking a lot about marrow. But I'm not sure that I might not have found that image in there, I don't know. Because it seems to me that you see how people inherit neuroses; migraine headaches seem to run in families, and they ran in my family—I don't happen to have them, but my grandfather had them and my father had them, at least I think that's what they were. And so these aspects of being unhappy, being anxious, unfulfilled . . .

LONDON: Those were the "heirloom" aspects. . . .

CLAMPITT: I thought of it as kind of a horrible heirloom, because it is passed down—it recurs in any case.

LONDON: In your essays, you have asked why sound receives so little attention in contemporary poetry. Looking through *The Kingfisher* last week we found these marvelous lines: "amber of Budweiser," "oleander stillness," "the in-mid-air resort of honeybees' hirsute cotillion." These are all auditory experiences, and the sounds are so magnificent: "ooze foreshortened into limestone." Now, in "On Refusing to Be Gorgeous," you talk a good deal about the prevailing flatness of diction today and what you call the "wholesale deafness to the sonorities of English." I wish you'd comment for us on the use of sound in your work.

CLAMPITT: I think it all goes back to the exciting poetry I read when I was very young. The first really great poetry to seize hold of me and never let go was John Keats, and the poem I particularly remember being seized by is "The Eve of St. Agnes," which is written in a Spenserian stanza that is just full of music. "By degrees / Her rich attire creeps rustling to her knees." There is just wonderful melody running all through that poem. Another one of my favorite poems in the world is "Lycidas." I don't like everything of Milton, but I love that poem, and it has been ringing in my head ever since I first read it. The sonnets of Shakespeare—another one of the great poems that struck me very early was the "That time of year thou mayst in me behold." There's a sonnet of Milton's: "Avenge, O Lord, thy slaughtered Saints, whose bones"—you know, you hear those sounds, and I don't know how you can want to be a poet and not want somehow to do something like that.

The background of "On Refusing to Be Gorgeous" is that I had been reading a biography of John Keats, by W. Jackson Bate. A whole dimension of the poetry of Keats came alive for me from reading that book. One of the things Bate does is to diagram the sounds in a stanza of "The Eve of St. Agnes" and point out how the different sounds connect. It was instructive to me. I don't think you can make a science out of it. I'm not sure how scientific Keats himself was; I think he just had a very good ear, and I think most poets who do write sonorous poetry do not do it by any science but simply hear echoes—one word will suggest another because of the sound. For me that's so, and I can't tell you how it happens, but I do write by ear. I'm an editor by profession—if I can call it that—and I edit by ear. I want to hear how the sentence falls; I want to hear a cadence someplace.

LONDON: When we were sitting outside talking, you sort of withdrew in horror when I said, "Must sound be an echo to the sense?" And you're still sort of shuddering at the sound of it. But don't you think that sound is always there to implement meaning? That, as Wallace Stevens says, "Without the weight of meaning, there is no flight." How much can one brocade a poem or embroider a line and not tread on very dangerous ground? When does the ear tell you to stop? We're all writers, and how do we, sitting at our typewriters, know how far we're allowed to go?

CLAMPITT: We can all make mistakes. Many people feel that the kind of thing I write is overdone. That it is lush. You have to learn to curb excess; you can't put everything in. I remember writing to a poet friend of mine, "Can it be that art consists of giving things up?" I think there's something in it. There are a lot of things going on at once when you write, there are various levels. Your ear is telling you one thing, but the ear is also plugged into your intention to say something in some way. I can't tell you how.

LONDON: What would you say if Ezra Pound were to walk in that door and say, "The contemporary poet must write nearer to the bone"?

CLAMPITT: I don't think poetry is a paring down to essences. I think poetry is in some way akin to music; it is disposing language in a way to give pleasure, and one way you give pleasure is by sound. I'm a little defensive on this because I'm obviously not a minimalist poet. There's a kind of poetry where you're expected to find your own meaning in the quiet spaces between the words, and I have been told that I don't leave any quiet spaces: "Your art got in the way of what you were saying."

LONDON: Moving from auditory imagery to the visual images that you use, we have a "suede meadow," we have "green velvet precipices." There are the "galleries of sheen," the "ponderous velour," and a "damask weave of luxury."

CLAMPITT: I'm just very much a sensualist. I like the way things feel. I think that's one thing that drew me to the poetry of Keats—he evokes all sensations, every one. I have a friend who's greatly devoted to George Herbert. I have never been able to feel a great closeness to the poetry of George Herbert, though I can admire it. I think the reason for that is that he's not really concerned about sensations; he's concerned about moral questions. Not that I'm not concerned about moral questions, but I can't get away from pleasure. The pleasure of the senses is something that is apparently more important to me than it is to some people.

LONDON: In a lovely poem, "On the Disadvantages of Central Heating" [from *The Kingfisher*] the last line is "the perishing residue / of pure sensation." I'm not sure that I know what the "residue of pure sensation" is, unless it's memory.

CLAMPITT: I guess what I'm saying in this poem is simply that I don't remember what we talked about when we sat around that coal fire. I do remember what it *felt* like to sit around that coal fire; I do remember what it was like in that house in Dorset where the sheets never got dry—I do remember that. It seems as though, for certain people anyhow, what you really preserve in the end, in memory, is not even emotion—it is sensation.

LONDON: So much of the sensation is also the sense of smell. In "Linden-bloom" [in *The Kingfisher*] "the aromas so intensely subtle, strollers passing under looked up confused as though they just heard voices"! Think of it.

CLAMPITT: That happens to me every time I come under a linden tree, or come to Central Park, or to the little park over here, which is the source of that poem, and the linden flowers are out. It seems so sourceless, and I forget what it is every time I smell it. There's something peculiar about that aroma, so that a whole lot of repeated experiences of smelling those flowers went into that poem. The sense of smell used to be very important for mammals, and once they got up on their hind legs it wasn't so important anymore, but it's still there, part of our equipment. I do think that mechanization of things has interfered with the enjoyment.

There are so many surfaces that are not interesting. I don't like the shapes of cars that are traveling along Third Avenue. I'm really more interested in things that are smashed; you know, the salvage, the auto salvage—because then they begin to get interesting textures, quite without intention. But I do think many things have been tooled in such a way as to be uninteresting; the whole idea is they look like everything else, and so the visual surface of things in the city and on television and almost anywhere you go have been flattened out in some way, just as music gets flattened out in the stuff they play to make you buy more things in the supermarket. I do think there's a problem here about pleasure; we have been deprived of a kind of pleasure that is there in things that grow.

LONDON: Over and over again, you redeem your poems from abstraction with very specific sensuous images, and yet there is so little use of the first-person singular. There's so little of the confessional voice in your work, of "I" or "me." How do you explain that?

CLAMPITT: Oh, I think it's probably because I've lived longer than a lot of people. When I was younger, I used "I" the way young poets generally do. It doesn't come naturally to suppress the first person. I don't intend to suppress it entirely. I guess if you spend a lot of time with something, you try to see what it's like and not just how you feel about it.

LONDON: What kind of permission do you give yourself to use words that send me to the dictionary? Like "eldritch," "droids," "wickiups," "pheromones." Our dictionary is an *OED* and it's very heavy, and I have to use a little glass—I find myself getting very worried about this.

CLAMPITT: If words are there, I want to find someplace to put them. I wrote a poem once that ends with "tortfeasors." Nobody will publish that poem. It's a legal term—a wonderful word. It is always a problem whether you're going to use a word that your readers will never have heard of. I can't defend it very well; if people don't like to look things up in the dictionary, I suppose I do go too far.

LONDON: In [the sequence of poems in *The Kingfisher* called] "Heartland," you say [in an epigram by Charles Olson], "The fulcrum of America is the Plains, half sea half land." And there's a wonderful obsession with oceans that goes throughout the poetry.

CLAMPITT: Reading that essay ["Call me Ishmael"] by Charles Olson that I quote from, [the idea of] "half sea, half land" was a kind of illumination for me. Because the Middle West, and particularly Iowa, where I grew up, didn't seem to be definable in any way. There was so little that had any shape there; it has been shaped largely by agriculture. What you see is fields and fences and little clumps of trees, woodlots and windbreaks, which were mostly planted. Every now and then where there's a stream, you'll have some woods. The horizon does not liberate you, it closes you in. You feel hemmed in by sameness. I could only think about the Midwest after I had figured out what it was.

That poem "Imago" to some extent was an effort to finally explain why I had so much trouble becoming a poet at all, getting hold of the subject that was really my subject and yet that had no form. How do you give form to a thing you feel has no form?

I only started seriously and also happily writing poetry as a regular thing after I began spending time on the coast of Maine. I had wanted to be on the ocean from the time I saw a lake for the first time, which was at about four years old. I still remember that experience of seeing a great sheet of water. I don't know what it was about being near a large body of water that was so attractive, but I do remember that experience and I always knew that I was going to come east and live near the sea.

Lucille Clifton

IN APRIL 1983, a month before her visit, Lucille Clifton wrote to Pearl London that she was sending drafts of a poem "from a series written trying to give voice to a young friend dying of leukemia." "chemotherapy," the poem London and Clifton discuss at length in class, would not appear in book form until *Next: New Poems* (1987), a finalist for the Pulitzer Prize along with *Good Woman: Poems and a Memoir, 1969–1980,* making Clifton the first poet to be nominated twice in the same year. *Next* embodies the empathy, lament, and elegy for which Clifton has become celebrated. "Artful, intense, Lucille Clifton's poems are made with an unerring ear and a burning mind," Adrienne Rich writes. "There are very large psychological reaches within this taut, spare poetry."

Clifton, distinguished professor of humanities at St. Mary's College of Maryland, was born in 1936 in Depew, New York, just outside of Buffalo. The men in her family all worked in the steel mill. Her mother, only in school till fourth grade, "was the educated one of my parents, in that my father could not write. [But] both my parents read everything that they could get hold of." Clifton went away to college at sixteen, first to Howard University, then Fredonia State Teachers College, where she began to write poetry. Her first book, *Good Times* (1969), became one of the *New York Times* best books of the year. Despite several bouts with cancer herself, Clifton has continued to write and win wide recognition, including a National Book Award for *Blessing the Boats: New and Selected Poems 1988–2000*.

"I feel very strongly a responsibility to my art, to my sex, to my family, and to my race," she says here. "And I feel a very strong responsibility to humanness. I don't know why I should feel it. Everyone does, I suppose. I often get asked when am I going to break out of black things and write real poems. Am I always going to feel bound? And yet I feel that I am freed by my culture because I do think about the whole language . . . a huge, living, vital language . . . all language is available for poetry."

"chemotherapy"

PEARL LONDON: A month ago Denise Levertov said that the woman writer today must be writing in the direction of what she called "a more public poetry." By which she means a political poetry. A poetry that deals with El Salvador and so forth. How do you feel about that?

LUCILLE CLIFTON: When I'm asked about writing political poetry I often quote Gwendolyn Brooks, who once said, "Whenever I walk down the street it's a political statement." I tend to write a more personal poetry but a lot of my personal life has tended to be political by virtue of my being a black woman. It's very hard not to touch on things that someone might consider political.

LONDON: Is there a subject matter that belongs exclusively to women? The subject matter of childbirth, menstruation, of attitudes toward marriage. Is there a responsibility on the part of the woman writer to deal with material that is indigenous to her?

CLIFTON: I think so. I hesitate to say that there is anything exclusively anybody's. But by the same token I think everybody has to write about that which they know. Certainly childbearing touches everybody. I've had six children. Menstruation—I've been doing that thirty-something years; certainly that has some kind of importance in my life. I think that women have some responsibility to say something about these things as being part of the human condition. Which is what we write about, after all. For too long women have believed that these things which are specifically female are somehow of lesser importance.

LONDON: Linda Pastan was here earlier this winter. She said the longest walk she ever took was from the kitchen to the study. What was your longest walk?

CLIFTON: My longest walk was certainly from Depew, New York, to Baltimore. I was born in Depew, which is twelve miles outside of Buffalo. It's a very small town. A Polish town, primarily . . . and then there was our family. We were there because there is a steel mill. My father, my grandfather, my brothers, my uncles all worked in the steel mill.

LONDON: Was that rough? Were you feeling insular there in a Polish town?

CLIFTON: Not at all. I didn't know any other place. In fact, as a teenager I worked in the Polish office of the New York State employment service because I understood Polish. I'm very lucky in my parentage, I think.

LONDON: That brings us to the poems about your mother. In *An Ordinary Woman* there is this: "i have dreamed dreams / for you mama" which I thought was quite beautiful.

CLIFTON: My mother dropped dead when she was forty-four. Both my parents were epileptic. My mother had grand mal seizures; my father had petit mal seizures. My mother had a brain tumor, my father also had a brain tumor. She was the most *wonderful,* absolutely wondrous, magical kind of person. Some of the things that this lady came up with, she probably was a bit mad. But she was wonderful.

LONDON: In one of the poems you say, "Mama, I have worn your name like a shield." I don't know about the madness, but she was also a great source of strength.

CLIFTON: Absolutely. She was the educated one of my parents, in that my father could not write. Both my parents were great readers. They read everything that they could get hold of. My mother, who only went to something like the fourth grade, read everything she could find about China. She had never seen a Chinese person face-to-face. She was just fascinated by China.

She lived with a husband who was a wonderful father, but he wasn't such a hot husband. My father had three daughters by three different women. And my mother raised all my father's children.

LONDON: Really? What an absolutely saintly lady.

CLIFTON: She was a saintly woman. After my brother was born my father and mother never slept together again—and my brother was twenty-one when my mother died, I think. Yet she adored my father. She was a great source of strength to us. She made us feel that we could do anything in the world we wanted. She always said that anywhere you are, you're there because you're supposed to be or you wouldn't be there.

We were raised in the Baptist church, and I can remember once at Christmastime I was there to do a recitation. I had gotten so tired of constantly going up front for recitations that I decided not to do it anymore. I stood there awhile—I was a very little thing—and everybody was looking at me, all the old ladies and deaconesses. And my mother marched up from the back of the church and said, "Come, baby." And she turned around and said, "Anything she don't want to do, she don't have to." She probably ruined me completely. But she was quite a marvelous person.

LONDON: Oh, I love that so.

CLIFTON: When she died I was eight months pregnant with my first daughter. My mother had gone to the hospital just for some tests for her epilepsy, and I went to see her. I had to wait for visiting hours to start, but then they wouldn't let me go to her room. And I kept saying, "Why? I don't understand." Finally my aunt and uncle came and they said, "Lu, your mother is dead." She had dropped dead fifteen minutes before I got there. She was forty-four years old. It was such a traumatic kind of thing that I began to say to myself, *Now I am going to live the rest of her life for her.* And so I started doing things that she enjoyed as opposed to things that I wanted to do. It took me about a year to figure out that she would not have wished me to continue her life but to continue mine.

LONDON: When did you actually decide to become a writer?

CLIFTON: I never did. One day, though, I'm going to decide that . . . [*Laughter*]

LONDON: After seven books.

CLIFTON: I wrote as a child, and my mother loved poetry. My mother used to recite "Abu Ben Adam." That was my mother's poem. Drop of a hat she would do that. Or "The House by the Side of the Road." All iambic pentameters. And when I would start writing she would always say, "No, baby, that's not a poem; I'll teach you how to write a poem." So I knew it as a thing one could do.

And things happened for me, I don't know why. I really don't. I just read something by [Czeslaw] Milosz, who said the reason he teaches Slavic poetry rather than poetics is because he doesn't know *why* or *how* this happens.

When I was little, in Buffalo, the only poets I ever saw were the portraits that used to hang on the elementary school walls. They were old, dead white men with beards. I had no relationship to anything there. So it just never occurred to me. Still, when I felt things—and I was always feeling things—I wrote them down. They didn't look particularly like the poems that I read in school and in books, but still I continued to do it.

LONDON: When did you actually publish your first writing?

CLIFTON: The first writing I published was a poem—a sonnet, I think—years ago in Buffalo. There was a period when I was doing sonnets. I was doing [Edna St. Vincent] Millay; I was *being* Millay, actually. And then I began to be Thomas Wolfe—because I read somewhere that he was tall, and at that time I was tall. Then I had a story in a little book called *Negro Digest*. I didn't publish anything else for years. Until I read that Robert Hayden was part of the literature panel of the National Endowment for the Arts. And I thought, Oh, this is a colored guy!

LONDON: He's a good poet.

CLIFTON: He's a wonderful poet and a lovely, lovely man. And I thought, Well, I'll send him a poem and see what he thinks of what I do. So I sent a couple of poems that later were in the book *Good Times*. And he wrote a wonderful letter back. He also took the poems to Carolyn Kizer—then Carolyn took the poems to the YMHA Poetry Center, and I won the Discovery Award. I received a telegram saying "Congratulations, you've won the Discovery Award." I had never heard of the Discovery Award. I also had no idea what the YMHA was. I thought it was a misprint—I had heard of the YMCA. I had six children, the oldest was six. It was all kind of a new world to me.

LONDON: When Stanley Plumly was here and talked about his father, he told us that he really didn't feel the earlier poems he'd written were very good because there was something corrosive in him. He had been filled with fear and hatred of his father, and that had colored and dominated his work. And it wasn't until he began to understand and have insight into his father and love his father and then forgave him that he really could begin to write. What he was saying is that one can't write as powerfully out of anger as one can out of love.

CLIFTON: I quite agree.

LONDON: But still, we have your poem "In Salem"—there's a lot of anger and that poem is gorgeous. What about anger?

CLIFTON: Well, first of all, I don't think you can get terribly angry with anyone or anything that you don't care anything about. I was saying to my class that black people *love* America—which is why they're so angry so often. Loving someone does not mean that they don't make you angry, that you don't see their faults. To pretend that things don't bother you does something awful to you. It seems to me that anger, perhaps like suffering, can be redemptive sometimes.

LONDON: Why don't we now start to look at the drafts for "chemotherapy."

CLIFTON: I should say that this is one of nine poems in the new manuscript that are trying to give voice to a person who has leukemia. I wanted to talk about not only the killing effects of the disease, but also the killing effect of the cure.

One of the tensions in this group of poems is between the girl, who was twenty-one years old, a beautiful, beautiful person, and her mother.

LONDON: There are a lot of changes.

```
chemotherapy

my days are pain.
my mouth is a cave of cries.
i am attacked by white coats
dressed like God.  what is this
chemical faith?   oh
mother mary where is your living son?
```

CLIFTON: Oh, yes. I write short poetry, fairly accessible poetry, simple poetry; and so sometimes people think, first of all, that I don't think about it; that I don't work on it. I work hard to chip away so that what I have left is the bare bones of the poem.

LONDON: Well, that's its power. If we turn to the first draft you have "my days are pain. / my mouth is a cave of cries. / I am attacked by white coats." And then in the next draft the "attacked" is left out, and you have "my room is filled with white coats." Did you feel that "attacked" was too obvious? Why was that omitted?

CLIFTON: "Attacked" was too purposeful. The white coats were doctors. In a place like Hopkins, which is a research hospital, they oftentimes will do things almost as if you were not a living person but were an object of research. But it is not hostile and purposeful, so "attacked" seemed too strong.

LONDON: In the earlier versions you have "my days are pain." In the final version you have "my hair is pain." Can you tell us about that?

```
my hair is pain.
my mouth is a cave of cries.
my room is filled with white coats
shaped like God.
they are moving their fingers ẍẍẍ along the wires.
 they are saying their chemical faith.
```

CLIFTON: It seemed to me that that made it more intense, and I wanted to center on Joanne's own suffering, her own feelings. The first poem in the series of nine ends "I call myself Gettysburg." Because it's almost like your body is having something of a civil war.

LONDON: Moving from "my days are pain" to "my hair is pain" seems very characteristic of your style and an enormously important lesson—the way you anchor the abstraction, the way you concretize these abstract things.

CLIFTON: I try to get to the specific thing which it seems to me illuminates the larger thing.

LONDON: I'd like to talk for a second about the line breaks. In the first draft, in your last line, you have "mother mary where is your living son" all in one line. You change it [in draft 3] to "child"; but what made you decide that you needed two lines?

CLIFTON: One of the things with these poems is that I did not wish them to be neat. Because leukemia is not neat. It seems to me that form follows subject. And I was concerned about being too neat with the lines.

```
chemotherapy


my hair is pain.
my mouth is a cave of cries.
my room is filled with white coats
shaped like God.
they are moving their fingers along
their stethescopes.
they are testing their chemical faith.
chemicals    chemicals    oh mother mary
where is your living child?
```


                        lucille clifton

LONDON: Let's talk about the use of colloquial language—idiom, vernacular, and so forth. Howard Nemerov says that he thinks poetry in English is coming to an end. He worries about the effect on our language of computer talk, jargon, slang, and all those "wicked impurities." Do you worry about that?

CLIFTON: No, I don't. I worry about Howard Nemerov now. One of the things I feel very strongly about is that American poetry should be written in the American language. Which is a huge, living, vital language. And I believe that all language is available for poetry. In the past only standard, written, formal English has been seen as suitable for poetry; I think that's ridiculous. The American language is wonderfully vital and alive, and poetry is dedicated to the life of language. It's a living thing.

I have written several children's books in a very strong black street language, and everybody talks about that. The people in the books are street kids, and it would be artistically ridiculous for me to have them speaking in a way that they don't talk. I also have some children's books written in iambic pentameter verse, but nobody ever says, "People don't talk like that."

LONDON: [Historian] Paul Fussell says, "the rhythm of a poem is the expression of the rhythm of a period." Of a culture and of a period, and that one can't get away from it. That the rhythm of a poem must move as the mind moves, and if that writer is a sensitive writer, he reflects the world he lives in. The rhythms in your poems change. In the early poems there's much more of a chanting going on. There's almost a kind of Emily Dickinson boldness and hardness and economy that comes into these later poems. What about rhythm?

CLIFTON: Our language is extremely musical; words have a kind of rhythm and music of their own. I'm very lucky in that I grew up hearing several uses of the American language. I heard the blues and I write to music.

LONDON: Really?

CLIFTON: Yes. I can't write if it's very quiet. I had four babies in diapers at once. When it got quiet I would start worrying. I listen to the blues, to Bach—Bach reminds me of poetry. I hear a lot of different music. That's why what Nemerov said is interesting to me. I think that black poets have been very important in opening up the language for poetry, opening up the music for poetry.

A writer who is not a minority thinks about the audience as people very much like him- or herself. On the other hand I am very much aware of the fact that my audience is of a number of cultures, a number of economic classes, and a number of colors. Black poets are always aware that the audience is very colored.

I feel very strongly a responsibility to my art, to my sex, to my family and to my race. And I feel a very strong responsibility to humanness. I don't know why I should feel it. Everyone does, I suppose. I often get asked when am I going to break out of black things and write real poems. Am I always going to feel bound? And yet I feel that I am freed by my culture because I do think about the whole language.

LONDON: One thing we don't find in your work is any use of myth or mythic figures. When Derek Walcott was here he was very interested in the use of myth to generalize and universalize his own material.

CLIFTON: Derek has a British education. America is a whole different thing. When he was in school they were educated to believe that the whole British experience was theirs. When I was in school, whatever we learned about anything, I knew darn well it had nothing to do with me.

STUDENT: Is there any justification from your point of view for the lack of capitalization and punctuation in your poetry?

CLIFTON: I like the look of it. I don't know punctuation very well, so I tend to punctuate as little as possible. And I like the look of the poem not capitalized. And the look of it matters to me a lot. I do sometimes capitalize. If there is a word that I think is important and needs to be emphasized, I capitalize it. I don't capitalize "I" very much.

LONDON: When E. E. Cummings didn't capitalize his "I" it was because he really insisted that his "I" stand in for Everyman, it was a kind of generalization of "I."

CLIFTON: Mine tends to be aesthetic. I like the look of it. I have a children's book that's coming out in May that is in iambic pentameter. And the editor added some commas. Some of them probably helped. But I had them take out the commas, because I don't care how grammatical it is, it breaks up my poem. Poetry, it seems to me, is not about sentences, it's about lines.

STUDENT: It's interesting that you don't capitalize first sentences. I had decided it had to do with the way you felt in relation to God.

CLIFTON: I do not think I'm religious at all. I don't go to church and all that. But I do write a lot about religious kinds of things. My own experience has taught me quite a bit about the experience of life and spirit and flesh and humanness—this is going to sound so bold and so arrogant—but I do not feel small in the face of God. So if I were going to have the G capitalized I would have a slightly less capitalized I. I wouldn't have a little one, I would have one that was a half step down.

LONDON: In those last poems in *Two-Headed Woman* there is a feeling of radiance that comes through the language.

CLIFTON: One thing that led to those poems was that Stanley Kunitz said to a mutual friend, "You know, I don't know anything about Lucille's inner life." And so I thought, OK, Stanley, are you ready for this?

LONDON: Was he ready?

CLIFTON: I don't know. He's never mentioned it.

Stanley Plumly

PEARL LONDON'S affinity for Stanley Plumly's poetry prompted more invitations to her class—five—than she extended to any other poet. He accepted in 1977, 1979, 1983, 1986, and 1993. The three visits for which tapes survive—1977, 1979 and 1986—neatly overlap an essential subset of his poetry, the collections *Out-of-the-Body Travel* (1977), which won the William Carlos Williams Award, *Summer Celestial* (1983), and *Boy on the Step* (1989). In 1996 Plumly described these books as a trilogy and said that the first of them centers on the suffering in his parents' lives. By the last book, *Boy on the Step,* "the world in which they are embedded is much more the issue, and that suffering and my own memory of it and my need to deal with it and transcend it, even faithfully represent it, show what I've learned." In all three books we see the mainstays of his lyric intensity and vision, the iconography of birds, trees, memory, and family. Robert Penn Warren has said, "Plumly established a new sort of ratio between the poet and his subject—or even his poem. It's a new turn of mind, behind the turn of language, in haunting, visionary pieces."

Plumly was born in 1939 and grew up in Ohio and Virginia's farm and lumber regions. Educated at Wilmington College in Ohio and at Ohio University, he has taught for more than forty years at institutions including Iowa, Princeton, Columbia, and the University of Washington. At present, he coheads the writing program at the University of Maryland and holds the Distinguished University Professorship there. He is the author most recently of *Old Heart: Poems* (2007), a National Book Award Finalist, and *Posthumous Keats: A Personal Biography* (2008), a project he first broached, years earlier, in Pearl London's company.

"Against Starlings"

LONDON: Marvelous poem. Back on your work sheet, you have [the first line] "a sound almost visible." You eliminated it. In the final version the first line is "their song is almost painful." I'd like to know your thinking.

PLUMLY: Well, I'll tell you. I think this is crucial. "The song is almost visible" isn't as true as "almost painful." I realized "painful" is motivation. It's truer as plot. "Visible" is not enough motivation. I don't know if you've heard a lot of starlings—it *is* painful; it's awful. That was the decision. I thought, Instead of announcing it, how can I make it visible?

LONDON: One other thing, right in there [lines 3 and 4 of the final poem], you have "A / wire." Nothing else. But if one goes back into the work sheets again, you have "the air with signals"—as though you were thinking of a wireless communication. And then you pared it down. Was that a part of it?

AGAINST STARLINGS

1

Their song is almost painful the way it
penetrates the air—above the haze and
level of the fields a thin line drawn. A
wire. Where the birdcall goes to ground. But I'd
stand anyway under the oaks lining
the road and whistle, tireless with chances,
tossing, by the handful, the crushed stone.
All of them answered, none of them came down.
By evening there'd be hundreds filling the
trees past hearing, black along the branches.
They'd go off with the guns like buckshot, black,
filling the sky, falling. I held my ears.
The holes in the air closed quickly, then healed.
Birds were bloodless, like smoke, wind in a field—

2

But not to be confused with the cowbird,
its brown head, its conical sparrow's bill,
nor with the red-wing, which is obvious,
even showy, blood or birthmark, nor with
the boat-tailed grackle—though at dusk, when they
gathered from the north, they were all blackbirds.
They were what the night brought, and the blown leaves,
and the cloud come down in the rain. The ease
of it, the way summer would be ending.
When I found one one morning it was the
color of oil in a pool of water,
bronze, blue-green, still shining. The parts that were
missing were throwaway, breast and belly
and the small ink and eye-ring of the eye—

FINAL TYPESCRIPT OF STANLEY PLUMLY'S "AGAINST STARLINGS"

3

Not to be compared with the last native
wild pigeon, trap shot high in Pike County,
Ohio, the fourth day of spring, nineteen
hundred--thirty years after the harvest
of millions filled the buffalo trains east.
They were, by report, 'the most numerous
bird ever to exist on earth,' what the
Narragansett called Wuskowhan, the blue
dove, the wanderer, whose flight is silent.
Not to be compared with the smaller, wild
mourning dove, which haunted the afternoon,
which you heard all day till dark. They
were the sound in my sleep those long naps home,
the last train calling down the line in time--

4

Sometimes, at the far end of a pasture,-
the burdock and buckwheat thick as the grass
along the hedgework, you could still find nests,
some fallen, some you had to climb to. They
were a kind of evidence, a kind of
science, sticks, straw, and brilliant bits of glass.
My mother had a hat like that, feathered,
flawed--she'd bought it used. It was intricate
and jewelled, the feathers scuffed like a jay's,
and so stiff you could've carried water.
The millinery species is over.
Those nests had nothing in them. Still, sometimes
I'd wait until the autumn light was gone,
the sky half eggshell, half a starling's wing--

5

Not to be compared with the fluted voice,
the five phrases in different pitches
of the thrush, the one Whitman heard, and Keats.
Sturnus vulgaris vulgaris—not to
be confused with the soft talk and music,
the voice that calls the spirit from the wood.
Those that stayed the winter sat the chimney
to keep warm, and cried down the snow to fly
against the cold. They were impossible.
They'd be dead before spring, or disappear
into the white air. —Not to be confused
with the black leaves whirling up the windward
side of the house, caught in the chimney smoke,
the higher the more invisible—

6

                              Black.
I saw them cover the sky over a
building once, and storm an alley. They were
a gathering, whole. Yet on the window
sill, individual, stealing the grain
I put there, they'd almost look at me through
the glass. Something magical, practical.
They'd even graze the ground for what had dropped.
I wished for one to come into the house,
and left the window open just enough.
None ever did. That was another year.
What is to be feared is emptiness and
nothing to fill it. I threw a stone or
I didn't throw a stone is one language—
the vowel is a small leaf on the tongue.

PLUMLY: That's all true. Again I opted for the concretion instead of the ideation. I also remembered a line in my first book—in a way, we're all derivative of ourselves, of our earlier work—I think the line is "a thin wire in the country." I've always thought, I like that line, but I never got it right. And I thought this was the chance to redeem that line. So in a way it's the anxiety of my own influence. I rewrote myself there.

LONDON: Small detail—in the very first stanza of the finished poem you have, "tossing, by the handful, the crushed stone." Much earlier in the drafts you talk about "tossing, by the handful, the shelled corn." It's so much less powerful.

PLUMLY: I've tossed both, actually. "Crushed stone" is from Peter, if you remember, the New Testament. Well, actually it was gravel. The corn wasn't working as well [in the poem]. But it ignited into something.

LONDON: I'm reminded, when I read "crushed stone," of an earlier poem of yours called "Heron." I don't know how many of you know it. I love that poem. In it you stand looking at the heron and you have stones in your hands. When we talked about it I asked you why you had those stones, and you were talking about the fear you had of your father. And you said—

PLUMLY: This is from when I was here another time? You remember this?

LONDON: I remember it well. "Heron" was one of the poems I loved best. But you said it was really dealing with your own aggression and your own hostility. I'm reminded of it with the "crushed stone." Is it aggression again? What do these starlings represent here? Rage?

PLUMLY: I don't think it's rage in the same sense. That was very focused. In the heron poem it occurs at a strategic point and [with the protagonist] as an adult. The strategy here is to get started and to go from doing it as a boy. One of the movements in the starling poem is from that to throwing a stone or not throwing a stone—and what difference does it make. Not anger so much as trying to change the space, the gestalt. Altering it in some way, and I did alter it. What difference does it make?

LONDON: Well, what difference *does* it make?

PLUMLY: Good question. "What is to be feared is emptiness and nothing to fill it." I don't know—stones fill it, or talk. Something has to fill it.

LONDON: Those wonderful lines at the end of the poem: "I threw a stone or / I didn't throw a stone is one language."
Let's take a look at a few more of the things that are happening here.

We have the wonderful use of "black" at the beginning of the sixth stanza. "Black" taken away from "invisible" [the last word of the fifth stanza] and brought down and left all alone at the head of that first line. And we have the blue dove [third stanza] and the cowbird with its brown head [second stanza] and the redwing [second stanza] and so forth. What is the symbolic value of color here?

PLUMLY: Oh, I don't know. That's a word that always scares me. I try not to think in terms of symbols, because everything is already that. One thing that has always bothered me is that the redwings and the cowbirds and the grackles and the starlings, et cetera, all got generalized. They were all the same thing for people—maybe even for me—and they aren't. I have other bird poems. The last poem I've written is a cedar waxwing poem. And of course the thrush isn't a blackbird at all. If there's any symbolic value, it has to do with trying to differentiate what was previously undifferentiated. To say, These birds are under threat—life is under threat—I'm under threat—if we don't make distinctions. They're not all the same. Once we make the distinctions, perhaps we don't shoot the starlings; we don't shoot the redwings.

LONDON: The nests, the starling's nests have nothing in them.

PLUMLY: I was always disappointed [about that].

LONDON: When we come to the fifth stanza some very interesting things happen. "Those that stayed the winter sat the chimney / to keep warm, and cried down the snow to fly / against the cold." That had originally been "cried down the wind"—what about snow there?

PLUMLY: I think "cry down the wind" is a cliché. The idea appealed to me, but it was just more of a cliché. I just wanted to get it out of there. They would huddle around that little chimney like a little fire or something. They were not going to make it. Why they didn't fly out of there, I never knew.

LONDON: In the final version you write "Not to be confused / with the black leaves whirling up the windward / side of the house." But in the work sheets, we have "not to / be confused with the soft talk and music."

"Soft talk and music" just doesn't compare. By what process did you eliminate it?

PLUMLY: "Soft talk" was a cliché. And I suppose that was part of it. But again it has to do with the process of differentiation. I wanted the reader to see the individual among the many. To see the particular in the general. Because poetry doesn't live, it seems to me, if it doesn't imply the single thing. Not the unique thing, but the single thing. The single thing is as unique as we're going to get.

LONDON: What is the difference between the single thing and the unique thing?

PLUMLY: There really isn't any. But a lot of people will seek out the unique thing and, I would say, end up inventing. They'll end up with clams playing accordions. They will invent into the object; they'll twist it, bend it in some way, distort it: they'll project into it to make it unique. That's where the mind has triumphed over what Rilke calls the certainty of the object.

Surrealism, to a certain extent, had a short life because of that. We learned a lot about objects from the surrealists. Most people learned about juxtaposition. That's where the newness was.

LONDON: Do you remember what Wallace Stevens said about surrealism? I think it was in *The Necessary Angel*—he said "Surrealism invents without discovering." I think it's the discovering that you're talking about.

PLUMLY: The last line in the starling poem, that's about as surreal as I get. Several things came together there.

LONDON: "What is to be feared is emptiness and / nothing to fill it." And then those wonderful last lines: "I threw a stone or / I didn't throw a stone is one language—" At some point you eliminated "the hard cicada." That sounded good—why did that have to go by the wayside?

PLUMLY: The trouble with cicadas is that they are too perfectly ono-matopoetic. They're so self-contained. I suppose they could be used in a poem—they have been in a lot of southern poems. [Robert Penn] Warren is fond of them. The whole Fugitive Movement is full of cicadas—as details, as a kind of atmospheric in a poem. But to put weight on them, I don't think they could hold it. It's one of those objects that when you sit with it for a while, it doesn't do much; it's too perfected. And too small.

STUDENT: When you started this poem, did you have that feeling that "what is to be feared is emptiness"?

PLUMLY: I have that feeling a lot. I must have had that feeling. I didn't have that language. But that was there, definitely. That was what really did start the poem.

LONDON: Before we leave "Against Starlings" let's take a look at the last line, "the vowel is a small leaf on the tongue." Back in those work sheets you wrote it differently. You wrote, "You knew this bird / you know that the vowel is human, and / vulnerable, a small leaf on the tongue." Could you comment on your thinking there? It's very interesting that you took away "human and vulnerable."

PLUMLY: Well, again, those were the announcements of the issue; they're not the issue. The issue was three words. My mind runs this way. Maybe I'm a latent symbolist—but words are objects, and I'll get them lined up in a certain equation. Change the equation, everything changes. The equation here was "vowel leaf tongue"; the rest is narrative. That's the lyric, that's what's at issue. The words are the embodiment or the enactment of those issues—the vulnerability and the human issue. And it had to be a small leaf, because the tongue isn't very big. I wanted it to be visible, with the tongue out, so you could see it. The kind of leaf you pick off a bush.

LONDON: I wonder what kind of leaf it would be . . .

PLUMLY: Maybe a pyracantha.

C. K. Williams

THE VISIT C. K. WILLIAMS made to Pearl London's class in March 1988 caught him at a vibrant period in his career and at a particularly key moment. He had turned fifty-one and his seventh book of poems, *Flesh and Blood*, had just been published and had become a National Book Critics Circle Award winner. Choosing a concise, eight-line-stanza form for its poems, Williams departed from the extremely long, Whitmanesque lines and stanzas that had become the signature style of earlier books like *Tar* (1983). That C. K. Williamsesque long line, we can now call it, has become one of the most recognizable stylistic reinventions of contemporary poetry and would return in the later books. Of his long line he has said that it liberated him to "write the way I thought and the way I felt." But with the transformation from *Tar* to *Flesh and Blood* here, he says, "[I] kept adding constraints, and each time it would generate new kinds of themes and meanings."

"I know of few diary-poems so moving and so full of incident as the eight-line poems in his book *Flesh and Blood,*" writes Dan Chiasson. "The ratio of sympathy to detachment here feels just right; documentary precision and the wide-angle embellishments of 'art' find perfect balance." The poems discussed that day in class found their way into *Selected Poems* (1994), with their close scrutiny of psychological states, of love and memory, and of "the self's relation to the larger world," as Chistian Wiman puts it. Charles Simic calls *Selected Poems* "one of the strongest and most original books of poems of the last few decades."

C. K. Williams teaches at Princeton University one semester a year, dividing his time between France and the United States. Born in Newark, New Jersey, in 1936, he attended Bucknell and the University of Pennsylvania. *Repair* (1999) would win the Pulitzer Prize, *Singing* (2003) the National Book Award for poetry.

"Medusa"

PEARL LONDON: I'd like to ask you what poetry must take into account. Wallace Stevens once said that the ultimate source of values for the contemporary poet and novelist is neither God nor society but imagination. Can we say that?

C. K. WILLIAMS: No. Frankly, Stevens bugs me when he talks about that. It's just not true. I'll give you a much better quote from André Brink, the South African novelist. He says we are living in the ruins of not one but two empires. The Western capitalist-Christian-industrial empire and the Eastern socialist empire. Then he says that in a time like this all the writer can do is to offer witness, or evidence. And then he says that the task of the writer is to keep alive human values. The work of the writer is to make clear what the basic human values are. He says it much more gracefully than that. And I like that kind of approach much more than Stevens's, where you sort of inject a little airy philosophy and make it sound as though everybody in the world is a philosopher, [but] they just don't quite know it. Which isn't true at all.

LONDON: Israeli writer Aharon Appelfeld has talked about how one who has survived the Holocaust can write as introspectively as he does, and he says, "Daily events do indeed knock on every door. But they know that I don't let such agitated guests into my house." Do you let those agitated guests into your house?

WILLIAMS: Into my personal house, too much; I get too upset by daily events and public events; sometimes I think I should just stop reading newspapers. In my poetic house, yes, too. Some of my earlier poems were overtly political.

I've been very concerned, as most Jews have, with what's been going on in Israel, and I have written some poems about the Holocaust that were very important poems to me. At a conference I attended recently, a radical lesbian poet asked, "Well, is anybody going to write anything about the Palestinians and what's going on with them?" And I was thinking, Can I do that? And do I have to—the way I had to write my poems about the Holocaust?

I don't know. I can't programmatically sit down and say, "Here's a worthy cause, I'm going to write about it." It just sort of has to happen. At the moment I don't know what I'll do about that issue. It might be I'm too far from it. . . . Maybe the Palestinians have to write their own poems.

LONDON: I'd like to ask about the concept of witness in poetry. Wouldn't you say it applies to internal as well as external events?

WILLIAMS: Yes, what interests me now is the witnessing of interior events. I don't feel particularly interested in offering the kind of witnessing that I offered in *Flesh and Blood* [1987]. In a lot of that book I was trying to look out and see others and make them a part of the poetic universe in a way that I hadn't been able to before. I still have a lot of unfinished poems left from it—another fifty or so—that I was still working on when I stopped, but when I go back to them they're of no interest to me. *Flesh and Blood* was the most exciting book to write: I'd just walk through the street and see poem after poem and my notebook would fill up and I'd be writing and writing. That's all gone now, and I feel totally bereft. The only things that interest me now are very introspective; the poems I'm writing have no details; they're almost pure language.

STUDENT: When you move from this external world of witnessing and giving evidence into the internal world of giving evidence about the workings of the mind, to what degree do you feel that you wind up in an elitist world? What happens to your audience?

WILLIAMS: That's an interesting question. There are poems in *Flesh and Blood* I realize are very difficult, very elusive. Some of the more interior poems like "Nostalgia" or "Resentment" can be quite difficult to follow. A lot of people won't necessarily get them. But those are the kind of things that interest me now. Maybe I am writing for a more select audience, though "elite" is a thorny word. The conservatism we have in America is really know-nothingism. But there are portions of culture that have to be conserved. Civilization, unless you keep recapitulating it, can die, wither away. And this has to happen in poetry, too. So if it's elitist in that sense, I find nothing wrong with it.

STUDENT: You're taking a different direction now, to bring up more of the inner view. And it's a leap into something you have not been writing. Is there . . . maybe is there a way of looking that you bring to yourself?

WILLIAMS: Well, when that happens, you often find that it's coming about maybe because of the influence of another poet. I've been very interested in some of John Ashbery's poetry over the last few years. And some of it shows in here, I think. Now, he has a specific way of doing that which I can't do and don't want to do. But in his big poems—"Self-Portrait in a

Convex Mirror" and particularly "The Wave"—he has a way of keeping track of what's going on in his consciousness that's absolutely awesome. Now, I can't do that, and, as I say, I don't particularly want to [do it] the way he does it, but I am interested in the phenomenon. So that for me to say, "Well, I decided that I was going to become more introspective" is really not quite true. You know, there's always this dialogue that's going on with other poetry. So ultimately one day I'll be able to say, "Well, this was mine." But the impulse of it, I would have to say, came from my studying him.

LONDON: Part of the thing that's been so interesting to all of us as we've been reading *Tar* and *Flesh and Blood* is the characteristic kind of eye that you bring to your work.

WILLIAMS: Are you speaking of "I" as a pronoun? Or—

LONDON: No, e-y-e. I don't dare approach the other "I." The eye that unlayers, that shades, that is continually finding in the perception various unshadowings, and so forth. I'm thinking very specifically now of "the blazing redness" of the apple in "Snow: II" in *Flesh and Blood*. What about this need to unlayer, to find, that falcon's eye. Is it always there? Is it consciously there?

WILLIAMS: I don't think of it in terms of the eye; I think of it in terms of the imagination. We see with our imaginations, we don't see with our eyes. And there are different ways to see with the imagination. The apple in the poem about snow is the imagination of memory; the poem is about memory as well as about love and the passage of time in love. The picking out of that detail of the apple has to do, really, with how incredible our love memory can be if we let it be.

LONDON: These extraordinary metaphorical leaps that your imagination takes. For example, now again, I'm thinking in "Love: Beginnings," that "faithful heart, snorting again, / stamping in its stall." That's so incredibly wonderful and right.

WILLIAMS: Yeah. I think so, too. [*Laughter*] Every time I read that poem I think, How did I get that? Where did that come from? I suppose I could try to trace back all the figures . . . I suppose I could, but in a way you don't want to, because then I'm afraid it will never happen again. Which it might never, I don't know.

LONDON: But you do it all the time. Let's talk for a minute about the evolution in form and shape from *Tar* to the eight-line stanzas of *Flesh and Blood*. What determined them? What were you groping for there?

WILLIAMS: Well, it was pragmatic. The poems in *Tar* would take three, four years from the time I started them to the time I got them worked out, sometimes. That was the way I worked. I just kept poems around a long time and I'd work at them. When I finished *Tar* I had a whole slew of poems left unfinished; some of them had been around on my desk for ten years. I was looking at one of them one day and I thought, This is never going to be a poem. It was about thirty lines long—thirty of the long lines. There was one stanza of about eight lines, and it occurred to me that it wasn't a bad poem in itself, and it became "The Park." Then I found "The Fountain" in the same fragment. Then I started going through all my old drafts, and I'd find what had been a twenty-line poem and make it eight; I'd find a four-line poem and make that eight lines, too. Then I really got into it, and the poems started generating themselves.

People often assume that a form is a constraint, something that you have to push and squash things into, but in fact a form is generative. And that eight line form surely was that for me. It took on a life of its own that was really exciting. I kept adding constraints—I decided that the end of a line would always be the end of a grammatical unit, decided to write some in one sentence, others I would divide in half; others are in couplets—and each time I would add one of these so-called constraints it would generate new kinds of themes and meanings.

STUDENT: You're using a line that's not common. In a sense you're at the cutting edge. How much concern do you have for where modern poetry is and where you'd like to push it? Or is it just your own concern about what you want to do?

WILLIAMS: It's more and more just my own concern about what I want to do. One of the benefits of becoming a middle-aged poet is that you really can't worry about that very much. I still have to struggle with the other questions: What have I done? Who am I? What is my audience? Although the basic struggle is always with myself. When I started writing that long line, people said, "That's not poetry, that's prose." And it was futile to argue. First of all, I didn't have the technical means to argue—I probably still don't. I just knew it was poetry. It's very satisfying to me to have people now accept that it is.

One of the things that has driven my poetry right from the beginning is the idea of not leaving anything out. When I first started writing I also wrote stories and plays and essays. And then I decided at one point that I wasn't going to do that. That I was just going to take any ideas I had for stories or plays or essays and find a way to put them into poetry. I'm becoming more and more of an intellectual as I get older. I feel as though this is a part of the mind that isn't usually brought directly into poetry—but in fact is a large part of the mind of many of the people who read poetry. People who read poetry also read anthropology or philosophy or linguistics. Why not be able to use that in poems?

STUDENT: Was there something that you felt that poetry could do for your ideas that stories and plays didn't do?

WILLIAMS: No, no. I just felt that I couldn't spread myself thin. I didn't have enough gift at the time. I just decided if I'm going to be a poet, I'm going to be a poet. I'm not going to distract my ideas into these other forms.

STUDENT: Could you talk a little about this idea of not leaving anything out? I think a lot of us have been taught to leave a lot out in poetry.

WILLIAMS: Well, that actually happened after my second book, which was published at the height of our Vietnam War despair and has a lot of poems in it that were very involved with that kind of sadness. That terrible hopelessness and rage became a kind of metaphysical despair about the insanity of the universe. And after that book I sort of collapsed. I've since found that I collapse after every book, but I didn't know it then. Also, my marriage had broken up, so my life was in terrible shape. And at one point I decided I wasn't going to write poetry anymore, because it was obviously destroying my life, that I had too much energy to be a poet; I was like a whirling top—I was just knocking everything in my life around. And then I wrote a couple poems—just as notes, almost—in these long lines. Not really thinking about poetry, because I wasn't a poet anymore; I had decided I was going to be a film writer and a film director. Then I went to give a reading one day, I read these poems and realized I was onto something, that these poems had taken into account portions of my consciousness that I wasn't using in the poetry I'd been writing. It came to me after a while that the poems I'd been writing were like rhetorical codes sent out from the poet I was towards people who understood how to decode them, and that I was leaving out an awful lot of people. And leaving out an awful lot of myself, too.

Another idea that came to me at the same time was that I wanted to speak in a voice that was closer to the voice I actually spoke in. Wordsworth said exactly the same thing, as we well know; that he wanted to write in the language that men speak. That line also seemed a way to get closer to that, too.

LONDON: Let me throw out something that Charles Simic said. I wonder if it disturbs you—as I have to confess it disturbs me. How would you reply to this: "For me, the feel for the line is the most mysterious aspect of the entire process. It took me years to realize that the line is what matters and not the sentence."

WILLIAMS: That's not a conflict, that's the history of poetry. That's just Charlie Simic's development. Everybody develops in a different way. The history of poetry is the tension between the line and the sentence, that's how it differs from conversational speech; it organizes language artificially. The line is an absolutely arbitrary unit, and that's what's fascinating about it. Just as in music it's absolutely arbitrary that we have a scale that has eight notes in an octave and some of them are divided into half notes—in India it's divided differently. Once you set up a convention, then there's something about the human mind that becomes exalted in the tension between the normal consciousness and the consciousness that is submitting to these arbitrary conventions. And in poetry the line is an arbitrary convention.

LONDON: I want to come back, if we may for a minute, to the concept of witness as against just evidence. Because I think that's a rather critical thing. When you speak of the witness of poetry, you're not really talking about just the external event; it's the internal event. So that, for example, when Milton says "dark, dark, dark amid the blaze of noon" he is writing a witness poetry, witnessing the condition of his own blindness. Isn't that maybe the direction that you're talking about?

WILLIAMS: That's clear. In *Flesh and Blood* I didn't really distinguish between the witnessing of inner events and the witnessing of outer events. It's sort of one of the tensions of the book. When I went to organize the poems to make an order for them it was very difficult. Obviously most of the poems that are witnessing also have to do with internal events. Because there's always transformation. It isn't ever just an imagistic sort of writing; in most cases there's some sort of intense imaginative transformation going on.

LONDON: That's the great thing that happens in the poem dedicated to Paul Zweig ["Le Petit Salvié" in *Flesh and Blood*]. Which I think is one of the really great poems.

WILLIAMS: That's nice to hear. Can you write that up? [*Laughter*] Galway [Kinnell] helped me write that, by the way. He gave me some great revisions.

LONDON: Did he really? In writing poetry which has pain at its center like that—and so much of it does—is it ever painful for you to write it?

WILLIAMS: I don't think there's a rule on this. When I was writing the elegy for Paul Zweig I would sometimes cry as I was writing. But that was the only time that ever happened to me.

STUDENT: Coming back to your long line—do you count beats at all?

WILLIAMS: No. I think the best way to describe my unit of measure is the weighted phrase. There's a book I read recently that analyzes [poet Sir Thomas] Wyatt and proposes that it's a mistake to try to count feet in Wyatt, that in fact he worked with phrases. I realized that's what I do, too. I'm always surprised when somebody actually counts up how many syllables there are in my lines because I never do.

STUDENT: Did you ever write anything in forms? Villanelles or sonnets—formal structure?

WILLIAMS: No. I once wrote a sequence of about fifty sonnets. Each one had a different rhyme scheme.

STUDENT: Were they published?

WILLIAMS: No, they were thrown in the garbage. They're gone. *Flesh and Blood* has one poem called "Medusa" that was really those fifty sonnets compressed down into eight lines.

Medusa

Once, in Rotterdam, a whore once, in a bar, a sailor's bar, a hooker bar,
       opened up her legs—
her legs, my god, were logs—lifted up her skirt, and rubbed herself, with
       both hands rubbed herself,
there, right there, as though what was there was something else, as
though
       the something else
was something she just happened to have under there, something that
she
       wanted me to see.
All I was was twenty, I was looking for a girl, the girl, the way we always,
       all of us,
looked for the girl, and the woman leaned back there and with both
hands
       she mauled it,
talked to it, asked it if it wanted me, laughed and asked me if I wanted it,
       while my virginity,
that dread I'd fought so hard to lose, stone by stone, was rising back
inside
       me like a wall.

STUDENT: Is there such a thing as fashion in poetry? Where some people write in short lines and then they turn and write in long lines?

WILLIAMS: There are certainly a lot of fashions in poetry, though I don't think those fashions have had to do with line length. Blake wrote in long lines, so did Christopher Smart, and then Whitman wrote in very long lines and nobody particularly followed them. It's not as though I invented the iambic pentameter with this line; I just devised something that was useful to me. When it was accepted as being verse instead of prose I was pleased, but the important thing was that I could do what I wanted with the line, that it becomes absorbed in the subject.

LONDON: What about the idea that a subject is utterly incidental to a poem? That any subject and every subject is your subject if you want it to be. Stanley Kunitz said that a poem is interesting not because of the technique, it's interesting because the poet, the writer, has understood something.

WILLIAMS: Well, you've asked two questions. The first question is, does the subject matter? And the second question is, is there a subject that then is understood? And there are really two answers. Up until the nineteenth century the subject in most poems really doesn't matter; a poem is a singing; it's an enactment of the human voice singing. And most poems are love poems; everybody knows everything about love, which is that you either have it or you don't. What's important is how the poet sings. It's like the composer—you don't care what theme Mozart starts with. Let him do anything. You want to see what he does with it.

Then there's the kind of poetry, which really begins in the nineteenth century, in which the subject becomes most important. And you get into the question of the historical function of the poem. For me the great thinkers on that are [Jules] Michelet and [André] Malraux. Malraux, in *The Voices of Silence*, talks about the change in the function of painting and sculpture in the nineteenth century, after God dies—whether God really dies, literally, or assumes a different place in our consciousness—and how art takes up some of the functions that religion had had as its purview. So subject matter has to become much more important. We see that really begin to happen in Blake and in Shelley. By the time you get to Whitman the subject of the work becomes enormous, and that Whitman can sing it is what makes him a uniquely great poet.

LONDON: One last thing. There's a point in "Some Remarks on Rhythm" [1960], a lovely little essay by [Theodore] Roethke, where he says the rhythm must move as the mind moves or the poem is lost. To what extent does the rhythm move as the mind moves?

WILLIAMS: I'd disagree with that a little, and turn it the other way around. The rhythm of the poem moves the mind, and rhythm generates meaning. That's one of the splendors of poetry, that it moves the reader's mind in a way it wouldn't move by itself. And maybe it's why we need poetry.

Molly Peacock

MOLLY PEACOCK was born in Buffalo, New York, in 1947. The first in her family to go to college, she attended SUNY–Binghamton and then the Johns Hopkins University writing program, where she studied with poet Richard Howard. For the next eleven years Peacock taught seventh-grade English at Friends Seminary in New York City and wrote two of her early books of poems, *Raw Heaven* (1984) and *Take Heart* (1989). Her visit to Pearl London's class in 1992 coincided with a self-described "tumultuous time," including the death of her mother and later her sister. She said she decided then "to become a freelance poet and to start teaching students independently, one to one. I left Friends Seminary and went completely out on my own."

Since that transition she has become something of an emissary on behalf of poetry: as a poet-in-residence at the American Poets' Corner (Cathedral Church of St. John the Divine, New York City), president of the Poetry Society of America, and a creator of Poetry in Motion, which for years put a changing array of poems on subways and buses throughout North America. Her own mature poetry has been noted for its reinvention of form—self-taught experiments with rhyme and meter, with sonnets broken down and built up again, as in "The Hunt," the many drafts of which she discusses with London. As Carolyn Kizer has written of Peacock, "She knows that form is needed to contain the pain and chaos of our lives." In London's copy of Peacock's poem "A Simple Purchase," from *Take Heart,* these lines are underscored: "and grope / toward form in our lives, / even if only the rhymes / of our mistakes survive."

Peacock's most recent books of poetry are *Cornucopia* (2002) and *The Second Blush* (2008); her prose works include a literary memoir, *Paradise, Piece by Piece* (1998), and *How to Read a Poem and Start a Poetry Circle* (1999). She is currently on the faculty of the Spalding University low-residency master of fine arts program.

———————

"The Hunt"

PEARL LONDON: I've been reading your work sheets you sent us and was so delighted about "The Hunt," that beautiful sonnet, and as I was thinking of Seamus Heaney's "Glanmore Sonnets," and then the China sonnets that Auden wrote, I asked myself, "Why the sonnet today? What does the sonnet offer you?" When Bob Hass was here last time he said to us that patterned form implies a patterned society. No matter how Elizabeth Bishop deviated from the thing—nonetheless, inherent in the sonnet is a kind of pattern. But we certainly don't live in a patterned society. Every day it becomes less patterned.

MOLLY PEACOCK: Patterned form comes from the premise that form is the *outside* of experience. My premise is that form is the *inside* of the experience, as a skeleton, not a cage.

LONDON: Not an encumbrance.

PEACOCK: Exactly.

LONDON: I was thinking about your poem, which I enormously like, called "How I Come to You." It's the first poem in *Take Heart*: "maybe you hoped / for rock solid through." And then some lines later you say, "I smashed myself" and then "This is how I come to you: / broken." Beautiful poem. And I thought to myself, My goodness—doesn't a smashed psyche, a rock broken through in that way, doesn't it demand a smashed form? Or if not, certainly not the neat, ordained, beautifully managed quatrains that we have here.

PEACOCK: The circumstances of my childhood were extremely chaotic. Nothing was delivered when expected. Promises weren't kept. Life was utterly, utterly unpredictable. (As a result it produced in me a state of hypervigilance.) As an adult this makes me the sort of hostess who remembers what everyone is drinking. That chaos made me love the so-called pattern that life isn't supposed to have. I clung to it. I escaped into art.

To go back to the sonnet: you might think of the sonnet as a wave. In the traditional Shakespeare sonnet, there's a part of the wave that goes out, then it crests and comes in. I don't think of the pattern as societal; I think of it as deeply internal both psychologically and physically. I have a physical sense of this form that is quite different from saying, "Oh, this form is not useful for us now because we do not live the way people lived in the fourteenth century." Indeed that is true, but we have the same physiology, and if not the exact psychology, we are certainly as human.

I went back to graduate school when I was thirty, and everyone was writing free verse, obsessed with line breaks. The whole workshop mechanism seemed to be going to these end words, and yet no one could tell me what a line was. I wanted to have an idea of a line. The only sense of the line as a unit I could have was looking at "traditional" poetry and seeing those units that had end rhymes. And I thought, Look at the density of this as opposed to breaking lines in these little prepositional phrases!

LONDON: You're not talking about meter.

PEACOCK: No, I didn't learn enough about meter until recently. "The Hunt" is more metered than my other poems because I simply didn't know how to do it before. You know how they teach you to measure out the meters? I could always do it when the teacher did it, but then when I was on my own my ear was different. So I decided, All right, I have to rely on my own ear. But I will count, and I'll count syllables.

LONDON: But you didn't write syllabic verse.

PEACOCK: I wrote a kind of loose ten-syllable line. Very loose. And because ten syllables in English sometimes falls into iambic pentameter, there are the metrical flashes throughout. So it's a mongrel mix. It's how I began to put these things together.

Take the opening line to *The Merchant of Venice.* Antonio says, "In sooth, I know not why I am so sad." He does not say, "In *sooth* I *know* not *why* I *am* so *sad.*" Each stress has a different weight in the line. And one stress is almost so light it's practically an unstressed syllable. There are those four more noticeable stresses and one almost unstressed stress. When I saw that, I thought, Well no wonder I could never count these things out! I felt that I had to listen to my own ear, and if my own ear was listening in some direction, I was simply going to go with that. I wasn't going to worry about being too perfect.

LONDON: I'm really glad you brought up the point of weight. The weight of a syllable really has to be measured in terms of the context. A syllable is not an absolute. It must be seen in the environment of its neighbors and its context.

PEACOCK: And in the case of "In sooth I know not why I am so sad," it's easy to see that each musical unit, in single-syllable words, is also a unit of meaning. But when you have polysyllabic words they go by more quickly than the time it takes to count out each unit of musical meaning in single-syllable words.

LONDON: I want to come back to the whole relevance of rhyme and form for the poet writing now. Because after all we are writing in a time of great tension and great dissonance, and that voice must also be heard. I thought about T. S. Eliot, who said, "Rhyme removed, much ethereal music leaps up from the word." Now, how are you going to answer that? Take away the rhyme and then you get this ethereal music. And he also says, "The rejection of rhyme is not a leap at facility; on the contrary, it imposes a much severer strain upon language." How do you decide at what point rhyme is going to fulfill your meaning and your purpose?

PEACOCK: I think he's right—for his own work. He combined rhyme and unrhyme. But the point that rhyme has for contemporary writers *now* is that very often free verse ignores music. The workshop aesthetic says that the notion of revision is excision. You have to take *anything extra* out. Get rid of it. [*Imitates voice of workshop instructor*] "Get rid of that syllable. Why have you got all those articles in there? Take out those "a's," "and's," and "the's."

LONDON: You sound just like Pearl London.

PEACOCK: And that's wonderful advice to get the student to really see the underpinnings of the language. But if you constantly overapply it, what happens is that you lose those unstressed syllables. And when you lose unstressed syllables, you begin to lose music. I've done some investigation into the metrics of free verse. And looked at the percentage of stressed to unstressed syllables, say, in a free verse poem. It's fascinating. There are always more stressed syllables in a free verse poem—the ones I've looked at. Especially in poems that have a medium to short line. Say Louise Glück—75 to 80 percent of her shorter lines are comprised of stresses without the relief of unstressed syllables. Getting from one line to the next feels like a very heavy experience. Part of that comes from the technique of excision. But for Glück this technique works so well because it's also an emotional formulation.

I began to be interested in shaping a line to retain my initial impulse in music. Because I found that when I revised, I lost the feeling. That part of the poem is very unconscious, the music coming out of you—that's your voice. I began to see these lines and the rhymes as a way to preserve my voice, the freshness of my own speech.

The system of the line in a poem is entirely different from the system of meaning. The line is strictly musical. The system of meaning in the poem is the system of the sentence. Prose only has one system—the system of the sentence. That's it. It can be very beautiful and lyrical and rhythmical, but just in terms of the sentence. The poem has the line, the rhythm of the line, *and* the rhythm of the sentence. So there are two types of music that are being dealt with. Very often in free verse, though, the poet goes only toward the rhythm of the sentence, and the rhythm of the line simply supports the rhythm of the sentence.

LONDON: Of course, this is what Wallace Stevens meant when he said, "A poem means in two ways." It has content—it conveys its meaning through content—and it conveys its meaning through language. That's what you are saying is very often shortchanged in the free verse form.

PEACOCK: Right.

LONDON: What I would love to hear you comment on is the use of grids in your thinking. The grids we lay with each other. The geometries of the architecture, [in Peacock's poem "The Lawns of June"] ". . . from here to the drug / store is forty-seven lawns, one hundred- / six lawns from here to the veterinary." That architectural approach, that geometry in mind.

PEACOCK: It is very much like music. I said there was the system of music, which is the system of the line, and the system of the sentence, which is the system of meaning; but there is also the system of imagery—the visual system in the poem. The visual system also, at least in my work, is as unconscious as I can make it. If I can get those images to rise up out of me and grab them I will do that. The grid hits me for the same reason; it's like a skeleton: it is the form inside things. It is what could govern chaos.

LONDON: That's what I'm getting at.

PEACOCK: And there is constantly in all of this work, in all of my life, that sense of chaos and that struggle to make sense of it. There's also a visual sense. I don't know whether you know the paintings of Richard Diebenkorn? He exalted suburbia in the sense of seeing from a helicopter view all of the various grids, the squares, the rectangles of the planned landscape. Nobody writes about suburbia. I grew up in it; I grew up in a place that people eschew, that's somehow not glamorous enough for poetry. Yet I saw that landscape as reflecting—to go back to Bob Hass—reflecting a need to have an experience, however unpatternable experience essentially is.

LONDON: "The Hunt" is a pattern.

PEACOCK: The most interesting page of "The Hunt" is the one that is nearly unreadable. The poet Lyn Lifshin once looked at a manuscript page of mine at Yaddo and howled—she thought it was the funniest thing that I actually wrote out the A's and B's and the rhymes like a schoolgirl.

LONDON: I was taken aback that with your ear they would have found their way into a list of that sort. "Howls," "vowels," "jowls"—and then there was one that you left out. What was it . . . oh, dear me, I've forgotten.

PEACOCK: I don't use a rhyming dictionary. I completely let my unconscious dictate the rhymes. So of course I leave things out. I must just block them—or I come onto something else. Do you see this *aba* pattern? That's the pattern of the triolet. Well, look at that. I start off and I'm thinking,

This is a triolet idea. Clearly it was not, because I abandoned the triolet almost immediately. The triolet is worse than a villanelle. It's like a tiny, tiny—

LONDON: Oh, I know what the word was; it was "prowls." And I thought, Why didn't she have it?

PEACOCK: You're right! "Prowls" would have been fabulous.

LONDON: We can add it. What made you think that the triolet was not going to develop here?

PEACOCK: By the time I got through the second line I realized that I was going somewhere, but I didn't know where I was going. I couldn't do that in a triolet because I was going to have to double back too much. You really have to know where you're going with a triolet and I didn't know. But I knew that I was trying for that moment when I'd get all the elements of the poem and could begin to drive them. It's like I would have all the horses harnessed and I would start going with them in my carriage. And because we're all going, somehow we end up in a direction and a destination—

STUDENT: Your work sheets are all really about the endings. The work sheets you gave us. The real working was on the endings, I found.

PEACOCK: Yes. That's absolutely the case with almost all of my work. First of all, I can't let the poem go. I couldn't write a poem like this in stages. I sat down and I wrote it right out. I wrote it out in an hour and fifteen minutes or something like that. I wrote it in bed, where I usually write. With a pencil on paper, like this. Getting up occasionally to get something and come back to bed. And this was one that just came out pretty much whole except for that ending. Where I keep struggling. I've had people comment on the ending, saying it's not the right ending, saying it's this, saying it's that.

LONDON: As we move on to the next [draft] page, you have "flung viscera my treated dog," and I'm not quite sure what you even meant by "treated dog."

PEACOCK: I meant that it was given a treat. I did change it. The dog is thrown viscera as a treat. Then "tamed" is my handwriting, because I saw instantly that that was a problem.

The   stubby, black-jowled dog inside me growls
and drools and warns and plants its crooked feet,
legs quivering, brindle-chest staunched, and howls
until approachers back off in defeat,
although a brilliant poacher sometimes cows
my dog, my heart, its bitten hope, with meat,
flung viscera which my treated dog mauls   tamed
and then protects, will guarding what I eat
while poacher raises rifle; and follows
my deer into my wood, calling me dear, fleet
beauty, and I run, wholly my wild soul,
while the dumb, bristled dog I too am yowls,
guarding empty gate and empty street
till hunter becomes me, and we repeat.

ack.
mirrored

I become hunter and worrpit

Molly Peacock

LONDON: When we move on to [another], "till hunter discards me and then we repeat"— there isn't very much change there. But if we move on to the [next] page, now the rhyme scheme is very clear; it's very unrelenting, it's very pounding: "till hunter discards me" becomes "till hunter becomes me" at the end. And of course now we have the "tamed dog."

How, as you looked at this poem and knew that you were approaching the final version of it, how important was the rhyme scheme at that point?

PEACOCK: Incredibly. When I took the material it was with the idea of a two-sound rhyme scheme. So I've got the "growl," "owl"—the "ow, ow, ow, I'm hurt, I'm hurt, I'm hurt" sound. And the "eee eee eat" sound.

THE HUNT

The stubby, black-jowled dog inside me growls
and drools and warns and plants its crooked feet,
legs quivering, brindle chest staunched, and howls
until approachers back off in defeat —
although a brilliant poacher sometimes cows
my dog, my heart, its bitten hope, with meat,
flung viscera my tamed dog mauls
and then protects, guarding what I eat
while poacher raises rifle: he follows
my deer into my wood, calling me dear, fleet
beauty, and I run, wholly my wild soul,
while the dumb, bristled dog I too am yowls,
guarding empty gate and empty street
till hunter becomes me, and we repeat.

                                   Molly Peacock

LONDON: Weren't you afraid of the "ow ow ow"? You know that wonderful story about Ford Madox Ford. When he was about seventeen his father took him to see Thomas Hardy. So he presented Hardy with his book, *The Brown Owl*. Hardy was then an old man and terribly kindly, and he looked at it. And he said [*disparaging the rhyme*] "Ow, ow, ow." And that was the end.

PEACOCK: [*Laughs*] I didn't say "ow, ow, ow," but there are people who have written about my work who do say, "This is relentless, this relentless rhyming—can't you stop it?" *I* almost can't stand to be inside the rhymes. And I chose them! The relentlessness seems to be the quality of this cycle of the dog, of the deer and the hunter. I loved writing it, because it seemed to me to be so deeply unconscious. I wanted to get at some very internal process that I myself did not truly understand, yet I knew that if I described it well enough it would be comprehensible, and other people would recognize its meaning yet not quite be able to state its meaning exactly. At least, that's how I feel about it.

LONDON: What we were saying at the beginning this morning—do you think that part of your use of this insistent sound in the rhyme was a part of a tremendous need to yoke the disparate parts together?

PEACOCK: It is a violent yoking together, yes.

STUDENT: I'm so fascinated by this diagram on the first [*manuscript*] sheet. The little grid you made with all these little *x*'s. Is it something that you doodle while you're thinking?

PEACOCK: I think I doodled it. But it's so much a piece of what this is And the other thing about this is, I didn't know it was going to turn into a sonnet.

LONDON: That's surprising.

PEACOCK: It surprised me, too. It just came out. I've written so many of them that it just happened. "The Hunt" is a perfect sonnet, but I very rarely write a perfect form. I wouldn't say that I actually deform the form, but I shift, sometimes I break, sometimes I prune the form to meet my needs. This I learned from Elizabeth Bishop, too. That she will work a rhyme scheme down and then she'll drop it. Then she'll pick it up later. And I thought—You can do that? Great. I'll do that, too. If it doesn't work I'm just going to drop it. Or sometimes the rhyme scheme will shift. I'll start out *abab* and there's some internal thing going on, then it becomes *abba*. And I'll go, "I wonder how that happened?" But I'll just let it happen. It's like being in an echo chamber often. So I don't even worry about it.

STUDENT: I was thinking about the ending. Where at the beginning you said "till I become the hunter," then you had an alternate, "till the hunter becomes me," and then "till the hunter discards me." Which would have changed the meaning of the poem.

PEACOCK: Yes. I was wrestling with the ending, too. And that was somebody else's suggestion, and I hung around with that for a while. I had to discard "discard."

STUDENT: And the difference between "I become" and "the hunter becomes me"—did you not want it that active?

PEACOCK: I went back and forth about it. But I think what I wanted was the hunter to act, and I wanted the play on "becoming," as in "that dress is becoming to you." "The hunter becomes me." The role of the hunter becomes me. I didn't like that aspect of myself. The aspect of me that wrote this is relentless and obsessed and—

LONDON: That's all right.

PEACOCK: I reveal myself to myself in a way.

LONDON: I'm not sure of that. I think all good poets are born in obsession. I do. But I have one last question that I must ask. In the line after the poacher raises his rifle, "he follows / my deer into my wood, calling me dear, fleet / beauty, and I run"—"deer" and "dear," one sound, two words, two meanings.

PEACOCK: It's the same interstice as "holy" and "wholly." And I'm drawn to it. It is utterly irresistible to me. I had to say it; I couldn't not say it. Because here I am the deer running away, and yet in that very gesture I am its reverse and am being endeared. It's the ambivalent meaning in one sound. It just makes my teeth itch; I have to do it.

Robert Pinsky

WHEN ROBERT PINSKY served three terms as U.S. poet laureate from 1997 to 2000, he was already something of an unofficial ambassador of American poetry. Much of his seemingly boundless energy and curiosity has always been directed outward, with books such as *Poetry and the World* (1988) and *Democracy, Culture, and the Voice of Poetry* (2002). His Favorite Poem Project encouraged and documented poetry's active role in American lives, and a 2008 essay slicing contemporary poetry into categories such as poets of self and poets of voice—fittingly, under the imprint of the

U.S. Department of State—puts Pinsky "among the most accomplished of the poets of history."

During his 1993 visit to her class, Pearl London, too, calls his integration of the daily news and the personally meaningful "one of the essential things" about his writing. Yet for all his "worldliness . . . and taste for tasks and assignments to which he devises ingenious solutions," as Louise Glück has said, few poets take more overt pleasure in the lyric than Robert Pinksy. In his brief book, *The Sounds of Poetry* (1998), he pushes for poems to become, again, spoken art, and he has recently edited an anthology of poems to be read aloud—*Essential Pleasures*. "The process is like getting an idea for a tune," he says to London. "You work on those few notes in a sequence, and change things, try out a harmonic structure for it, write a C that goes with the A of the tune. The idea of the words may have been there, but it becomes a poem at the moment you start feeling that sensory, melodic version of it." The poem he brought to class the day of his visit, his much anthologized "The Want Bone," merges meaning and sound into one of his purest lyrics with, as London says, a "beautiful, beautiful last line."

Pinsky has taught at Berkeley, Wellesley, the University of Chicago, and Boston University. He was born [in 1940] and raised in Long Branch, New Jersey, a down-at-the-heels former resort town. The grandson of a some-time bootlegger, he earned a bachelor's degree at Rutgers and a doctorate at Stanford. In addition to ten books of poetry, he has published acclaimed translations of Dante and Milosz. Robert Lowell once wrote, "It is refreshing to find a poet who is intellectually interesting and technically first-rate. Robert Pinsky belongs to that rarest category of talent, a poet-critic."

"The Want Bone"

PEARL LONDON: One of the essential things about your writing—and we've been talking about it here for two weeks—is the idea of the poet as one who yokes together the disparate parts. The ability to look at that which is the daily news and integrate it into a context that is meaningful to you. This is Eliot: "When a poet's mind is perfectly equipped for its work, it is constantly amalgamating disparate experience." And this is Pinsky: "Modern poetry that means the most to us seems to create essential energy from that fusion or disparity." What brings it together in your mind? Where does it begin?

ROBERT PINSKY: We could describe it aesthetically or theoretically, but I prefer to describe it practically and socially.

LONDON: Well, do it.

PINSKY: This country's genius has to do with mixing. I am a mix. You are a mix. I would like to write works of art that include the vocabulary and the idiom and the manner of speaking that I grew up with in a—what you could almost call a less-than-working-class neighborhood. A neighborhood with no one-family houses in it, and on either side of us rooming houses. I would like to include that but not stylize my speech, so I simply was posing as a tough street-boy poet. I would like to include also the fact that I have a Ph.D., and I have read a good many books, and I have a lot of very smart friends, people who know many languages. I would like to include also the part of me that watches television and the part of me that . . .

LONDON: Reads John Donne.

PINSKY: Reads John Donne. Poetry too for me is the hybrid of particular moments and circumstances. We speak the world's most bastardized, mongrelized language with, I believe, the world's largest vocabulary. The English dictionary is fatter than the dictionary of other languages because the language itself is the product of yoking. Legend has it there's a hill in England called Torpenhow Hill. In one Germanic language a *hough* or *how* is a high place. In a Scandinavian language a *tor* is a high place. A *pen* in a Celtic language is a high place. So one set of invaders comes in a kills and rapes one set of people and says, "What do you call that?" "Pen," they answer. "That's Tor Pen!" the invaders say. And then some other people come in and rape and kill and torture them and say, "What do you call that?" They say, "Tor Pen." "That's Torpen Hough!" the new invaders say. So in England today Torpenhow Hill [can be translated as] Hillhillhill Hill. We happen to speak a language that is unusually rich in calamity and accretion.

LONDON: Robert Pinsky, when I talked to you the other day, I said to you that I went to the *OED* to look up "want bone." And gosh—

PINSKY: It said there, "A word invented by Robert Pinsky in 1989."

PEARL: Now that, to me, was sort of wonderful. And I wanted to talk with you about that, about the poem and about the word itself. Because "want," when we think about it and as we've been talking about it, is deficiency, desire, need. . . . It's all of these things, it's craving, it's life—loving—and it's also insufficiency and hunger. And lack, as in death, maybe.

PINSKY: The want bone, the actual shark bone, is an impressive object. And it does remind you that wanting is kind of a hole or space, like a letter O. I first saw the object at a friends' place, on my way to Martha's Vineyard—

LONDON: The object being the jawbone of a shark, the mouth of it.

PINSKY: Yes. They are beautiful. Maybe especially the tendons in the corner, in an hourglass shape made of string but twisted into a helix: "pleated like a summer dress." And along the lip, a honeycomb texture. And the jaw is frozen open, gaping like the embodiment of wanting. I was on my way to a writers' conference on Martha's Vineyard when I saw this thing on someone's mantelpiece. The beach—an important setting for me. And I have desires myself—there are things that I want! So you look at the object and you do say, "Yes, this looks like Robert to me." You want something. Empty, frozen, dry. A feeling that is sort of gorgeous or sopping and sort of helpless and dry.

[READS]

The Want Bone

The tongue of the waves tolled in the earth's bell.
Blue rippled and soaked in the fire of blue.
The dried mouthbones of a shark in the hot swale
Gaped on nothing but sand on either side.

The bone tasted of nothing and smelled of nothing,
A scalded, toothless harp, uncrushed, unstrung.

The joined arcs made the shape of birth and craving
And the welded-open shape kept mouthing O.

Ossified cords held the corners together
In groined spirals pleated like a summer dress.
But where was the limber grin, the gash of pleasure?
Infinitesimal mouths bore it away.

The beach scrubbed and etched and pickled it clean.
But O I love you it sings, my little my country
My food my parent my child I want you my own
My flower my fin my life my lightness my O.

LONDON: A gorgeous poem.

PINSKY: Thank you, Pearl. The process is like getting an idea for a tune.
You work on those few notes in a sequence and change things, try out a
harmonic structure for it. And write a C that goes with the A of the tune.
The idea of the words may have been there, but it becomes a poem at the
moment you start feeling that sensory, melodic version of it.

LONDON: It's that yoking. It's that great yoking of the conceptual and the
sensory.

PINSKY: And it's speech, talking, that we do all day. Speech is in the body:
this is hot air! And I'm shaping that vibrating air with all kinds of mem-
branes, a special organ in the throat, and the tongue, lips. . . .

LONDON: Why did you use the word "swale"? S-w-a-l-e: again, a swampy,
marshy kind of place. But why? It's an archaic word in this context.

PINSKY: Well, it rhymes with "bell." I got the idea that it would be useful
in this poem . . . usually you rhyme on the B and the D. On two and four,

again, just like in music. And it's satisfying: "brrrrrrrrrrrr the end, brrrrrrrrrr my friend." In this poem, it was more "rrrrrr yes rrrrrr, rrrrr but." It was a more tentative or unsatisfied movement. So I rhymed on A and C rather than B and D.

And I like the word "swale" because it reminds me of "bronze" and "brazen," those other words you were talking about in [my poem] "The Ghost Hammer," including "hammer," which drives something home, it homes things. "Swale" is an old word, and it means a low place, often a wet low place, though in this case it's a dry low place, so it might be a gully running through the beach. I also like the word because it reminds me of "swell," its opposite.

LONDON: Ah, I didn't think of that.

PINSKY: And there's a certain tumescent, swollen quality to this poem. Clearly "want bone" makes you think both of a penis and perhaps of a vagina. A penis in the word "bone" and a vagina in the shape of the jaw. This thing of tongues tolling in bells. And "swale" is a sexy word to me: it suggests "swell" and "swollen" and means "low and wet."

LONDON: We were talking about the word "O." This beautiful, beautiful, beautiful last line, "my fin my life my lightness my O." This brought to mind Melville, where he says, "Oh my world, Ah my world." There are two ways—the tragedy of it and the wonderfulness of it. What happens . . . what is the "O" here? Is it "Ah my world wonderful, Oh my world tragic"? Is it a composite?

PINSKY: Well, "O" is emotion, fullness, a sound that registers abundance or excess of all kinds of feeling; but it's also a zero, an *O*. So I guess it's paradoxical. One of the things about this "want bone" is that you can see through it. You can't fill it up, because it's hollow, open—how can you fill up the jawbone? It's like filling up an *O* or a ring, you just pour things through it and they fall out, go somewhere else. So I suppose in that sense there's some sense of desire's futility, the notion that desire . . . you know, we sing to hear the song end; desire is self-defeating in a certain way. You desire to stop desiring. So the fact that it's an "O" means it's very full. "Ohhh, I'm full." But also it's an O, it's empty. It's that conundrum of wanting and of pleasure, that riddle or paradox of wanting.

I like noises. I've always envied Renaissance poets and even nineteenth-century poets for being able to say "Ah" and "O." It's one of my secret desires to get some of the things they do in doo-wop songs—*ah, oh, da doo-ron-ron*—into poetry.

LONDON: But you also like emptiness. It worries me. Emptiness is present.

PINSKY: Well, I'm impressed by entropy. They tell me that the world is a clock that's running down.

LONDON: There's this whole concept about the bent toward abstraction on your part. This is one of the things that I think we all have been talking about at considerable length.

PINSKY: When I began writing, partly under the influence of Eliot, partly the deep-image poetry of the seventies, the one thing that seemed most *un*poetic was abstract language. And to do what is not expected is always more glorious and pleasurable than to do what is expected. So to write a poem that had a lot of abstract language in it, in a theoretical way, simply would be gratifying. . . . To do what you were not supposed to do. This was personal, too, because I never did very well in school. I was in "dumb class" in the seventh and eighth grades. Expelled, at one point. I didn't like doing what I was told to do.

LONDON: I think they sent you to the wrong school.

PINSKY: No choice, for that family in that time and place. I found I could even read, say, *Julius Caesar* as long as it wasn't assigned. And if it was assigned, then I could read *anything* else. So finding a grain to go against is perhaps a personal matter. Also, my cultural background, a certain kind of lower-middle-class Jewish background, tends to value patter—fast, rapid, improvised talking. When I see Robin Williams—a Gentile military brat, I believe—improvising a performance, a shtick of some kind, he more or less explicitly alludes to that tradition. If I listen to Ornette Coleman improvise choruses over and over on some simple chord structure, I feel that's not so different from what I want to do with talking.

This may be chemical or temperamental. I like to think about five things at once. I get bored by one thing at a time. Someone else might make something great by thinking about one thing at a time. I like seeing how many balls can go in the air at once.

I like teasing, I like running fast. I like dodging and changing direction. . . .

LONDON: This raises a very critical question. Before we talk about a poetry of witness, before we talk about the poetry of evidence, don't we, to a very large extent, choose the evidence that we are going to see? Isn't it true, as Roethke said, "We see what we believe"? And if that is so—and I'm playing the devil's advocate right now for a minute—what are you going to say about answerability? To whom are you answerable? Is it to your past—Grandpa Dave? Is it to your daughter—[in the poem] "An Explanation of America"? Is it to your extended world—the community? Is it to your internal world, the moral world of Isaiah, or non-Isaiah, whatever that's going to be?

PINSKY: I believe I'm answerable in poetry and in my life—"What did you do with your freedom?" It can panic you, when you think about quite young people, because they seem, superficially, to be so completely taken by cultural definition that they wear brand names, logos of corporations, on their shirts. Sometimes their speech seems completely made out of things they've been taught to say by advertising or by mass media—but that is a form of camouflage. Inside, underneath, something is unique.

As in every era, we have a partly controlling culture that we can make into an instrument. In [the poem] "Ginza Samba," the saxophone for me resembles this English language that forms me, controls me—but I can use, try to make mine—clearly, some of each. In theory, if I think about all those shaping things, all those ancestors—literal ancestors of my body, figurative ancestors of this language, of this art of poetry or music forming me—what do I want to do with all that they gave me? In a word, I would like to make it my instrument.

I am answerable to that idea. How much of what you did while you were alive was you, and how much was created by your circumstances? How much have I been determined by everything that determined me, and how much did I act back on it, maybe remake it? Make something new.

I decline to believe that Charlie Parker and Lester Young simply produced what was determined by their circumstances. There was something in them. There was art, in a word. Some spirit that made something new, that had not been there before. And that making required an act of mind, an act of intelligence, an act of—

LONDON: Transformation.

PINSKY: Transformation. And I'm answerable: Given my opportunities and my circumstances, did I transform it? Or did I say, "Oh, I bet I know what an audience would like to hear." Or "I know what goes down." Or "This will sound like what they need." I'm answerable.

Edward Hirsch

AT THE TIME Edward Hirsch visited Pearl London's class in October 1993, he had published three books of poetry: *For the Sleepwalkers* (1981), nominated for a National Book Critics Circle Award; *Wild Gratitude* (1986), which won that award; and *The Night Parade* (1989). The central beauties of his poetry, described by Stephen Dobyns as an "emotional richness coupled with a precise sense of language and metaphor," have been a recognized part of his poetic repertoire from the start. That emotional richness seems to be expanding through his seven books, whether about the history of a city or about poets and painters from the past. It can also be felt in Hirsch's critical works, from the best-selling *How to Read a Poem: And Fall in Love with Poetry* (1999) to his *Poet's Choice* (2007), a compilation of his poetry columns for the *Washington Post Book World*.

In this conversation with London, one can see something else, too: the agile intelligence reflected in both poetry and prose. London and Hirsch are clearly enjoying each other's company, even (or mainly) as she probes for the roots of his affirming nature, for his meaning of the absolute, for his core vocabulary of metaphor. London describes Hirsch's recent work as "terribly wounding, dark poems," but marvels that, even still, "everything is forgiven." Their conversation extends into an exploration of the title poem to his volume *Wild Gratitude*, a particularly candid give-and-take about the process of creation and revision.

Hirsch, born and raised in Chicago, discovered poetry at age eight when he opened a random book in his basement and read Emily Brontë's poem "Spellbound." He taught for eighteen years in the writing program at the University of Houston, then left for New York City in 2003, when he was named president of the Guggenheim Memorial Foundation. He was elected a chancellor of the Academy of American Poets in 2008.

"Wild Gratitude"

PEARL LONDON: We live in a society that is deeply aware of its uprooted-
ness, of loss, of alienation in all forms and shapes. You often use the word
"praise" in your poetry, and you quote Auden's "affirming flame." The feeling we can find in your three books is of something deep-seated, something very shared and rare in this society. But I ask myself, What is there to
praise that is so powerful? With all of the ineptness and all the wounding in
society, does this praise come from your sense, as you put it, of "surviving
the nightfall"?

EDWARD HIRSCH: Well, you've raised the idea of alienation. And loss. I
believe that that's the beginning of poetry. Poetry begins with alienation,
and poetry speaks against our vanishing. The lyric poem in particular
seems to me to have the burden and the splendor of preserving the human
image in words, as the most intense form of discourse. Poetry speaks
about and against loss in its root function.

I see the writing of a poem as a descent. The descent is psychological.

That which is darkest in human experience. It can be in yourself, it can be in others, it can be in the death of someone you love. It's a descent into the unconscious. You try to unearth something. You try to bring something to the light. In terms of my own vision of things, it's in the movement from the third section of *Wild Gratitude* to the fourth section, from the darkest moment in that book historically into something else. That's what I mean by an encounter with the worst. To face what Elizabeth Bishop calls "our worst century so far" and still come out. To find what ground we can still praise, to celebrate our survival.

LONDON: In *The Night Parade* you talk about "putting the night away." You couldn't have said that in your first book.

HIRSCH: I think a first book is extremely hard to conceive of as a book; it's kind of a best hits. Because you write it over such a long period of time and you're not entirely convinced you'll have a book. You're just writing poem after poem. You're trying to make it be a book at some point, but it's a little unwieldy. I have a firmer idea of a book as a thing now. Robert Frost says that if there are twenty-nine poems in a book, the book itself is the thirtieth poem.

LONDON: Did he? Oh, I love Frost. I sit at his feet.

HIRSCH: I still write poems individually. Not so much thinking about a book at the beginning. But at a certain point the poems start to cohere in some way, and you start to arrange them and think about them and make an order; you start thinking about that thirtieth thing.

LONDON: When, at the very beginning of *The Night Parade,* you talk about the absolute—we must "stave off the absolute"—and then, in the next-to-last poem, again we hear "the cold slopes of the absolute," what do you mean by "absolute"? Is it absolute annihilation, the darkest places?

HIRSCH: I'm using "absolute," as you say, as annihilation, as the terrifying infinite spaces between stars, as Pascal says. The absolute erasure. The terrifying invisibility.

LONDON: Well, this was the thing in Robert Frost again. That he walks in darknesses not of woods only. That terrible feeling there's no design, no architecture in this universe.

HIRSCH: Exactly. The poem of Frost's I'm totally crazy about is "Desert Places," if you know that poem.

LONDON: Oh, yes, it's wonderful.

HIRSCH: It ends: "they cannot scare me with their empty spaces / On stars . . . where no human race is / I have—"

LONDON: People don't understand Frost. They think he's a pastoral poet who writes about green trees and I don't know what—

HIRSCH: They're completely wrong. Our Frost is Randall Jarrell's Frost. It's the darker Frost. Frost is unblinking. And that Frost gives me courage, because he's remorseless in his willingness to look at the darkness.

LONDON: He had lots of darknesses to look at. His son.

HIRSCH: Wife, his marriage.

LONDON: His sister was crazy.

HIRSCH: The mental illness in the family. But also there's something—this is where I hear the Americanness in it. "They cannot scare me with their empty spaces / On stars"—there's a little bit of the tough guy in it—"On stars where no human race is." Now there's a little bit of joke in the rhyme:

where no human *race is.* "I have it in me so much nearer home / to scare myself with my own desert places." There's a tone I hear in this that I have tried very hard to get in my own work, which is a—I don't know why it's so moving to me—but it's a combination of desperation and playfulness.

LONDON: We were talking this last week about the core vocabulary that we keep finding in your three books—

HIRSCH: I feel unmasked! I want to put my jacket on.

LONDON: In Auden's essay on Frost, he counted the number of—as a metaphor for the desolation and the loneliness—

HIRSCH: I feel something unhappy coming here.

LONDON: He counted the number of empty barns and the number of wintry landscapes, and so forth. And I think there were—I wrote it down— twenty-seven poems in which the time is night and twenty-one in which the climate is winter. These are all aspects of desolation. So the other day when we were talking about Edward Hirsch, we had three words that we wanted to ask you about. One is "purple." I found "purple" on pages 14, 18, 51, 69, 73—and another is "forehead." "Forehead" I can't even explain to my students, but it's all over the place: 3, 29, 81, 75—I don't know.

HIRSCH: Oy!

LONDON: But mostly, "fire." So I thought we would ask you in terms of this core vocabulary—before we talk about the imagery itself—to com- ment on that for us.

HIRSCH: I don't have a symbolic scheme here. Not in the way that, say, Wallace Stevens did, where blue always represents something, and red always represents. But I am immensely attracted to several situations in poems. One that I like most has to do with insomnia. I mean, I am an insomniac—I'm lots of other things, too, that I don't write about—but I like the situation dramatically. It creates a sense of isolation and darkness, outer darkness. A sense of everyone else being asleep while you are thinking. I like the dramatic situation it sets up in a poem. I like dawn and I like dusk. I like transition. That moment is immensely powerful to me. I don't even know exactly why, but this is where purple comes in, the moment of transformation from light to darkness. I think purple is a bruised way of getting from brightness to darkness or from darkness back out.

LONDON: I'll never wear purple again.

HIRSCH: I don't mean I sit down and think about purple and this is what I encode. But I like this moment, when things are changing, transforming, suspended.

LONDON: But isn't that really making purple into a metaphor? When you say it isn't like Stevens—now, Stevens's great metaphor was blue. One of the lines I love more than anything is in one of his very late poems, when he's looking at the blue sky and questioning what he can praise in life, and he says of the sky: to be blue there can be no questions asked [from "The Ultimate Poem Is Abstract"]. That's a metaphor of the first order. And I think your purple is.

HIRSCH: Well, now you've got me there. You're absolutely right.

LONDON: I am right; yes, I think so, too.

HIRSCH: What I mean is that it's descriptive—don't gloat—

LONDON: Forgive me, I'm sorry.

HIRSCH: —it's descriptive with metaphorical overtones. The only reason I'm resisting this at all is because I don't think it always means the same thing.

LONDON: Blue means the same thing in Stevens, you can be sure.

HIRSCH: In Stevens, blue means the same thing. For me it shifts a little bit from poem to poem. In a root sense, you're absolutely right. That is, as soon as you start talking about transitions being emblematic, or liking the situation of insomnia rather than just anecdotes about insomnia, you're talking about metaphor. You're moving from the descriptive to the metaphor, and that's a Frostian thing. Thinking by metaphor, using the description to lead to metaphorical thinking. That's the same thing with "forehead."

LONDON: Why?

HIRSCH: Because it's almost always used, for me, imagistically. You know, the forehead of a house. It's a kind of metaphor about mental processes. About thinking.

LONDON: Let's come back to Stevens and praise.

HIRSCH: Remember his idea of the American sublime that must come out of the bare place. It's Edward Hopper.

LONDON: Yes, that's right.

HIRSCH: This is an American—

LONDON: It's what we're talking about in your work.

HIRSCH: This is a line that I see myself as part of. An American line of romantics, perhaps, seeking the spiritual out of the darkest conditions of our lives.

LONDON: And that tremendous combination, or dichotomy, or whatever you want to call it, of both prayer and praise. Which brings me to your poem "Wild Gratitude" and Christopher Smart and his cat Jeoffry. I'd like to know how you came to Christopher Smart.

HIRSCH: Christopher Smart I've known about for a very long time. I'm crazy about him. Nice word, "crazy." Especially "Jubilate Agno." I'm very attracted to these eccentric . . .

LONDON: "In Praise of the Lamb."

HIRSCH: OK, so I'm thinking about this poem, and I'm thinking about the strangeness of this poem, thinking, What is so immensely moving about this? Why is this extravagance so funny and so moving? And why isn't it just funny? Why does it seem crazed and desperate?

LONDON: It is.

HIRSCH: It is. And I came to feel that Christopher Smart was someone for whom daily life, ordinary life, was completely alien. That he holds on to the most ordinary things with a kind of desperate tenacity because they're completely lost to him. This is someone who is spending his life in a mental hospital, thinking about daily life. It's as if it's on another planet. The only poet who even comes close to this tone, in a way, is James Schuyler. Who is also very crazy in his poems and has a certain frisson. But anyway, this is so immensely moving and so extravagant because the most daily things seem completely miraculous to him, because they're all being totally lost to him. I wanted to write about that. And so, I think, I'll associate my little cat Zooey with a famous cat out of literature and see what happens.

LONDON: "He purrs in thankfulness, when God tells him he's a good cat" [from "Jubilate Agno"].

HIRSCH: That's right, exactly. You see, I think the playfulness always comes from how far you can push it. Frost has a tremendous essay called "Thinking by Metaphor." Every metaphor breaks down at some point, and the idea is, how far can you push it? This is pushing it.

LONDON: You came right to the brink.

HIRSCH: You go right to the brink, exactly—I'm going to take my cat Zooey and I'm going to play with my cat Zooey on the same day that I'm going to have an anniversary poem about Smart. I'm going to go back and forth, back and forth between Christopher Smart in 1749 and me in 1981.

I wanted to think about this thing of holding on to daily life from the outside with a kind of tenacity. That's where I got this. Also, I was immensely moved by something that Dr. Johnson said about Christopher Smart. Boswell tells the story that Smart—he was called Kit Smart—that he was going from house to house asking people to kneel down and pray with him. It was completely crazy. And Johnson says, in a wonderful way, "One would have to be mad not to want to pray with Kit Smart."

LONDON: Really?

HIRSCH: I think it's so splendid. And I thought, I want to pray with Kit Smart, too, and here's my way of doing it. I'm going to make it as extravagant as possible in the spirit of this thing. This is what I mean about the comic as well as the desperate, because there seems to me something funny about it, going back and forth.

LONDON: Before we look at the manuscript, throughout your work, in all of these terribly wounding, dark poems, everything is forgiven.

HIRSCH: You're completely right. There is a very strong commitment in my work to face the worst and come out of it. The affirming flame, which you've talked about. Emerson's optative mood.

LONDON: Or in the revisions. To understand, to find the reasons.

HIRSCH: In the revisions, absolutely. And the gesture of, despite all of this—in the [poem "Dawn Walk" at the] end of *Wild Gratitude*—"we are here, / Yes, we are still here." That's the ground on which you praise.

STUDENT: In the several drafts that we read of "Wild Gratitude" it remained a block. No stanza breaks until the final version [broken into six stanzas]. I was wondering, at what point do you make that decision? In your poetry you very often have four-line stanzas or six-line stanzas that you really stay with. Do you feel pressed to maintain six lines when it wants to break on the fifth line?

HIRSCH: Yes. I think that a form, though, which is what you're talking about to some extent, is a series of expectations. It's a contract that you set up, as a musical form, a series of patterns and expectations and fulfillments and thwartings and movement, and your task is to work through the form so that the reader can follow. Many poets do something that drives me up the wall. They'll do five lines, five lines, five lines, five lines, *four* lines, five lines, *six* lines, five lines. Formally, it doesn't make any sense to me. I believe it has to make sense.

I always begin with a stanzaic idea. That is, I try to write by the line as a unit of meaning and by the stanza as a unit of meaning. Sometimes that's regular and sometimes that's irregular. I follow it through. Sometimes when it's operating well, it fulfills itself; other times it's not fulfilling itself, so you have to change it. Or something feels radically wrong to you—as it began to feel with "Wild Gratitude" as a big block. So I had to fool with it. Each poem is different, but what I would say about it overall is that I have a stanzaic idea to get me going. If the poem is not alive, if something is not happening, then I change it. And I decide the way Marianne Moore decided her stanzas. She wrote one, and if that seemed attractive, she kept going and kept patterning it like that.

This will be a good question to ask Robert Pinsky. Because Robert Pinsky almost always, ninety-nine and three-quarters percent of the time, writes formal stanzas. He has tremendous difficulty writing irregular stanzas.

LONDON: I'd like to look at two drafts of the manuscript of "Wild Gratitude." The poem changes title from "August Thirteenth" to "Wild Gratitude."

In terms of the actual process of writing, in line 6 on the first draft, you had "tender poet," but the word "tender" was omitted in the second draft. What was your thinking?

HIRSCH: Not only is "tender" dropped, but so is "of madness" ["tender poet *of madness*"].

LONDON: Yes.

HIRSCH: I was thinking it felt like a telegraphed punch. It felt like an editorial. I was telling us that Smart is a poet of madness, [but] shouldn't the whole poem enact that? "Tender" seemed to me unnecessary. So I thought, I'm a little overdoing it here, let's cut this out, let's just call him "the poet Christopher Smart," that's what he was, and let's not editorialize.

You can see [line 12] where I looked up how "Jeoffry" was actually spelled. See that? I'd been working for weeks, and I realized I had misspelled it until I looked back here.

LONDON: As we move down the page [line 21, in the first draft]. "This morning I realized just how much he loved to hear—" and of course you

August Thirteenth

Tonight when I knelt down next to our cat, Zooey,
and put my fingers into her clean cat's mouth,
and rubbed her swollen belly that will never know kittens,
and watched her wriggle onto her side, pawing the air,
and listened to her solemn little squeals of delight,
I was thinking about the tender poet ~~of madness~~, Christopher Smart,
who wanted to kneel down and pray without ceasing
in every one of the splintered London streets,
and was locked away in the madhouse at St. Luke's
with his sad religious mania, and his wild gratitude,
and his grave prayers for the other lunatics,
and his great love for his speckled cat, Jeffrey.
All day today--August 13, 1981--I was thinking
~~how~~ Christopher Smart blessed this same day in August, 1759,
for its calm bravery and ordinary good conscience.
This was the day that he blessed the Postmaster general
"and all conveyancers of letters" for their warm humanity,
and the gardeners for their private benevolence
and intricate knowledge of the language of flowers,
and the milkmen for their universal kindness.
This morning I realized ~~just how much~~ he loved to hear--
as I have heard--the ~~small~~ clink of the milk ~~bottle and~~
on the rickety stiars in the ~~very~~ early morning,
and how terrible it must have seemed
that even this small gift was denied ~~him.~~
But it wasn't until tonight when I knelt down
and slipped my hand into ~~my cat's~~ waggling mouth
that I remembered how he'd called Jeffrey "the servant
of the Living God duly and daily serving Him"
and for the first time understood what he meant.
Because it wasn't until tonight when I saw
my own cat roll over on her fluffy back
that I realized how much he loved to watch/Jeffrey
fetch and carry his little wooden cork
across the talk grass in the back yard, patiently
jumping over a high stick, or calmly sharpening
his paws on the woodpile, rubbing his black nose
against the ~~nother~~ of another cat, stretching, ~~and~~
slowly stalking his traditional enemy, the mouse,
a rodent, "a creature of great personal valour,"
and then dallying so that he could escape.
~~And it wasn't until tonight~~ that I understood
it is Jeoffrey--and every other cat like him--
with his sly "mixture of gravity and waggery"
~~who~~ could teach us how to live; purring,
in his own strange Greek, measuring the/music
with his footsteps, ~~slipping through the tall~~ grass,
wreathing himself in the living fire.

Wild Gratitude

Tonight when I knelt down next to our cat, Zooey,
and put my fingers into her clean cat's mouth,
and rubbed her swollen belly that will never know kittens,
and watched her wriggle onto her side, pawing the air,
and listened to her solemn little squeals of delight,
I was thinking about the poet, Christopher Smart,
who wanted to kneel down and pray without ceasing
in every one of the splintered London streets,
and was locked away in the madhouse at St. Luke's
with his sad religious mania, and his wild gratitude,
and his grave prayers for the other lunatics,
and his great love for his speckled cat, Jeoffry.
All day today--August 13, 1981--I remembered how
Christopher Smart blessed this same day in August, 1759,
for its calm bravery and ordinary good conscience.
This was the day that he blessed the Postmaster general
"and all conveyancers of letters" for their warm humanity,
and the gardeners for their private benevolence
and intricate knowledge of the language of flowers,
and the milkmen for their universal human kindness.
This morning I understood that he loved to hear--
as I have heard--the soft clink of milk bottles
on the rickety stairs in the early morning,
and how terrible it must have seemed
when even this small pleasure was denied him.
But it wasn't until tonight when I knelt down
and slipped my hand into Zooey's waggling mouth
that I remembered how he'd called Jeoffry "the servant
of the Living God duly and daily serving Him,"
and for the first time understood what it meant.
Because it wasn't until I saw my own cat
whine and roll over on her fluffy back
that I realized how gratefully he had watched
Jeoffry fetch and carry his wooden cork
across the grass in the wet garden, patiently
jumping over a high stick, or calmly sharpening
his claws on the woodpile, rubbing his nose
against the nose of another cat, stretching, or
slowly stalking his traditional enemy, the mouse,
a rodent, "a creature of great personal valour,"
and then dallying so much that his enemy escaped.
And only then did I understand that
it is Jeoffry--and every creature like him--
who can teach us how to praise--purring
in their own language, measuring the music,
wreathing themselves in the living fire.

omitted "just how much" [in the second draft]. Again, what tells you when you want to move into the minimal statement or the most economic way of writing? Because "just how much" is obviously more excessive than "this morning I realized he loved to hear."

HIRSCH: I don't know. It seems obvious in retrospect, but when you're working it doesn't seem so obvious. You're trying to get it right and trying to get it down. And I was thinking—

LONDON: And you have it again [deleting "very," line 23] in "very early morning."

HIRSCH: Exactly. Especially when you've got a poem that's extravagant in its very idea, so you're just finding moments where it seems overwritten. I'm just going back and cutting back on that which seems adjectival or not doing anything—

LONDON: I'm glad you said that. Now tell us, because we are writers, how do you feel about adjectives? I always keep saying they're the stuffing in a big Victorian sofa. What do you feel about them?

HIRSCH: To some extent you're right, in the sense that they don't usually do much work. You're trying to have the language work for you—and Pound is right to put them under proscription. Although when I say [line 27] "though I slip my hand into Zooey's waggling mouth"—

LONDON: Yes, that's nice.

HIRSCH: —I don't say "into Zooey's mouth." "Waggling" seemed to me to do some work. Whereas "small" in "the small clink of milk bottles" isn't doing any work.

LONDON: Well, "clink" is nice there.

HIRSCH: So you go back and say, well, "clink" does the work, but you don't need the "small." "Clink" tells you "small."

LONDON: Do you set out to look for verbs that are going to be muscular?

HIRSCH: Not so consciously. You do it, but you just keep repeating the poem to yourself like a mantra as you keep thinking it through and typing it through. Page 12 is the first typing, actually; I've been writing it over and over again. Really, what I've given you is a very elided version. Because there are hundreds of other ghastly pages in between.

STUDENT: Do you ever have an idea of a phrase in your mind that should be a certain rhythm and you put adjectives in—?

LONDON: For the rhythm.

HIRSCH: I do. And I realize that's always a mistake. Because you're filling the form. If you're filling the form to fit the rhythm, filling with words, the words aren't working. You hear a music, but you have to make sure the words are doing the work, not the underlying musical structure. I think you can overstate the "never any adjectives" rule, but you do find that they're most expendable in your own work. Looking at it here—we're at a pretty late stage in this poem. This is really almost done. Now it's about honing down, seeing what you can cut. You're going through words one by one, saying, "Do I need 'tender,' do I need 'madness' "—or with "sad" religious mania, do you need "sad"?

LONDON: What made you *add*—not delete—[in line 14] "whine"? "Because it wasn't until I saw my own cat whine and roll over." But in the earlier version you don't have "whine." Well, cats don't have to whine.

HIRSCH: I wanted to elongate the experience of playing with the cat. I wanted to extend the experience, the amount of time you're spending doing it. You're slowing down the poem, in terms of the perceptions. I like the "whine and roll" because I like the way it divided it into two actions. I'm trying to slow down the poem at that point to focus it very specifically on the cat.

LONDON: Now, there's one more line, third from the bottom [of the first draft]. "In his own strange Greek, measuring the music." That is omitted. Now, why? I liked "strange Greek."

HIRSCH: This is the hardest thing for me. It fit the poem in the beginning. You can see where you get the idea of Christopher Smart praying in some foreign language and the idea of measure. But it seemed to me the poem had set up a logic that no longer accommodated that line. "Strange Greek" introduced something three lines from the bottom and it had you thinking about it. It shouldn't be the focus anymore. If it doesn't fit the poem, it must go.

Frank Bidart

FRANK BIDART was fifty-four years old when he visited Pearl London's class in March 1994. While his first two books of poetry, *Golden State* (1973) and *The Book of the Body* (1977), won him considerable praise, his third book, *Sacrifice* (1984), cemented for many critics a sense of Bidart as master of reworked forms, particularly the long dramatic monologue, with jump cuts, shifting voices, and idiosyncratic punctuation. The poem he brought to London that day was "Confessional," from *Sacrifice*. At the time the poem was published, he said, "I have just been through hell with a long poem, 'Confessional.' Six years ago I wrote the first part of [it]. I felt immediately that it wasn't complete. . . . Well, it took me six years to discover what the second half must be." About guilt, forgiveness, and his relationship with his mother, "Confessional" was called by the *Nation* "one of the most intelligent and moving poems on family relations." London calls it "one of the very great poems."

Bidart was born and raised in Bakersfield, California, where his father was a successful potato farmer. He attended the University of California, Riverside, and in 1962 moved east to start graduate studies at Harvard. He has lived in Cambridge ever since and has taught at Wellesley College for more than thirty-five years. *Desire* (1997), his fourth full book of new poems, was nominated for a Pulitzer Prize, the National Book Award, and the National Book Critics Circle Award, and at the time of *Star Dust* (2005), he won the Bollingen Prize in American Poetry from Yale University.

"When I write a poem," Bidart tells London, "I can always hear a voice, whether it's my voice or another character's. The question is, How do you get that thing on the page so that the reader can hear it?" For Louise Glück, "the importance of Bidart's work is difficult to overestimate; certainly he is one of the crucial figures of our time."

————————

"Confessional"

PEARL LONDON: Around the time of your first book [*Golden State*] you say, "I realize that things with which the world had confronted me had to be at the center of my poems." And at that point you said your poems had "to dramatize the moments when I felt I had learned the terrible wisdom of the past (so I could unlearn it)." So learning is a kind of unlearning?

FRANK BIDART: First of all, applying ideas to one's life is inescapable. You cannot live without doing that. Because in fact life is a chaos and a nightmare unless you understand.

I think in the world I come from—I'm from Bakersfield, California— there is a terrible, overwhelming poverty of ideas that people have access to in terms of their experience. And I'm talking about the world of Bakersfield in the fifties. I don't know what it's like now. And I think, in the case of my parents, it was a terrifying disparity; it was a very painful—for me, in terms of my mother, a tragic disparity, because she's somebody who had a great desire to understand her life and very few tools to do that. Not that I understand my life, I mean, all these things are relative. But I am not quite as at the mercy of some things as I think she was.

LONDON: And way back in 1973 what was the critical moment—what made you know not to be at the mercy of the past: did that happen when you came to Cambridge and met Robert Lowell?

BIDART: You know what really happened? This is a story which I've never written about. I went to Catholic high school—and I wanted to be a Trappist monk. My mother, who was divorced and remarried and in the eyes of the Church living in adultery, was horrified by the prospect of her only child becoming a Trappist monk. She fought ferociously, and at the time, of course, I was furious with her. In Bakersfield, the sort of Catholic college you want to go to if you want to go to what you imagine is the best Catholic college is Notre Dame. It was June, I graduated from high school, she was just in a complete rage, and what I wanted to do was go to Notre Dame and as quickly as possible escape to a monastery.

Anyway. She found out that the University of California was having weekend seminars, three-day things you could simply sign up for and listen to UCLA professors, and she talked me into going up there. I really thought that if you were earnest and serious you had to be a Catholic. You know, look at T. S. Eliot. There was this whole thing about converts to Catholicism and intellectuals becoming Catholics in the thirties and forties and fifties. So I agreed to go up with her. And a man named Abraham Kaplan, to whom I will be eternally grateful, did a three-day course on Socrates, Plato, and Aristotle. I had been given and accepted this idea that to be serious was to be a Catholic, and to discover there could be such serious and earnest minds that were not was overwhelming. Suddenly the idea of one truth being the only truth was impossible.

And it's Socrates talking about the unexamined life not worth living. It's not worth living because you can't live it. It's too painful, intolerable, too self-destructive; it's too destructive of others—in some sense all the conceptualizing in my poems is the attempt to get out of that.

LONDON: To get out of it, yes. And when you finally come to Cambridge you meet Lowell. You're twenty-six, and Lowell was forty. What interested me was, in the examined life, you realized you could not write your *Life Studies* in the same way Lowell could.

BIDART: The motor of Lowell's poems is not dramatizing the attempt to apply conceptual structures to the world. It's not that there aren't conceptual structures—there are many in his work—but the motor of the poems is not that act. I felt that was *my* subject. Lowell is a great genius at giving you a physical world that is pregnant with meaning and also resists meaning. And those poems in *Life Studies* about "my father's bedroom," "my mother's bedroom," the way the objects that people own reflect their nature, their world, the contradictions within their feeling and nature. But that's not what I wanted my poems to do, what I needed my poems to do.

LONDON: They had to be that drama of process.

BIDART: No sensibility is going to see into everything . . . There are inherent contradictions within human feeling. There are contradictions between what we promise and what we can perform. We both love and hate our parents, and it's difficult to accept that because we would like only to love them, and they certainly want us only to love them.

People fail each other. People do not do what they want to do for each other, because we constantly feel contradictions. On the one hand, we want to be a good husband; on the other hand, something else in us says, "But you have the injunction to fulfill yourself." Sometimes fulfilling yourself and being a good husband—you cannot do both. And we feel pain at the pain we inflict, so human beings feel remorse in relation to each other.

I mean, I do in relation to my mother, for instance. I felt a tremendous desire to be the son that she wanted and needed. She was this very bright, serious person, full of sensibility and feeling, stuck in a kind of wasteland. At a certain point, in 1972, I decided to buy an apartment in Cambridge. When I told her this on the phone, she got tremendously upset. And then it came out that she had thought that sooner or later I was going to move back to Bakersfield and live down the street. Well, that would have killed me. And that's just a kind of outward embodiment of her desire to repeat a connection that we had throughout my childhood—that could not be repeated and could not be returned to. I could not save her. Or if I tried to save her, I would have killed myself. That's a source of guilt. It doesn't have anything to do with a God.

LONDON: Now. That brings us to "Confessional," which I think is for me, personally, one of the very great poems. In "Confessional" there are several premises. One is that you felt badly, or tragically badly, because you knew you had wanted to be the center, the focus, of her life.

BIDART: Yes. Absolutely did. When I was a kid, I was, and I loved it. And then it was a prison.

LONDON: And you also felt that you had been, as you say, in an enterprise together. This joint thing. And then you say, "TO SURVIVE, I HAD TO KILL HER INSIDE ME." The question comes up of forgiveness in that poem.

BIDART: Right. Absolutely.

LONDON: [*quoting from the poem*]

> Her plea, her need for forgiveness
> seemed the attempt to obliterate
>
> the ACTIONS, ANGERS, DECISIONS
> that made me what I am . . .
>
> To Obliterate the CRISES, FURIES, REFUSALS
> that are how I

came to UNDERSTAND her—; me—:
my life . . .

Truly to feel "forgiveness"
to forgive her IN MY HEART,
                    meant erasing ME . . .
—She seemed to ask it to render me paralyzed,
and defenseless . . .

Now that I no longer must face her,
I give her in my mind

the "empathy" and "acceptance"

I denied her, living
Why are you angry?

Now this is the part that I have to . . . I've read this poem now several times. And what is forgiveness? It seems to me that forgiveness has to be— here you've been telling us that you left prayer and came to insight. Forgiveness is a large portion of insight.

BIDART: Should proceed from insight. Right.

LONDON: A great deal of it. It also assumes compassion. So if . . . let me put it this way: if the compassion and the insight are being deepened in you, then you are not being erased; you are being, if anything, enriched. And why would that forgiveness mean erasure? I think you could have had it in you to forgive her.

BIDART: I couldn't while she was alive. It's easy to forgive when somebody's dead. Relatively easy. But when she was alive, whatever insight I felt or thought I had, I still felt anger. To forgive her—at least in the ways you are taught what forgiveness means—you are supposed to have gotten over the anger. So it meant lying to both myself and to her about what I was feeling. And also, people use forgiveness as a weapon, you know. There's a wonderful line in Lowell, "Christ, our only king without a sword, who turned the word forgiveness to a sword."

LONDON: Where is that?

BIDART: That's in the sonnets. It's the last two lines of a sonnet.

If I, in my own mind, had said I forgave her, and if I had tried to act thoroughly to reassure her that I did . . . if I internalized wholly the idea of forgiveness, I would have felt disarmed. Because then I would not have had my protection. You know, holding on to my anger was partly a way of protecting myself. And I felt I would have been swallowed up without that. People want to say the slate is wiped clean, we can forget. And then you're at the mercy of them all over again.

It's more than ten years after her death—but as time goes on and the person is not in some sense threatening and you can understand more truly the way they are at the mercy of patterns, one can come to something like forgiveness, I think. But boy, I didn't. And I know that I felt I would have been disarmed and rendered helpless if I had. But also . . . see, I think, sure, we can forgive relatively small things. But the biggest things, I don't think you do. If I were backing out of the driveway of my best friend's house, and if I didn't see their child and ran over and killed their child, I don't think they would ever forgive me. I don't think it's possible. If they were to say they had forgiven me, I think it would be a lie. If a couple is married for thirty years and the husband leaves the wife for a woman thirty years younger, she probably never forgives him—if she wanted to stay married. There are some hurts that are so large and so fundamental. . . .

LONDON: So maybe that's one of the necessary thoughts that one must deal with. Because you say at one point—I forget which poem it's in—"the way to approach freedom is to acknowledge necessity." And that is the acknowledgment of a very painful necessity.

BIDART: And the idea is if the conceptualizing in the work of art is attempting always to account for the fundamental situation in it, the conceptualizing will have a kind of necessity about it. Now, it doesn't mean that that conceptualizing resolves everything or is wholly satisfactory. Or there couldn't even be another paradigm that you could apply to the situation that would be better. But it would have a certain logic, a certain cogency in the relation between ideas and the action . . . and you can participate in the work in a far deeper way.

LONDON: You have these lines: "The past, in maiming us, makes us." And then you have, after that, that wonderful arrangement on the page: "fruition is also destruction." That is where I need you. Of course the past maims us. We know that. We are wounded and crippled and mutilated by it.

BIDART: Right. Would I choose now to have a different past? I know when I was a kid I certainly would have chosen to be in a different world. But everything I know is a response to everything I have experienced. It would mean giving up everything I think I know. So I can't will to undo it.

LONDON: But "fruition" has not been "destruction" for you. It has been a very positive thing. It is the making of you the writer, the poet, the artist.

BIDART: You know, there's a period when you can inhabit that poem, and then it's no longer where you're living. It's no longer satisfying. It's no longer the order one would make. First of all, there are a thousand other things that invade one that you can't make an order out of. And, I mean, when I am depressed, and certainly sometimes I'm depressed, I don't pick up this book [*holds up his book*], and this doesn't cheer me up! [*Laughter*]

It represents an attempt, which was as serious and earnest as I could make it, which when you have to face it later has not solved your life. It destroys the optimism you had that this one structure, this poem, was going to get it all right.

LONDON: We would like to know why, in "Confessional," this terribly anguishing poem, why you had to add the hanging of the cat, which didn't really happen.

BIDART: Right. I'm not sure why I felt I needed it, but I felt I needed it. I think it has to do with embodiment. It's not adding something that fundamentally, for me, isn't true. It's an emblem of something that, for me, is true. What is it about? The mother is talking and she has this dream about the cat, and in it she wants to save the cat: the only way to save the cat is to strangle it. There's a quotation from John of the Cross, which Eliot uses, "to divest ourselves of the love of created beings." To teach the child that the child must not fix its attention on the things of this world. But it's mad, utterly unacknowledged . . . the aggression, the violence, the jealousy in it are utterly unacknowledged. See the top of page 55:

[READS]

> For years she dreamed the cat
> had dug
> its claws into her thumbs:—
>
> in the dream, she knew, somehow
> that it was dying; she tried
>
> to help it,—
>
> **TO PUT IT OUT OF ITS MISERY,—**
>
> so she had her hands around its
> neck, strangling it . . .
>
>   Bewildered,
>
> it looked at her,

        KNOWING SHE LOVED IT—;
    And she *DID* love it, which was
    what was
        so awful . . .

The joining of love and hurting that person, where the act of saving them becomes the act of hurting them. These were meanings that were not true to what was fundamentally true in my relation with my mother. I needed some outward embodiment of them. And—

STUDENT: Did this come in a dream?

BIDART: Well, it's a joining of two things. The hanging of the cat is a story that a travel writer said happened to him when he was a child. You know, it's almost a Victorian thing of cruelly teaching the child something. But the dream about the cat digging its claws into the thumbs is a dream that a friend of mine had after his cat died. He told me the story of the dream and that horrible sense of feeling that, in order to save the cat, he had to kill the cat. It sat in my brain for years, really, until I was writing this poem and things came together that had not existed.

STUDENT: One poet was here, and he had a very beautiful poem about a disadvantaged brother who wandered off into a silo, went up on this lad-der, and could easily have killed himself by jumping off. It's a very beauti-ful and affectionate poem, and he told us it wasn't true. And I felt cheated. If this were an [invented] "persona" poem, I could have accepted it. It's just that it's in the first person, very intimate, and you feel that you've been told a lie.

BIDART: Well, OK. First of all, I think one has to understand that all art is artifice: it's made. And as something made, it isn't just a report. I've said before that "the aim of art is to make life show itself." How can you make things show themselves? When does life show its essential nature? If I thought the story about the cat were fundamentally a lie about my mother, I would feel I had betrayed her. [But] I feel at some fundamental level it is true; that is, its essence is true; what it's about is true; it did not literally happen. And you can say—one can say—well, the fact that it didn't literally happen matters. But I am hoping within the world of the poem that it reveals something that not only is true but also that I needed in some way to reveal.

But also—I understand absolutely the emotion you're talking about. I agree with you. I would feel I had betrayed my mother if I had put in a story that in its essence was not true. That is, if I were faking it in some way. There's a famous interview with Robert Lowell in the *Paris Review* where he talks about this. Because it turns out many of the things in *Life Studies,* or a certain number of them, are invented. Did not literally happen, he's saying. But the reader has to have the illusion they are getting the real Robert Lowell. And that illusion is one of the ways a work of art *works.* I think he would say that it is not an illusion, because these things are at the service of something he did feel; were fundamentally true. But part of the illusion is the use of the first person, a mode of writing that we understand as autobiography. And in that sense autobiography is a genre, it's a fiction. It's a fictional mode.

LONDON: In "Confessional," the syntax, the punctuation, the caps, the italics, proceed from the demands of the voice. My feeling is that it is not only the voice of the character that is really being heard but also the voice of an age: fractured, disjunctive, discontinuous. In many senses an echoing of where we are.

BIDART: Somehow for the fiction to work there has to be some fundamental authenticity of voice. When I write a poem I can always hear a voice, whether it's my voice or another character's. How do you get that thing on the page so that the reader can hear it? I found that when I set my poems down in the sort of usual ways, the voice wasn't there. One could not hear it—hear what I heard in my head, or hear an equivalent. So I struggled and struggled and would retype pages hundreds of times in order to make that movement embody the voice I heard. *I felt if I lost the voice I heard, I had lost the poem.*

Now this is a very grand parallel, but when Stravinsky wrote "Sacre du Printemps" he said he heard things that he did not know how to write down. And that's why he kept changing the way it was set up in terms of bars—because he heard things that the notation would not embody. I heard a voice, and when I changed language in order to make something that looked like good lines of poetry, the voice disappeared. And that voice was absolutely crucial. It's almost a visual phenomenon—I know when the page is working for me, I have a kind of illusion that the voice is hovering like a quarter of an inch above the page.

In the case of a great poem by Bishop or Lowell, it's all in the words— it's in those lines, the way the lines sit on the page; there's a kind of adequacy, in some sense, of language to gesture, language to spirit. [But] I don't think that's true of my poems. There are the words and then there is a set of tensions, a subtext at war with those words. That illusion of hovering a quarter of an inch above the page has to do with feeling the voice in its relation to the words. Feeling, say, that if there's a dash followed by a semicolon there's a kind of gesture that is cut off and held in suspension. The words themselves, alone, don't do it.

Now, you could say, "Well, they should do it." But I don't know how to do it that way. The only way I've ever found to do it is by creating a force . . . a set of dynamics on the page that embodies the subtext. And if you can put it together—the signs on the page in this way, where you feel the war between the words and the tone or the gesture—I think the page works.

William Matthews

THE ARC OF William Matthews's career—eleven books of poetry from *Ruining the New Road* (1970) to his posthumous *After All* (1998)—coincided almost exactly with that of Pearl London's seminar at the New School. London admired Matthews and his work in equal measure, and she invited him to her class three times, spanning their working lives: an unrecorded early visit, a midcareer discussion of poems from *A Happy Childhood* (1984), and a final conversation about his poem "My Father's Body" from *Time &*

Money (1995), two years before his death at age fifty-five. Excerpts from the last visit follow.

Born in Cincinnati, Ohio, in 1942, Matthews went to Yale as an undergraduate and to the University of North Carolina for his master's. He taught at a variety of colleges and universities, including Cornell, Iowa, and the University of Washington, in Seattle, in the end directing the creative writing program at City College of New York. Matthews played an increasingly public role in the world of poetry, serving as chair of the Literature Panel of the National Endowment for the Arts and as president both of the Associated Writing Programs and of the Poetry Society of America, where he served alongside Pearl London.

Throughout his career, Matthews's poetry was distinguished by his understated voice, lasting metaphors, and an almost instinctual sense for the music of the line. "I'm overeducated, and one of the things you learn when you get overeducated, if your heart is in the right part of your chest, is never to sound like William F. Buckley Jr.," he says here. But in his later work he also exhibits an increasing facility for more formal poetic structures. In the introduction to *Search Party: Collected Poems of William Matthews* (2004), a Pulitzer Prize finalist, Stanley Plumly writes, "The full heart behind the poems becomes more and more available to the luminous mind making them. Too often honored for his wit alone, Matthews is a poet of emotional resolve, enormous linguistic and poetic resources, and, most especially, a clarifying wisdom."

———————

"My Father's Body"

PEARL LONDON: Now, here are all these great new poems. What has he invented here? What is it that has changed? Because change isn't just external, it's internal; something had to have happened for that kind of renewal. And I began to read these new poems, asking myself, What has deepened, what has been enlarged, what has been transformed, and what has been, I think, transcended? So I come back to that very general question I wanted to begin with. How, Bill, do you think these new poems differ from the earlier ones?

WILLIAM MATTHEWS: *Time & Money* in some sense starts literally with the title. I realized at a certain point that I was growing tired of hearing my male friends my age talking about time, because what they really meant was time left, and there was something boring about hearing anxious jokes by bright men about mortality all the time. There were other ways of thinking about time. Of course it's the case, as one of these poems in the new manuscript suggests, that my father had died; and so these thoughts about mortality and so forth were not far from me. But I mean, one more prostate cancer joke and I was just going to leap out the window. There's never quite enough time and never quite enough money, but that's not an interesting way to talk about them. I said to myself, I think I'll write a book in which I try to talk about these things in more interesting ways than that.

LONDON: Let's turn—can we, Bill—to "My Father's Body" and talk about how you come to [the word] "time" at the very end. You have said that a poem had a form it had to become.

MATTHEWS: Something's worth saying about this point. There's a castle outside Edinburgh, a writers' retreat. I went there because it was exotic, because I like Scotland, and because it's rather near where my mother lives in England. My father had just died, and I thought it would give me a chance to check in on my mother. I was there for a month surrounded by wet sheep. I don't know if any of you have ever sent yourself off for a month someplace to write, but one of the things you discover early on is that those places work much better for painters and composers and novelists than they do for poets, because, you know, you get up and you work really hard for three hours and you think, OK, I've had it, that's it. I'm a sprinter. I work in these intense bursts and then I'm done for the day. So it's noon. And you look out the window and there's thousands of wet sheep.

But I had anticipated this as a problem and took something along to work on: translations of the [Roman poet] Martial, which are now a book. Because of the problems of translating Latin into English—Latin being an inflected language and English being a word-order language—you have to invent equivalents for some of the rhetorical things that Latin can do that English can't. A lot of those were formal. So in order to translate the Martial I was writing more in forms than I had done for a long time. The pleasure of doing that, which I had forgot about, was great. I've written more poems in traditional forms since then; it's always been the case that I've written both, but the proportion has shifted a little bit, because I discovered when I was working on the Martial that I really loved some of that formal fuss. I had forgot how deep and erotic my relationship to it was.

LONDON: Even sonnets?

MATTHEWS: There must be, I don't know, ten sonnets in *Time & Money*.

LONDON: Let me come back to "My Father's Body," because here was Bill Matthews saying that a poem had a form it had to become. And I thought to myself, I wonder if that is valid and true for "My Father's Body." And looking at it, what deepened that form? The momentum of the line, certainly; the fact that there are no stanza breaks, this is cumulative; the fact that there's no predictability in it; and that last word without rhyme, without metrical pattern, that word "time," which really, for me, just blows up enormously. So I really began to ask myself about the form there and about the poem itself. To what extent did it have a form waiting to see the light of day?

MATTHEWS: Well, these decisions are intuitive. Afterwards when you talk about them you sound as if you're much more knowledgeable about your own procedures than you actually are. So that caveat is an important one to make. When people do retrospective articles about you, they make it sound as if you had a series of decisions: at 3:00 a.m. you went and knelt in a chapel with your sword and prayed to the Virgin and you were granted your Blue Period.

But the truth is that a lot of those decisions get made when you say, "I'm sick of writing short poems, I'm going to write long poems now"; "I'm sick of writing yellow poems, I'm going to write blue poems." A lot of these decisions are made at the muscle level. And it seems to me that I made some intuitive decisions about this poem that were smart.

What I would say now is that the poem imitates in its lack of relief through stanza breaks, in its monolithic size, it imitates the way a death takes all the oxygen out of a room and becomes the only thing you can

My Father's Body

First they take it away,
for now the body belongs to the state.
Then they open it
to see what may have killed it,
and the body had arteriosclerosis
in its heart, for this was an inside job.
Now someone must identify the body
so that the state may have a name
for what it will give away,
and the funeral people come in a stark car
shaped like a coffin with a hood
and take the body away,
for now it belongs to the funeral people
and the body's family buys it back,
though it lies in a box at the crematorium
while the mourners travel and convene.
Then they bring the body to the chapel, as they call it,
of the crematorium and the body lies in its box
while the mourners enter and sit
and stare at the box, for the box
lies on a pedestal where the altar would be
if this were a chapel.
A rectangular frame with curtains at the sides
rises from the pedestal,
so that the box seems to fill a small stage,
and the stage gives off the familiar
illusion of being a box with one wall torn away
so that we may see into it,
but it's filled with a box we can't see into.
There's music on tape and a man in a robe
speaks for a while and I who am so good with words
speak for a while and then there's a prayer
and then we mourners can hear the whir
of a small motor and curtains slide
across the stage. At least for today,
I think, this is the stage that all the world is,
and another motor hums on
and we mourners realize that behind
the curtains the body is being lowered,
not like Don Giovanni to the flames
but without flourish or song
or the comforts of elaborate plot,
to the basement of the crematorium,
to the mercies of the gas jets
and the balm of the conveyer belt.
The ashes will be scattered,
says a hushed man in a mute suit,
in the Garden of Rememberance,
which is out back.
And what's left of a mild, democratic man

FINAL TYPESCRIPT OF WILLIAM MATTHEWS'S "MY FATHER'S BODY"

```
will sift in a heap with the residue of others,
for now they all belong to time.
```

think about. You wake up and you say, "This is the third day that my father's been dead. I have to go down and fill out some forms, and my mother is staring cross-eyed at these insurance forms and I think I'm going to wind up doing that," and on and on.

It seemed clear to me fairly late in the first draft of the poem that the poem would end with the word "time." And that therefore I was glad I hadn't engaged in any kind of pattern in the poem because I wanted the word "time" to be inevitable, without any support from metrics or rhyme.

LONDON: And that's what happens. That's exactly what happens.

MATTHEWS: If "time" were the B word of an A-B rhyme, there's a sense in which you could hear it coming, and it would be compelled by the form; I know there are people who think that would be an elegant effect. It seemed to me in this poem it would be more truthful—I'm not against elegant effects, as I hope some of these poems have made clear—but in this poem I wanted "time" to be inevitable without any support from a formal pattern. I didn't want it to complete a series of rhymes.

The other thing about dealing with a death is that it's a little monotonous and repetitious. And the anaphora of having: first they come and do this, then they do that, then they do that. The recurrence gave me a kind of form that didn't happen at the right-hand side of the page [the line endings]. Most of this poem's formal effects happen on the left-hand side, which is a little unusual, but which was fun. It's not a poem that isn't carefully shaped, in its way; it's just that you can't predict its shape mathematically. Most of it happens at the side of the poem; we're not used to looking for formal organizers.

LONDON: Well, that's its great impact and strength. But I must tell you, the first time I read it—and I don't know how all of you felt about it—I came to the lines just before we come to "time" where you're talking about everything that has happened, that Don Giovanni without flames and so forth, and then you have the line "mild, democratic man." I was very, very unhappy, because what I really wanted to hear about were his rumpled shirts, and maybe a frayed eyeglass case, something much nearer to the human condition. And then, I began to think about this. Somewhere along the way you had written: "the more lovingly remembered and painstakingly rendered a loss is the more, on the one hand, it is ours, and the more, on the other hand, it is already given to memory and art, which have, each of them, their own uses for loss." Now that put it in its context that I needed. At that point, as you moved toward the word "time," it became art; it took on another dimension. What about that? What about not having that rumpled shirt in there? Was that something that just came out of you? That you knew you had to move into a larger dimension?

MATTHEWS: Well, in some ways what I admired about my father was a kind of crazed, midwestern friendliness. Or desperate midwestern friendliness, as I called it somewhere else. I used to travel with him occasionally, and we'd get to an airport and we'd have a forty-five-minute layover, and I would open a book and I would look up in twenty minutes, and my father would be having a brandy in the bar with somebody and their only common language was German, and they each had about five hundred words of it. He had a way of making himself equal to everybody he met, no matter what adjustment was required. There seems to me a kind of moral courage and achievement in this—on top of whatever psychic longings and gaps drove him to be compulsively friendly. I'm not sure this was all his choice, but if he was stuck with it, then you have the possibility of making it into something which is not just a tic of your unconscious but is something that you can shape and put to use. He ran an international student exchange program—so his idea of life was that if you picked people up and put them together good things would happen to them. There was a sense in which the "mild, democratic man" is a shorthand reference to what seemed to me most durable about him. People who know him, when they read the poem, always comment on that line: "Oh, that's particularly just."

LONDON: Coming back to the body of the poetry, wouldn't you say that right from the beginning, all of the poems—somewhere, somewhere—are living in a moral universe.

MATTHEWS: I think of the issue of equilibrium, both as a sense of personal poise or balance and also the notion that you can't deal fairly with the world if you don't have the ability to make yourself equal to people. These are notions that have seemed to me important.

And it seems to me that in writers like Stevens and Nabokov and Bishop the real love is for the ability to experience the physical world. And to make connections by means of elaborate linguistic patterns that imitate in some way the profusion and inventiveness of the creation. In one sense it's about order, but in another sense it's about the unbelievable diversity of the world that we can apprehend with our senses.

If you imagine what an expiring Nabokov or an expiring Stevens is most annoyed at, at three minutes before death, it's "I'll never make another metaphor." They're not thinking, "Oh, my idea of order turned out to be really interesting." I'm not particularly interested in ideas—which have wrecked lots of poets. I think they ruined Ezra Pound. His fascination with ideas turned a great lyric poet into a kind of raving village idiot.

LONDON: Robert Frost said that a poem must have in it the colloquial. The jargon, the healthiness, the ruggedness of the jargon. I know Frost has been a great influence.

MATTHEWS: Oh, I'm much taken with Frost. What didn't interest me in, say, Stevens and Nabokov was the slightly mandarin tone. I'm my father's child. I didn't want to sound like my education.

LONDON: Yes, in Stevens it's not *slightly,* either.

MATTHEWS: So I wanted to figure out a way to talk with all this compression and so forth but in a way that sounded equal to whomever I might be speaking. So Frost was great for me. The discovery that you could write poetry that sounded like convincing speech and in the mouths of New Hampshire white trash—these were not educated people. And they're really interesting to listen to. It's poetry and it's human speech and I thought, Oh, this is for me. Because I want to be able to do both. I'm over-educated, and one of the things you learn when you get overeducated, if your heart is in the right part of your chest, is never to sound like William F. Buckley Jr. [*Laughter*]

LONDON: When did you discover Frost?

MATTHEWS: I guess I read Frost when I was in high school. The first poet I read all the way through was Auden, and in a peculiar way, Auden led me to Frost. Auden has a kind of magpie intelligence. He just picks up things. There's also something chatty, something conversational, in Auden that was of interest to me. Here's a case of an overeducated person who knows how to talk to you as if he were a person rather than a book or a representative of a superior class or a superior education. I liked Auden's tone of voice. I think I went instinctively from Auden to Frost because Frost, as an American voice, sounded more recognizable to me.

I meant it with all seriousness about a low boredom threshold. It's been a real advantage to me. Having a high boredom threshold would be a different advantage to a different kind of poet; you have to use what you're given and make an asset of it. That's what an artist is. You're born with a limp and figure out a way to run fast with a limp. If you think, I don't like the sound of my voice when I do this, that's information . . . it's exactly the information that you need. I mean, the thing that I feel more and more as a writer and as a teacher of writing is that you really have almost all the information that you need to solve your problems right in front of you. Within four feet of you. If you can teach yourself to look around and find it. Don't let the clues go by. It's really everything you need.

LONDON: For all the great splurging of language, there is distillation all the way through. We mustn't typecast even William Matthews.

MATTHEWS: That's why I've never wanted to write a novel.

LONDON: Why?

MATTHEWS: The low boredom threshold. The distilling is the fun. To write a novel well—I have a couple friends who are good novelists and I love what they do and admire it enormously, it's just very different from what I do. When their characters cross the street it's a good street and they know what the stores are, they know what people wear on that street; and I don't care. I want to write a description of what it feels like to cross the street and I don't care about the stores and I don't care what the people are wearing. I mean, in a sense, everything is distillation.

Paul Muldoon

IN 1951 PAUL MULDOON was born into a Catholic family in County Armagh, Northern Ireland, his father a farm laborer and his mother a schoolteacher. He studied English, Celtic, and philosophy at Queen's University in Belfast, where he was befriended by Seamus Heaney, a tutor there. At the time of his graduation he had published his first book of poems, *New Weather* (1973). He was only twenty-one years old. His other early collections include *Mules* (1977), *Why Brownlee Left* (1980), and *Quoof*

(1983), which he wrote while working as a radio and television producer for the BBC.

To this March 1995 conversation with Pearl London and her class, Paul Muldoon brought along thirteen draft pages of his poem "Cows," from *The Annals of Chile* (1994). The book has been credited with a more directly personal tone than the earlier works even as the lines, rendered so brilliantly, catch his most recognizable traits: word lists and wordplay, postmodern breaks of form, wit, shifting technique, and the widest net among poets for the sounds and catchphrases of other poems, other poets. ("Some little nod in the direction of Ted Hughes," he says here about "Cows.") If the aim is not clarity, the effect is clearly powerful. "Between the two electrical points," Muldoon says, "between the positive and the negative, the A and B, whatever it is, a spark might leap between these . . . two points . . . somehow in the midst of it all the hope is that some connection is made, some shape is made in the world."

Muldoon was forty-four when he visited London's class, and seven years away from the Pulitzer Prize he would win for *Moy Sand and Gravel* (2002). He currently lives with his wife and two children near Princeton, New Jersey, where he teaches and chairs the Peter B. Lewis Center for the Arts. He edited *The Faber Book of Contemporary Irish Poetry* (1986), and in 2007 was named poetry editor of *The New Yorker*.

———————

"Cows"

PEARL LONDON: I want to read you something that you said about the essential Byron. You're talking about *Beppo*, one of Byron's great poems, and you say, "In that poem, we see Byron at his brilliant best—witty, wise, at one moment stepping on the gas and cruising along the narrative equivalent of a six-lane highway, at the next, content to pull over and make a leisurely digression down some back road or blind alley." I said to myself, My goodness, isn't that a way of describing your own writing in the *Annals of Chile*. Is that far-fetched?

PAUL MULDOON: One of the things I like about Byron is his sense of humor. For many people, of course, poetry and humor, anything that smacks of less than solemn, equals some kind of lack of seriousness. Byron is a writer who gives the lie to that immediately. But I do really admire, to go back to that quotation, his narrative urgency and thrust, but also his wonderful ability to digress. Of course he's not the first writer to have digressed.

But let me see now, I'm not sure if I'm really answering this question. I'm not sure if I'll answer any of these questions, I have to tell you.

LONDON: You're going to be answering them before we're through. [*Laughter*]

MULDOON: OK, well, let me say about the Byron—as you know when writers speak about other writers, they're usually, in many cases, speaking of themselves at some level, you know? Not that I equate myself with Byron or anything like that, but I think often what they're saying is really about themselves.

LONDON: Is a poem for you what Frost said, a feat of associations?

MULDOON: Well, that happens in some of the poems, absolutely, that one goes from one stepping-stone to another. I can't really think of a decent metaphor for it. But between the two electrical points, between the positive and the negative, the A and B, whatever it is, a spark might leap between these at least two points. And it's usually with at least two thoughts or images or phrases that these poems begin. They're quite often quite heterogeneous ideas, to borrow that term from Johnson, so that one takes a piece of ice on the top of a barrel, and a memory of the school photographer coming around, and that photograph, and puts them together and somehow in the midst of it all the hope is that some connection is made, some shape is made in the world. A more familiar phrase of Frost is that a poem be "a momentary stay at confusion." I suppose that's my sense. That somehow I'm making a shape, making a little construct in the world, which is after all what a poem is, a made thing in the world. Where something will be clarified for a moment, where one's sense of the world will be revised, if only for an instant. Not necessarily in any earth-shattering way, but so that one will never quite look at whatever it is we're dealing with in the same way.

Which is a rather tall order, but I'm afraid it's the order I set myself anyway, and I'm sure many writers do, that at some level one wants to come out of the poem changed.

LONDON: It's the word "momentary" [in "a momentary stay at confusion"] that I dispute with Frost. That's not momentary, that's part of the evolution of you as a poet.

MULDOON: Right, but I guess that what Frost is thinking in an uncommonly self-effacing way for him, and I suppose which I was picking up on, is that one makes that little shape in the world and, at some level, one would hope one might make as grand an impact as that and it would help one to live one's life. But you know, I'm not sure, even if it were to do that, that it's true for anything more than an instant. And you know, the person who wrote "Yarrow" [in Muldoon's *The Annals of Chile*], or through whom it was written, it's ancient history, one has moved on, one is trying to do something else. It did make sense of things for me for a moment, or made sense of how little sense things might make, which is maybe just as important. I'd be delighted to think that someone else might take something away from it. I have to believe in the efficacy of poetry in some way, that it does make something happen. But the fact of the matter is that it's difficult to see exactly what it might be for, most of the time.

LONDON: All of us these last two weeks have been looking at various underlying questions about what orders these poems, and we considered the undermining of traditional forms, what somebody called "the crumbled sonnet," and then your use of terza rima in "Calves," and then of course the absolutely staggering incredible half rhymes. My favorite one was in the "Incantata" when Paul Muldoon says, "That's all that's left of the voices of Enrico Caruso / from all that's left of an opera house somewhere in Matto / Grosso." That's marvelous! Whoever in the whole world except Paul Muldoon could do that? Yet as I've really been thinking about all of this, it seems to me that the essential thing that brings it into a cohesive work is the interrelationship, over and over again, between the imaginative and the actual.

MULDOON: Well, certainly, I mean one wants the poems to have, not only some relationship to the world as we know it, but also some evident relationship. A poem like "Incantata," perhaps even more because it's more than demi/semi-autobiographical—and because the speaker of the poem is much more like the historical figure who would sign a check "Paul Muldoon" than in many others—I suppose it looks as if it's truer or more real than poems in earlier books. I mean certainly one wants the poems to mean something.

LONDON: And there are these big polarities that become great polarities in your work. This beautiful, wonderful obsession with language on the one hand, enormous outpourings of language, of metaphor, all these great unburdenings. And at the same time, there is a reticence. You have on the one hand a very brash vocabulary and, on the other hand, a very unbrash sensibility. Sandy [poet J. D.] McClatchy found somewhere in Whitman, who's always telling you about the self, "No one will ever get at my verses." Well, isn't it rather interesting, that whole inner inaccessibility, and Frost: "I've written to keep the over-curious out of the secret places of my mind, both in my verse and in my letters." I don't know to what extent the reticence and to what extent these enormous, glorious profusions of feeling and language are polarities. Maybe they're not.

MULDOON: Well, I think there is something in that. I don't know if it's reticence. Certainly some of these poems are quite difficult to get at. But that's not as if—

LONDON: That's not reticence.

MULDOON: No, it's not, it's not. I mean, you—

LONDON: What makes them difficult?

MULDOON: Well, all I would say is that if there are difficulties, as I think there are with some of them, it's not as if I get up in the morning and set about putting them in. I mean, I think it varies from poem to poem. Sometimes it may be a matter of reference or allusion or just the landscape of the poem, or the cultural impediment of the poem. Or it may be of vocabulary, or it may be that sometimes these poems are written in a kind of telegram-ese and they move, I think in some cases, quite smartly over the points.

LONDON: But always within the disciplines of the thought. Or if you're departing from the disciplines of the thought, you're doing it deliberately.

MULDOON: Well, I hope so, yes. But again, my aim, as I'm sure it is with most writers, is to end up with something that will be available to the first or second reader. I suppose the first reader is oneself trying to make sense of what's coming out there. If the style of some of these poems is quite telescoped, the style of many others is very available, at least on some surface level.

STUDENT: Do you write drafts, lots of drafts?

MULDOON: Yes. I've always worked on a typewriter for the most part. Now I mean, you have a few lines written out [in the drafts of "Cows"]. The poems begin in all sorts of ways. And in fact, when we come to look at this, you'll see that sometimes it's a phrase, an image—sometimes, because I often write in traditional forms, they start with little rhymes, or at least they're fueled by rhymes. Rhyme, I believe, is something that's not imposed on the language in some sort of cookie-cutter way but is integral, intrinsic to the language, and at least I find it a way of making discoveries and finding out what this poem wants to say in the course of events. So they can start in all sorts of different ways.

Now, conventionally, with a poem that's a page or a couple of pages long—your average poem insofar as there is such a thing—I would try to write it in one sitting. By one sitting I might mean a week. I'm very bad at coming back and revising. That's not to say I don't revise—of course, I come back and I change phrases and lines, but that tends to be the exception rather than the rule. Now, as I say, that's not to say that I don't come back to poems a week, six weeks, six months, or a year down the road and say, "How could anyone have produced such garbage?" I just find it very hard to revise in the Yeatsian mode, for example. So what I try to do is to write one line at a time. This is a piece of advice that I sometimes give to my students that they find mind-bending. You write that line, and then you say, "Oh, but you know there's so much that I want to get down there." One line at a time, and I try to get that right, and then I go on to the next one and I don't leave that until I think it's right.

"Cows" was written over quite an extended period. I started it in County Monaghan in Ireland where it's set. I was staying in a writers' colony there, and it's set in the area around there and I just couldn't get it started at all. The first page I'm pretty sure was . . .

LONDON: "When God put all his eggs in one basket."

MULDOON: That's right. Now I had a typewriter, I know—

LONDON: I love that line, and I want to know why you didn't keep it somewhere.

MULDOON: I honestly don't know; I think the first thing I had . . . I was making a few notes, so I must have decided that the poem would be called "Cows," and it's dedicated to a man called Dermot Seymour, an artist who was knocking around at the time, and he's really the other person in the poem. As you can see [on the cover art for *Selected Poems: 1968–1986*], he makes super-realistic paintings, often featuring cows and generally some surrealistic landscape set on the border into Northern Ireland, often with a

COWS

FOR CLASSROOM USE ONLY

for Dermot Seymour

When God put all his eggs in one basket

drumlin trampoline
cough human
best bib and tucker one in a tuxedo
tie-dye
gas-masks goggles
glamorous claymores
group scarab
methane gas they run on

helicopter gunship which comes out in the poem itself. So this part of the world is drumlin country, you can see a couple of—there's "drumlin" and "trampoline." To say where the poem began is very difficult. I mean, one can see certain things, but one can never quite work out necessarily the sequence in which things happen.

LONDON: No, not the sequence, but we can hear where the sounds are, the importance of the music of the language. Certain things surface that perhaps aren't mathematical, but in "drumlin" and "trampoline" we already hear a relationship.

MULDOON: I think where the poem actually begins is the "cough," like a human cough. It's with that image the poem eventually begins.

LONDON: I would love to know what the peripheral imagination is doing when jotting down the side notes.

MULDOON: I have no idea. I might have been reading Yeats at the time. Maybe it was something to do with the Indian cows, the sacred cows. . . . One thing that you will see here, if you look right up to the top right-hand corner of that page, you can see . . .

LONDON: "Parable"?

MULDOON: And beside it there—I'm afraid I cut it off because I wasn't careful enough when I photocopied—you can see the phrase "spot where a cow has lain."

LONDON: That's the end of your poem.

MULDOON: And that in fact was another image that really drove the poem. I don't know if any of you have spent time with cows at all, but they have a little area where they've been lying . . . there seems to be a spot.

LONDON: "Where a cow has lain," an indentation in the grass. . . .

MULDOON: So that was an image that started me off. You can see I was sitting around . . . I would make the odd little note, and this really isn't typical. What's typical, you know? You can say I was just letting my mind play around. You can see there are the "claymores"—"claymore" means a big sword, but it's also a type of land mine. A bomb. And there, the "group." It's usually not a group of people, but it's where cow dung accumulates. And there you can see the scarab, which turns up as "oscaraboscar" [in the finished poem], and that's why there's a double dung beetle, as you know.

LONDON: In the next draft, that first typewritten line is, "even as we speak, there's a smoker's cough / from behind the hedge," but in the final version of the poem you've added "whitethorn" to "hedge." Tell us about that.

MULDOON: Any thoughts yourselves?

STUDENT: You later on use "Hawthorne."

MULDOON: Yes, but here it's a particular allusion to something. The great poet of County Monaghan is Patrick Kavanagh, whose great claim to fame was that he made the distinction between the parish and the province, and the parochial and the provincial imagination. There's a famous poem of his called "Epic" in which he talks about Homer making the *Iliad* out of a rise such as the one he's describing between two farmers. That's the parochial imagination. And the provincial looks to some center; believes that the heart of things is elsewhere. He talks about it in another poem, that he will never die unless he goes outside these "whitethorn hedges."

I think part of the plan is—you mentioned the vocabulary earlier on— these are not the nice words in the right order, but they're the right words in the right order. And one of the reasons why they're here is that rhythmi- cally "from behind the whitethorn hedge" actually stops you, then "we stop dead in our tracks," which is the classic case of a cliché. This is aiming to take a little risk.

LONDON: Now, pages ahead, there are four typewritten stanzas and on the bottom lower left corner you've written "BCB, CDC . . ." the [rhyme scheme of] terza rima.

and the other flicker-fade

till all that's left is a faint glow of tourmaline

set deep less in jet than jasper or jade?   *then sprouts*

                    -oOo-

That smoker's cough again. We share a trampoline

ccups and humps and heaves squiffy bevy hi-fi

as cow after cow

                              C humped doifs

    b

    c

    b
                              Devon

    c

    d   *inshes and*
                              rajwont
    c

MULDOON: Could I say a word about terza rima? On another page I have "even as we speak, there's a smoker's cough / from behind the hedge / and what might be the click of a safety catch." You can see that the terza rima as a form wasn't there from the outset. . . . I believe in the poem determining its own formal structure, and of course that happens fairly early on. But given the setting of this poem, there were reasons why terza rima would be, might be, effective.

Conventionally, as you know, terza rima is associated with Dante. I suppose it is in the sense a kind of nightmarish journey, a descent into some . . . I mean, once you begin to talk in these terms, you sort of see yourself becoming slightly idiotic, but you know what I mean.

LONDON: Let's look at this line here—in the third stanza [of the draft] you have "and the other flicker-fade / till all that's left is a faint glow of tourmaline / set deep less in jet than jasper or jade?" And in the final version, the printed version, the last line is "set in a dark, part-jet, part-jasper, or -jade?"

That after-image, you see, it was flickering and fading. You ordered your line to reflect the caesuras, the breaks, "in a dark, part-jet, part-jasper, or -jade" which is much more of a flickering and fading than that earlier, lovely "set deep less in death than jasper or jade." Do you think that was part of the thinking that went into it? Because that's what Wallace Stevens does, puts in all those commas and those caesuras to give you the sense of not-fulfillment.

MULDOON: Probably, I'm sure that it's meant to be slightly mimetic, as you say. You can see where I ran out of steam there at the bottom of that same page . . . I got into this terza rima and then I didn't know what to do, so I just put in BCB, CDC. . . .

LONDON: I want to know how you got to "emphysemantiphon." What was happening there? "That smoker's cough again: it triggers off from drumlin / to drumlin an emphysemantiphon," I don't know how to say it.

MULDOON: "Em-phy-seman-tiphon," I say it. You asked where I was stuck before. It was just there [in the previous excerpt] at: "That smoker's cough again. We share a trampoline"? So I had to do something. After "it triggers off from drumlin / to drumlin"—[and I chose] an "emphysemantiphon / of cows."

```
That smoker's cough again: it triggers off from drumlin
to drumlin an emphysemantiphon
of cows. They hoist themselves on to their trampoline
```

LONDON: I love it. It's echoing down.

MULDOON: You know, I would say this is what happens when cows are coughing in unison across to each other. And can I just say a little bit more? There's a danger in using a word like this one, a neologism like this, and one of the main dangers is, of course, that people say, "This guy has OD'd on Joyce." (*Laughter*) That's basically what's going to happen . . . and then you get to "metaphysicattle" and then by the time you get to "oscar . . ."

LONDON: That's what I'm coming to. "Oscar . . ."

MULDOON: "Oscaraboscarabinary." Have we moved on to that now?

LONDON: No, we haven't gotten that far.

MULDOON: "Emphysemantiphon." Any thoughts here? This poem is, as you know, set on a terrible night. I don't know if you've ever heard—and of course, that's where it begins—heard a cow cough behind a hedge. It's very scary.

LONDON: Is it?

MULDOON: Yes. It sounded like somebody lurking in there. I don't know if you get the sense of this country that I'm describing here, perhaps some of you know it . . . I mean, it's a very dangerous part of the world, basically.

LONDON: It is indeed, and that's why that last line is so marvelous, that in this place of ominous unspoken danger, we lie down for a little while where a cow has lain. It's a marvelous poem. And I'm terribly pleased—where is it?—where you finally say, "This is no Devon cow." Ted Hughes.

MULDOON: "This is no Devon." It's kind of tongue in cheek. I mean, it's a little unfair because Ted Hughes, he writes wonderfully about cattle. I suppose in a way what those lines are meant to be saying or suggesting is one can't quite write a poem about cows in 1990, or whenever this poem was started, without having some little nod in the direction of Ted Hughes, who—I don't know if you know any of his poems, "Moortown," for example, diaries of his life and time as a farmer, are absolutely brilliant poems about the birth of cattle and dehorning. Do you know them at all? Brilliant.

LONDON: Finally, please tell us why "a Tuareg." This has been bothering me.

MULDOON: Oh, you know, it's so dreary. What do you think of this word, "oscaraboscarabinary"?

STUDENT: I don't really like it.

MULDOON: What has it ever done to you? [*Laughter*]

STUDENT: A little bit too whimsical and silly. I mean, before it, "Again the flash. Again the fade." It's kind of organic and repetitive and a little bit . . . nicely heavy . . . and then the image I get in my mind is just jumping off the page.

MULDOON: Of "oscaraboscarabinary"? But I wonder if that isn't perhaps what one's meant to get? Or something along those lines. Let me ask, how seriously do you take the speaker of this poem, who for example goes into the etymology of the word "boreen"? He's not exactly to be taken seriously. There's a little element of the pompous . . .

STUDENT: Right. I find a little element of it attractive . . . it just seems a little too . . .

MULDOON: Overdone?

STUDENT: I mean, that was just my impression.

MULDOON: Well, that's fair enough.

STUDENT: I'm so stuck on the word that I'm not into the world of the poem.

MULDOON: But you know, I think we're talking about the same thing, if you don't mind my suggestion. I think that that's partly what one's meant to do, is to stop with it and to be stopped for reasons that are less than rewarding. What the poem is trying to do towards the end is say, "Look, let's cut this out." What does one do—let's leave off from the froth. . . . I mean, I agree with you, I just want to wonder. And this is my variation that you don't necessarily have to accept at all. What the poem is trying to do at the end is to say, "All of that is fine and well, but it's really nothing compared to the reality of facing up to the fact that there's this truck up the road which could be . . ."

LONDON: A truck of death.

MULDOON: Quite dangerous. And—

STUDENT: But it also acknowledges how hard that process is. It's not just a simple process from turning from froth to something else. You set it up with however I might allegorize and then you kind of give an example of what you're allegorizing.

MULDOON: That's the hope.

STUDENT: And then you keep going, implying that it's just not a simple matter of turning from a complicated view of the world to a simple view, when you're a complicated person.

LONDON: Good point.

MULDOON: But it's risky, and I think one of the risks it takes is that it might turn people off. And I think in fact that's one of the risks that all these poems on some level take, and it's quite understandable that some people might just want to throw the thing out. Life's too short.

STUDENT: Well, it is a challenge. It's the kind of challenge that made me read ahead and say, "What's going to happen to this, what is this?" A reader doesn't have to like every element of the poem for the poem to be successful for the reader. If I didn't like it and that's part of it, then that's good.

MULDOON: That's what I was trying to suggest, that it may actually be aiming to do what you're recognizing it as doing.

LONDON: I have to come back to the Tuareg, which really kept me up all night.

MULDOON: You know, Tuareg, it's the whole association of "Arab" in "scarab" in the North African dung beetle . . . the dung beetle in the scarab . . . which is where the "-carabinary" comes from, and the word is a metaphor based on the beetle looking like a little firing party.

LONDON: Aha, thank you, that's good.

MULDOON: So in other words, I mean, it's just as this lady here suggested. It is a kind of condensed looney tune, you know?

[PUBLISHED VERSION, "COWS"]

> Even as we speak, there's a smoker's cough
> from behind the whitethorn hedge: we stop dead in our
>   tracks:
> a distant tingle of water into a trough.
>
> In the past half-hour—since a cattle-truck
> all but sent us shuffling off this mortal coil—
> we've consoled ourselves with the dregs
>
> of a bottle of Redbreast. Had Hawthorne been a Gael,
> I insist, the scarlet "A" on Hester Prynne
> would have stood for "Alcohol."
>
> This must be the same truck whose tail-lights burn
> so dimly, as if caked with dirt,
> three or four hundred yards along the boreen
>
> (a diminutive form of the Gaelic *bóthar,* "a road,"
> from *bó,* "a cow," and *thar*
> meaning, in this case, something like "athwart,"
>
> "boreen" has entered English "through the air"
> despite the protestations of the O.E.D.):
> why, though, should one tail-light flash and flare

then flicker-fade
to an after-image of tourmaline
set in a dark part-jet, part-jasper or -jade?

That smoker's cough again; it triggers off from drumlin
to drumlin an emphysemantiphon
of cows. They hoist themselves on to their trampoline

and steady themselves and straight away divine
water in some far-flung spot
to which they then gravely incline. This is no Devon

cow-coterie, by the way, whey-faced, with Spode
hooves and horns: nor are they the metaphsicattle of Japan
that have merely to anticipate

scoring a bull's-eye and, lo, It happens;
these are earth-flesh, earth-blood, salt of the earth,
whose talismans are their own jaw-bones

buried under threshold and hearth.
For though they trace themselves to the kith and kine
that presided over the birth

of Christ (so carry their calves a full nine
months and boast liquorice
cachous on their tongues), they belong more to the line

that's trampled these cwms and corries
since Cuchulainn tramped Aoife.
Again the flash. Again the fade. However I might allegorize

some oscaraboscarabinary bevy
of cattle there's no getting round this cattle-truck,
one light on the blink, laden with what? Microwaves? Hi-fis?

Oscaraboscarabinary: a twin, entwined, a tree, a Tuareg;
a double dung-beetle; a plain
and simple hi-firing party; an off-the-back-of-a-lorry drogue?

Enough of Colette and Céline, Céline and Paul Celan:
enough of whether Nabokov
taught at Wellesley or Wesleyan.

Now let us talk of slaughter and the slain,
the helicopter gun-ship, the mighty Kalashnikov:
let's rest for a while in a place where the cow has lain.

Li-Young Lee

WHEN LI-YOUNG LEE visited Pearl London's class in March 1995, he was thirty-seven years old and had written two books of poems. His visit coincided with the release of a third book, his prose-poem memoir, *The Winged Seed: A Remembrance.* In lush language, the book unfolds Lee's extraordinary biography: his father was for a time Mao's personal physician, but on the establishment of the People's Republic his parents fled to Indonesia, where Lee was born in Jakarta in 1957. The following year, with Indonesia becoming increasingly anti-Chinese under President Sukarno, Lee's father was arrested and imprisoned for nineteen months. After his release the family traveled in exile for five years, moving from Hong Kong to Macao to Japan before arriving in the United States. Lee's father then attended seminary in Pittsburgh and settled the family in the small town of Vandergrift, Pennsylvania, where he became minister of a Presbyterian church.

The themes of memory, father, language, God, selflessness, and humility that animate Lee's memoir play out as well in his first book, *Rose* (1986) and even more deeply in *The City in Which I Love You* (1991), honored as best second volume of poems by the Academy of American Poets. In London's copy of this second volume, one line in "The Cleaving" is marked with especially urgent asterisks and underscoring: "What is it in me would / devour the world to utter it?" In their conversation London asked Lee about that line, and Lee's response illuminates his impulse toward the visionary: "As I was writing the poem," he answers, "I wanted to write from a place of unknowing, not from knowledge. . . . My wish was that the poem would move toward a kind of ecstatic utterance."

Lee, who studied biochemistry before shifting to poetry in his senior year at the University of Pittsburgh, now lives in Chicago with his wife and two children. Over the years he has worked in warehouses and as a karate teacher, and he has taught poetry at Stanford University and the University of Iowa. Since his visit to London's class he has written two additional volumes of poetry, *Book of My Nights* (2001), which won the William Carlos Williams Award, and *Behind My Eyes* (2008).

"The Cleaving"

PEARL LONDON: I must say that *The City in Which I Love You* is a wonderful odyssey of interiority, a pilgrimage in search of the self. What's extraordinary to me is that if one compares it with some of the great pilgrimages in literature—like Byron's "Don Juan"—there's so little solipsism in your pilgrimage. Don Juan's world is completely centered around himself; and your world isn't that centered. What do you think is the explanation?

LI-YOUNG LEE: Writing for me is an act of love, and poems are shapes or forms of love. It seems important for me that the poem graduate—from a lower form of love to a higher form of love; from a sense of personal love to a kind of indifference or impersonality.

I found that as I was writing *The City in Which I Love You* I was interested in who was actually there, writing. I'm interested in the evolution of the personal pronoun "I" in literature. Not only in literature, but in our culture—what is the "I"? Who is it?

LONDON: That's very important. Because one really wonders to what extent the "I" embraces a whole community of people, of ideas.

LEE: What became interesting to me was the very inexactness with which we live every day with this self. At some point I thought, I'm going to have to be a little more naked. I thought an actual self with all the inexactness and all the confusion of memories, that was more interesting, that was somehow more true, more naked, than very neatly trying to assemble this Frankenstein monster and saying, "This is me." That somehow felt dishonest to me.

LONDON: Do you now feel—now, grown and father of two children and so forth—do you now feel a sense of identity which is utterly your own?

LEE: No. No, I don't. I feel more than ever that there is no "I." That's where I am today—I might feel differently five years from now. All the versions of personhood—that my parents have given me, the culture has given me, my brothers and sisters, wife, children, friends—one is greater than all of those versions. And that greater someone can't be nailed down with a pronoun like "I."

LONDON: "I" could be a universe.

LEE: Then that "I" is the "I" I'm interested in writing toward. That "I" which is the universe. I'm trying to move toward an ecstatic state in which the small "I" is extinguished and merged into a larger "I."

Part of me does feel that if I keep writing and living according to afterimages, then I'll always be late . . . for my own life, somehow. If I'm living dependent on who I thought I was, who my parents told me I was, all of those things seem to me cumbersome—they're obstacles toward something more immediate, something more naked. For the longest time I've walked through the world thinking, Well, I'm this, I'm that, while there was always a voice inside of me that knew I was nobody. In the way that Emily Dickinson said, "I'm nobody; who are you—are you nobody, too?"

LONDON: Don't you think a great part of this had to do with the fact that you had this extraordinary childhood? The upheavals were so vast and monumental and earthshaking. Sukarno putting your father in prison, the escape from Indonesia, and then coming to a small western town in Pennsylvania after all of that. It takes in its stride vast worlds of experience. In his book *The Anxiety of Influence,* Harold Bloom says that every writer ultimately must overthrow his literary fathers in order to reach a voice of his own; he must also overthrow the fathers that he loved and respected and revered in order to become father to himself. Do you feel that that would apply? I mean, how can we overthrow a father who has suffered so much for you? Who rowed his family to safety. Who stayed in a terrible prison. How do you overthrow that? Can one overthrow it?

LEE: To this day, the margins of my father's life seem a little outside my own compass. And I do feel the need to see myself not just in the context of this figure who is sometimes overwhelming. But I also have a firmness, an intuition that I'm as large as that—even if it doesn't feel that way right now.

LONDON: In his preface to your first book, *The Rose,* Gerald Stern writes that "understanding and coming to peace with a powerful, stubborn, remote, passionate and loving father . . . is the critical event, the critical myth in Lee's poetry." Do you think that's true?

LEE: I don't know that that's entirely true; I know that the father figure is powerful in my work and in my life. I keep struggling with the idea of a personal father and an impersonal father. And I guess it's that struggle that I'm most engaged in. The idea of an impersonal father in the universe, and the idea of it embodied somehow in a personal father.

LONDON: In "Furious Versions" you say "the past / doesn't fall away, the past / joins the greater / telling, and is." The past is right there in the present; you can't relegate it to some other history. The past *is*. You can say the past *is,* but also, don't you have to realize that the past changes as you change? Isn't the past also a material that takes on other colorations in the light of where you are in life?

LEE: The difficulty of representing the past brings me to interrogate even the nature of representative language. It isn't the past that you're writing about, so what are you writing about? It's fiction. I'm not interested in writing fiction. I don't want to live by any more fictions. Not my parents' fictions, not my culture's fictions, not my own fictions.

LONDON: You really want to get to the nitty-gritty of the fear in you and the hope in you.

LEE: I really want to know who it is sitting and doing the writing. When I realized that the past, the way I recollected it, was very different than the reality, what do I do about it? The conclusion I've reached now is to stop writing about the past. Because you can't recollect it; there's nothing to recollect. There's nothing there.

STUDENT: I heard you on the radio just last week talking about your memoir, and you said something to the effect that you wanted to find the child—that person, that voice, and write from his perspective.

LEE: I want to achieve a voice, a language in poetry, that is utterly childlike, utterly naked. A firstness.

STUDENT: It seems that when you are talking about fictions you're talking about interpretations that you see as no longer valid. But in order to write, you must interpret; you must choose. Choices involve interpretations. If you feel that your past interpretations are now fictive to you, how are you going to avoid that? The instant that you grow, your interpretations will change. So if you view past interpretations as fictive, there is no truth.

LEE: I feel a poetic truth is closer than any truth that we can approach. The closer something is to poetry, the closer it is to reality. Let's just take the lyric poem as an example—the manifold quality of a lyric poem, the instantaneousness of a lyric poem, the feeling that many consciousnesses are simultaneously being enacted—that is closer to reality. The lyric moment is reality. But we don't always live in that reality. The lyric moment is closer to the truth, to me, than a narrative which is a fictive process.

My hope when I was writing this book was that I could proceed by a deeper compass than narrative fictive logic. I don't think I escape narrative in this book, but I wish I could.

STUDENT: But you're not just referring to the past or remembering the past—you want to do it in a more spiritual way, a less visual way.

LEE: I want to get beyond representation, which is appropriation of reality. I don't want to appropriate reality. I want reality to occur on the page, I want a new reality, a new interiority to occur at the level of the language.

LONDON: In "Arise, Go Down" you say, "unable, thank God, to see in each and / every flower the world cancelling itself." We have that rose, and we also know that you have seen that rose with aphids in it, the petals shriveling, the world canceling itself. What concerns me here is that yes, this is the metaphor or the symbol of the world canceling itself. But the world also regenerates itself. Nature is prodigious, and survival is an underlying force. You know much more about survival than I do. And yet in that rose you see cancelation; in that rose you see endings. Is there not some other part of you now, moving away from that childhood and that terrible history, that also sees not cancelation but proliferation?

LEE: Well, I do. I do see a positive aspect. The cancellation that I bemoan is the cancelation of the specific. That's where the heartbreak is.

LONDON: It's the loss of one father.

LEE: It's a specific house, a specific yard, a specific man.

LONDON: That probably is the answer that we needed to hear. Because it is that one house, that one door that hurts so much.

LEE: And, again, that's the struggle between the personal and the impersonal. Impersonally speaking, I see that there is a rejuvenating and constantly renewing process going on. But personally speaking, I say—all the specificities, where are they?

LONDON: In "This Hour and What Is Dead," you write "Someone tell the Lord to leave me alone." How did you reconcile that with your own ideas about God?

LEE: The God I was addressing in that poem was very much the God of my father, which is a God of the Old and New Testaments. A very Christian God. A very patriarchal figure. Already very embodied. Kind of entrapped and encrusted with anthropomorphic features.
    Right now I'm wondering about the possibility of writing a religious poetry. A genuinely religious poetry. Because I feel we live in an age of secular poetry.

LONDON: Can one write a really religious poetry today?

LEE: I'm wondering about that. Maybe not a religious poetry but a poetry whose spirituality isn't ironic. Which is genuine, sincere, hungry. It would have to be the real thing. I'm just curious what that would look like, what that would sound like. Because for me secular poetry isn't enough.

STUDENT: It's really hard, because in Herbert and Donne's day there were shared assumptions about what the furniture of religion was. But now there aren't any. So if you write a poem that is open to a lot of different assumptions it might be rejected by some people because it says "Jesus" if you're a Jew, or . . .

LEE: So it would have to avoid using the signposts that we recognize when we say religion. And the poem would have to proceed by an intelligence that is entirely new, distinct from the intelligence that we use in a secular poem. That's what I'm interested in: what is that new intelligence?

LONDON: I have a very good friend—he's a brilliant critic—and he maintains that there is only one important religious poet writing today. He says it is A. R. Ammons. Because, he says, Ammons sees the universe as an absolutely integrated, coordinated system of relationships between people, between atoms and stars, between all of the phenomena of nature. He's seeing this as an utterly bound-together world in which man and atom and stars all have a relevance and a real meaning for each other. And that is, for him, godlike.

LEE: I think Ammons is a very great poet. I have a real quarrel with him, though.

LONDON: What?

LEE: He's too rational for me. His poems proceed with a great, brilliant, rational mind. And for me . . . there's no peril in there. The irrational and the rational together make the kind of peril that gets enacted in poetry.

LONDON: I wanted to ask you a few specific questions about "The Cleaving." "What is it in me would / devour the world to utter it?" We grasp that premise, right? And then you say, "I would devour this race to sing it / this race that according to Emerson / *managed to preserve to a hair / for* *three or four thousand years / the ugliest features in the world."* And you go along and say, "I would eat Emerson, his transparent soul, his / soporific transcendence."

[READS EXCERPT, "THE CLEAVING"]

What is it in me would
devour the world to utter it?
What is it in me will not let
the world be, would eat
not just this fish,
but the one who killed it,
the butcher who cleaned it.
I would eat the way he
squats, the way he
reaches into the plastic tubs
and pulls out a fish, clubs it, takes it
to the sink, guts it, drops it on the weighing pan.
I would eat that thrash
and plunge of the watery body
in the water, that liquid violence
between the man's hands,
I would eat
the gutless twitching on the scales,
three pounds of dumb
nerve and pulse, I would eat it all
to utter it.
The deaths at the sinks, those bodies prepared
for eating, I would eat,
and the standing deaths
at the counters, in the aisles,
the walking deaths in the streets,
the death-far-from-home, the death-

in-a-strange-land, these Chinatown
deaths, these American deaths.
I would devour this race to sing it,
this race that according to Emerson
managed to preserve to a hair
for three or four thousand years
the ugliest features in the world.
I would eat these features, eat
the last three or four thousand years, every hair.
And I would eat Emerson, his transparent soul, his
soporific transcendence.
I would eat this head,
glazed in pepper-speckled sauce,
the cooked eyes opaque in their sockets.
I bring it to my mouth and—
the way I was taught, the way I've watched
others do—
with a stiff tongue lick out
the cheek-meat and the meat
over the armored jaw, my eating,
its sensual, salient nowness,
punctuating the void
from which such hunger springs and to which it proceeds.

LEE: I love Emerson, I just had a problem with something I read in his journal. He was talking about Asians. Chinese, specifically. He said they had no culture to speak of, no music. He said they're not even as good as the Africans, who are at least willing to carry our wood. And he said that they've done nothing useful except manage *"to preserve to a hair / for three or four thousand years / the ugliest features in the world."* The poem begins by looking at the face of this butcher. So it's about that—it's about countenance, and it's about what the culture defines as beauty or ugliness.

It's a weird wrestling I'm doing with Emerson. I can't imagine me without Emerson. And yet there's this thing about him that gets to me. That's deep in the culture.

LONDON: That's right. Because inherent in your work there is a certain transcendentalism. Your kind of transcendentalism may not be a replica of Emerson's, but it is very essentially there. In "The City in Which I Love You" you say, "I'm famished for meaning." I feel that about your work throughout. You are famished for meaning; you are searching for meaning.

LEE: I'm just always hungry. Writing is about hunger. And the object of the hunger keeps eluding me, as it does in that poem.

LONDON: Tell us about "The Cleaving." That was a very difficult poem for all of us, I think. "What is it in me would / devour the world to utter it?" This voracious appetite to devour everything, to embrace everything in order to give voice to it, to utter it—wonderful. And then, the almost last lines: " . . . at every / moment of our being. / As we eat we're eaten." Please comment on that for us.

LEE: As I was writing the poem, I wanted to write from a place of unknowing, not from knowledge. So I don't know that I knew what I was talking about when I said that. But my wish was that the poem would move toward a kind of ecstatic utterance.

LONDON: It does. It acquires body as it goes. It's a poem that takes on real inner momentum. I want to know why we are eaten, though. Do you mean, finally, that we are perishable?

LEE: I suppose. And that our hunger is immense. It sometimes feels to me that the proposition is—hunger.

LONDON: We have this butcher shop, the pork, the fish. What were the circumstances of your writing that? And why "The Cleaving"?

LEE: My feeling is that living in this country is a violent experience. It's violent to the soul. There's a violence to living in a material world. And I somehow want to account for that violence. Or write from it.

STUDENT: Participate in it.

LEE: I do feel sometimes that, like it or not, I participate in it. So this is a way to come to terms with that.

STUDENT: Could you say more about the unknowing?

LEE: It's writing from a state of unknowing. When you're writing along and you think, I'm not sure I made sense—don't ask. And that's hard to do. It meant I had to outwit or outrun all these voices in my head, all these critical faculties. It meant writing the poem from start to finish over and over and over and over to get into that place.

STUDENT: You wrote "The Cleaving" over and over and over again?

LEE: Yes. And each time I would go a little farther and a little farther.

I would like to make a sound that is just pure telling. I was sitting on my back porch a few months ago, and I was listening to the wind for a long time until I realized: that's the sound I want to make. I don't want to *write* about that, I want to *do* that. Whatever that is—the wind in the trees. We've heard that sound before. It's oceanic; it's huge; it's on the verge of meaning. If you listen long enough you feel there's definitely meaning there. Then you realize it's just wind in the trees. I want to make that kind of noise. *That* big. *That* elemental. *That* dark. *That* fresh. *That* raw. *That* mysterious. Right on the verge of human meaning. Entirely nonhuman. I would like to make a noise like that. Full of sound and fury—and maybe signifying nothing, I don't know. It's that sound I want to hear.

LONDON: You're talking about plumbing the depths of the unconscious.

LEE: Exactly.

LONDON: Moving in on something much more complicated than the daily narrative of events. You really would like to be able to record the psychological events.

LEE: Right.

LONDON: But writing is different from painting and different from music. Writing must be grounded in content. Content must be there as an impetus, as a groundwork. And then if you can take off, fine. But the groundwork in literature, in writing, is what words have to do. And they do have to have connotations. Don't you agree with that?

LEE: I do, but I guess I'm going past content straight to meaning. I would like to be right at that place where meaning itself is being made; to hear language at that level. I know many poems that have a lot of content but no meaning; and I know many poems that have a lot of form but no content. I would like to do away with all of that and go straight to meaning. Just meaning staring at you from the page.

Charles Simic

FIFTY YEARS DEEP into his career, Charles Simic has created a new category of poetry, one that is easier to describe than name: dark and irreverent, it has an abiding humor, an underlying mysteriousness if not mysticism, a deceptively plain line and diction and often a plain subject, such as a knife, a spoon, or the title subject of the poem he brought in draft form to London's class in 1995, "Official Inquiry Among the Grains of Sand."

Born in Belgrade in 1938, on the eve of World War II, Simic lived through bombings, periods of hunger, the ten-year exile of his father, and the imprisonment of his mother. "Hitler and Stalin conspired to make me homeless," he has said. Not until he was in his midteens was his family reunited, settling in the United States. Simic began writing poetry as a high school student in the Chicago suburbs.

One aim of his poetry, Simic says, is "to restore strangeness to the most familiar aspects of experience." To London he says that "the foundation of poetry is based on chance," and as chance can run toward violence, violence, too, is at an edge not far away. "Official Inquiry" and its grains of sand run together with a snooping seagull of "a secret government agency." But even as Simic describes line by line the making of the poem, he laughs when London suggests that he might have an overall vision. "No. No, I never had a vision," he says. "Sometimes awkwardness is inevitable— and important."

Simic was still making "Official Inquiry Among the Grains of Sand" at the time of his visit. "Here's a little poem I'm working on," he wrote to her weeks earlier. "This draft will change, so I'll have another version when I come." The poem eventually appeared in his 1996 volume, *Walking the Black Cat*, a National Book Award finalist and one of five books of poetry he published in the 1990s. Simic, who has taught at the University of New Hampshire since 1973, became the U.S. poet laureate in 2007.

––––––––––––

"Official Inquiry Among the Grains of Sand"

PEARL LONDON: You have said, and said in many ways in many contexts, that the successful poem is strangely anonymous. And in the poem you've sent us, "Official Inquiry Among the Grains of Sand," you write in the first line of the final version, "You're wholly anonymous." Is it a meditation on the idea of incognito?

CHARLES SIMIC: How this poem starts, it's really hard to know. I had the phrase "official inquiry," and then I think my wife said, "How come we have all this sand in the house? We live in the woods of New Hampshire." So I looked, and it's true. We've got a lot of sand. It makes no sense. We're some distance from the ocean. So she says, "The dog brings it in." That was puzzling, too, because there wasn't a sandlot nearby. So you suddenly make an idiotic connection between "official inquiry" and "among the grains of sand." This particular poem starts like that. Then some language begins to form slowly; you have no idea where you're going.

My point of saying every poem is finally anonymous is that, after many, many versions—you've only seen, what, three or four; I probably will have more versions—this thing progresses; you discover things in it that are lurking that you can't see. By the end, well, in a way you have written the poem, but in a way the poem and the language of the poem, the situation, has sort of written itself. You were somebody who discovers the poetry in the situation, in what was there developing. Because at some point it isn't that I have something to say anymore. What's happening on the page is more interesting. I look at it and I see, Aha! It can go this way. You know, let it go this way—I don't care. Next version we'll see what that means. Then one day you look at it and you say, "Well, it's really not going anywhere; I was deluded here and had it wrong." Then you stop. Then you have a new idea, and so forth. It's a process that eventually emerges or evolves into a kind of thing where I feel, well, the poem is my poem—it is *my* poem, I suppose—

LONDON: You say it several times and in different places, "good poetry honors the here and the now." And yet—and yet—you do not name places, you do not name locations, you do not have dates. In your poetry of the period of Vietnam, Vietnam as such *isn't*. It's full of all the pain but as such it *isn't*.

SIMIC: Well, my subject is always contemporary history. . . . The reason I don't name names is because I think names mean nothing.

LONDON: We come back to the anonymity.

SIMIC: You know, it's not the anonymity. If you read some classic Chinese poem about some great military campaign and you find out that one hundred thousand brave warriors died, these sorts of names are not too interesting for me. It's the event. The names also give a kind of phony authenticity. I'm always reminded of certain mystery writers, somebody who says, "I lit the Chesterfield, I tapped it on my Rolex." They continue to tell us what shoes they have. Robert B. Parker—I mean, I love this kind of stuff but it's almost a parody. It also has to do, going back to the fifties, with a certain kind of academic poetry that my generation just hated. You had these sorts of poems about traveling to Europe when they see a great painting in some museum in Venice. They tell you all that, and "Titian," they say, "what a great painter Titian is." They give you the name of the painting. It's dropping names for the yokels back home. This is an overreaction, I know. But for a long time in my poetry I would never name anything—on purpose. I always wanted a really clean poem. No distractions. Just the experience itself and take it or leave it.

LONDON: We were reading last week "Butcher Shop," which is one of your very early efforts. With its "great continents of blood" and so forth. And we began to look at the introduction of violence in so many of these poems. Somewhere along the way you said that violence is really a pathetic attempt to feel.

SIMIC: Well, I think I probably changed my view about that.

LONDON: Why?

SIMIC: That was a time with perhaps a little simpler solution. There's no question a lot of people in the world enjoy violence; and the notion that somehow violence is against human nature is really absurd. Naïve. There's so much killing in the world at any given time, and it's not that these people are going around feeling tremendous pangs of conscience. Especially if you're young and full of pep. If you're old and you've already got a lot of aches, violence is not so much fun—because who wants more aches? Otherwise, how to explain the tremendous violence in the world? The implication that all is owed to bad leaders who have misled this wonderfully innocent and peace-loving humanity for the last three million years and who said, "Oh, gee, if I only had a chance to cultivate flowers I would have done that; I wouldn't have killed my neighbor"? I'm not excusing it, and I'm not approving of it. It's just the way it is.

LONDON: So, too, in the body of your work, the role of chance: "I believe in the deep-set messiness of everything." That's lovely.

SIMIC: Well, chance is a given. I have always been open to the god of chance. Anybody can offer me some words, suggest something, I'm open. A lot of things that occur in writing are a product of chance. Something pops into your head, and you have no idea how it pops into your head. The foundation of poetry is based on chance. You cannot *will* a good metaphor, or even a crummy simile. "Compare your fingers to something in some brilliant new way"? All I could come up with now is "My fingers are like breakfast sausages." Which is terrible. You cannot will a great figure of speech; they happen. So at the foundation of poetry there is that element of chance, of accident, of something that cannot be . . . so one is always open, one is always—

LONDON: What would you say to those who say that, in art, chance happens only by necessity? That whatever line, word, concept, metaphor, is introduced has to be so organic that it is necessary, no longer chance.

SIMIC: This is the idea of Yvor Winters, at one time a great literary critic who, I suppose, some thought a great poet. He used to say that whatever element you have in a poem, including figures of speech, has to be paraphrased and defended intellectually. There has to be a good reason for the choice. That's why he was a lousy poet. Because that's not how great inspired metaphors and figures of speech have occurred in the history of poetry since Homer. Not to mention the Chinese. There are things that cannot be paraphrased but are extremely understandable, too. Try to explain my black cat walking across the room; I have a beautiful black female cat. I mean, just the way she moves. If I were to attempt to sum her up I would betray her complexity and her beauty. The same thing about a good figure of speech. There are things we understand without having to reduce it down to a kind of problem, to reduce the imagination.

LONDON: We all went through the several versions of the new poem until we got to that wonderful "rat-infested." "A weed-choked / rat-infested, / And vacant seaside villa." In one of your essays, you write "The rat is my totem."

SIMIC: When I'm writing something like that, at that point, I'm not really seeing a rat-infested world. I'm struggling. I have a particular seaside villa in mind. I have an idea and I can't quite get it right. What I'm interested in [is] the notion of a grain of sand in a sea of humanity. We are all grains of sand. So it's an "Official Inquiry" into the lowest common . . . totally anonymous, anonymous . . . somebody who looks like anybody else. But I started writing the poem, and at some point I thought of this beach. My friend used to have a house nearby, and there were these wonderful Victorian villas on the Maine coast. But I don't like the poem yet, the way it's coming out. I need something better. What I wanted is this huge abandoned structure, right? You can take it symbolically [as] representing something of the past. Maybe I should put in the turrets or verandahs. I don't know. Something that would quickly convey. . . . What happens in poetry is that you really have to do this quickly. You can't spend lines and lines talking about this seaside villa. It's got to be quick. The reader has to see it— bap! That's it. I just don't have it yet. It's not the way I want it. I want to be behind the villa to the sea where there's all this sand.

LONDON: In the earlier poems you allowed the poem to be dominated by a sequence of images. In these newer poems the single image consolidates the poem. I think that's a big difference.

SIMIC: Yeah. I didn't understand something when I was young—it's a good thing I didn't. The poems we liked had a lot of wonderful images, crazy images, you know? I realized years later that we didn't really know how to read a poem. Basically, if we saw a poem of a friend of ours in a magazine, you'd say "Wow! Some incredible image," you know? You wanted a poem that had incredible images. It's a terrific impulse, just to have one image after image after image.

LONDON: You said, "In my poetry, images think." I love that.

SIMIC: This has always been true—if you have a good image, a memorable image, you remember it. Think of Wallace Stevens's "Thirteen Ways of Looking at a Blackbird." More than a few of the images are wonderful. You begin to tinker about them after a while. It isn't just the visual thing itself. You realize, there's more here than meets the eye. Depending what the relationship is, a metaphor could be symbolic at the end or simple. . . . But a good image leads to some intellectual content.

At the end that's why you stay with it. It won't let you go, if it's a good image. I'm sure when Kafka had the idea of that penal colony machine he knew—"Nothing to worry [about] here now, this is going to write itself." Or the castle. Certain things like that are just invitations to endless reverie. But once you find it you have this moment and say, "Ooo, this is going to take a long time to work out, but I like this, I have to stay with this."

STUDENT: In looking at the different versions of "Official Inquiry" yesterday, I stumbled a little bit over the words "rat-infested *and* vacant seaside villas." And when I read the poem again today I also realized that you have "a previously unknown *and* secret government." Now, when we study writing with Pearl, she usually says, leave out connecting words. Use commas instead.

SIMIC: It does sound a little prosy. Sometimes you want to put it in. This is still just a version. I mean, "and" is a perfectly fine word. Sometimes you put it in.

STUDENT: It doesn't have a specific reason.

SIMIC: No specific reason. You try to get the movement of the thing; you're working with description, you want to get the thing right. What happens in these poems, at this level, is still pretty much unconscious. You go by hunches. You see a thing developing in a certain way and it's only later, when you feel that you have more or less what needs to be there, that you begin to notice two "and's" in the first stanza, which is probably awkward. Makes it kind of sound prosy. But I'm tentative, thinking, Well, God knows what's going to happen to that vacant seaside villa; it might take some other form. Maybe some other detail is going to—

LONDON: When is it finalized? When do you know that this is exactly the way you want it? Because you can go on.

SIMIC: Not always. Sometimes you realize this is all you can do with it. You get tired of it, too, sick of it. What happens, I think, in earlier versions—even this version, I was looking at it today on the plane—the syntax is a little plodding. It needs a little more snap. I don't hear the snap yet. Because too many things are pulling in my mind. I'm trying to find some details that are missing . . . which I intuit are there, but I can't quite summon them at this point.

LONDON: Charles Simic, you said, "It took me years to realize that the line is what matters and not the sentence."

SIMIC: Well, the problem with the sentence is it's a Cartesian structure, a logical thing. There's an object. You want to get to the end of the sentence to find out what the sentence is saying. It's a complete thought; it's this or that; it comes to a period. [But] in poetry, you really think of lines. A line of poetry is a unit of attention, a rhythmic unit; you want to hear the line bounce, or one line after the other. And at some point as one fools around with these things one has a kind of musical insight—that I still don't have in this poem—which has to do with that snap. It's like a stand-up comedian.

He talks in lines; he doesn't talk in sentences. He says, "This . . . this . . . ," bits of language separated by silences, which send you in certain directions.

Hopefully, it all comes together to make this thing visible, to tell my relationship to the content. That's what determines the line. If you're lying under a tree after a great picnic lunch on a perfect day, when the sky is blue, the world is at peace around you, and you want to write, you're not going to write short lines. You're not going to say, "I am / lying / here." You're going to say "I am lying here under this great banyan tree," and you're going to go on and on—it's going to be a huge line. You really have no idea what is happening, in a sense. Which way it's going to go. It's going to find itself, hopefully.

LONDON: Do you become obsessed with it?

SIMIC: I have a lot of poems that I'm obsessed with.

LONDON: Now, one of the poems that I adore, one of your most complex and beautiful, is called "White." There is a sense of obsession there.

```
OFFICIAL INQUIRY AMONG THE GRAINS OF SAND

                                    ?
You're anonymous,
You believe yourself thriving/incognito
In the rear of a vacant,                    li~ b~~?
Rundown seaside villa.

The flea, like the informant
Of a still unknown secret service
Is on its way
With a pair of tiny binoculars. magnifying glass

Aha! The sunflower seed.
The long-lost dog hair.            > on the junction of visible-invisible,
A sugar crumb
In all that sand.
```

SIMIC: I rewrote that many times. "White." But I have many things like "Official Inquiry" that I put aside and, later, look at again—

LONDON: Let's look at the genesis of it, then. [After version 1 on page 300] in version 2 [see page 302], you have added [in handwriting] "head to foot, / heart and soul, / utterly and completely, / the indistinguishable you."

And then, in the third version [see page 303], which may not be the final version, there are very drastic changes. We have this entirely different thing: "At the junction of / Visible-invisible, / Past the long lost. . . ." All this specific detail, very visual images—"the solitary sugar crumb"—and, finally, the jolt "There, with your pants down, / Clutching your mouth in horror. / Without a shadow of a doubt, / The indistinguishable you!" How different that is. What happened between?

SIMIC: It's just that the language is more interesting. To think of the grain of sand clutching its mouth in horror—totally unlike all its billion neighbors. Another grain of sand, discovered by the official inquiry, located finally, they say to it, "You! Aha! You, mister. We got you." So of course this grain of sand is a little shocked, astonished. I just thought it sounded better than the other thing. The other thing is kind of awkward. I was groping, not knowing quite what I was doing—

LONDON: What about the very emphatic: "With your pants down, / Clutching your mouth in horror."

SIMIC: I mean, the whole comedy of the thing, of course. After all, it's a grain of sand we're talking about. But even this grain of sand doesn't like to be known as a grain of sand, right? "Leave me alone—I'm just a grain of sand. Go to some other grain of sand. Why me? You've got all these other grains of sand, you know? Why bother me?"

LONDON: I don't know if you remember that lovely essay that Borges wrote when he saw the Pyramids in Egypt for the first time. He stood there, absolutely awed by the sight, took some grains of sand, and let them

Mother Version
Version 2.

OFFICIAL INQUIRY AMONG THE GRAINS OF SAND

WHOLLY

You're anonymous.
You believe yourself ~~living incognito~~   *making do*
In the rear of a r~~undown~~ ~~twice~~ ~~the~~ *vacant*
And v~~acant~~ seaside villa.   *weed-chocked*
A ~~Some~~ *gull* ~~Some fbw~~, like the informant   *prowling*
Gray   Of a st~~ill~~ unknown secret service,
Is on ~~its way~~ *stepping aloud importantly*
With a magnifying glass.

Aha! The sunflower seed.
The long-lost dog hair.
? 2.At the junction of visible-invisible
{ A sugar crumb,

There ...
~~Head~~ *not then ...* *head to foot,*
Heart of soul,
utterly or completely —
The indistinguishable You.

drift through his fingers and said, "Now I've modified the Sahara." But let's come back to this. What about the gray gull? We find him in many versions . . . once he's like an informant, and then you use the word "snoop." He's a snoop. Why?

SIMIC: Although we are twenty miles from the sea, they come to my town dump and snoop around. You go and throw your garbage, and they

OFFICIAL INQUIRY AMONG THE GRAINS OF SAND

You're wholly anonymous.
You believe yourself living incognito
In the rear of a weed-choked,
Rat-infested,
And vacant seaside villa.
A gray gull, most likely the chief snoop
Of a previously unknown
And secret government agency
Is tiptoeing around importantly.

Aha! At the junction of
Visible-invisible,
Past the long lost dog hair,
Past the solitary sugar crumb,
There, with your pants down,
Clutching your mouth in horror.
Without a shadow of a doubt,
The indistinguishable you!

3rd Version

Simic

go around, look at you [and say], "Loser." They have this kind of view, always conspiring to come over and say, "What's happening?" But the informant, snoop, I changed that. First it was a flea with a magnifying glass, and I thought that was just too surrealistic. First thing that popped into my head. Then I started really seeing much more just the way a seagull looks. The way it moves around. The notion is that the seagulls are in the service and they work for some agency going around. Interviewing a grain of sand.

LONDON: The lost sunflower seed has "Aha!" at the junction. But early on, I didn't quite see why it was relevant.

SIMIC: Well, I was trying to find some small items, the kind of stuff that you would find at the beach. In the sand, bottle caps, the grain of sugar. Imagine somebody drops a grain of sugar in the sand, how are you going to tell them apart? And of course there are always dog hairs everywhere. But that will change, too. Something will come the next time I go to the beach. . . .

LONDON: Why did you decide on two stanzas instead of the four quatrains [in the second version]?

SIMIC: The stops were unnecessary. It became a little slow. If you have a poem of four stanzas, clearly in each stanza there has to be something that can occupy the reader and so it's necessary [for the poet] to make the reader stop and take it in. This is not very complicated stuff that is being conveyed in the poem. If there's a rich image—of such richness that the reader has to dwell on it, and you want the reader to dwell on it—that doesn't make sense here. If you have too many pauses, they create a false melodrama. You know, you stop after every line as if something tremendous is being said; it's not.

LONDON: Chekhov always said, "May my pauses be accurate."

Let's come back for a minute, though, to the long leaps of language. "Visible-Invisible": tell us about that. Because I'm not sure that if some of my students had written "Visible-Invisible" I wouldn't have said, "Go home and make it simply 'invisible.' "

SIMIC: And maybe "junction" is wrong; maybe it should be *"line* of Visible-Invisible." [The published version has "intersection."] There's a line, obviously, where you squint, and there's a line where if you're looking at something—I don't know if you ever looked at a grain of sand, somebody loses a pearl earring, some little item on the beach, and everybody goes nuts trying to find it. It's amazing how hard it is to see in the sand. So I was thinking of that kind of thing. Once you look at the sand on the beach you're amazed at what's there. You would find, for example, on this minute level, as your vision becomes microscopic, what is obviously a piece of green glass reduced to just a shard, to a *tiny* little fragment.

LONDON: Is that "Visible-Invisible"?

SIMIC: If there was a line between the visible world and the invisible world, this is the Visible-Invisible; this is the place where they cross, the junction.

STUDENT: You go down to the beach and all of a sudden this thing is transformed by metaphor.

SIMIC: I was thinking, I don't have the words yet, it's almost like I was at the address: at "the junction of." If you said to someone, "Where do I find this particular grain of sand I'm looking for?" [He would say,] "Well, you got to make a left, go right, and then when you come to the junction of, over there, just where the invisible is on the verge of turning into the visible—there! Look! There's the one."

LONDON: That's nice.

SIMIC: Again, the language is not yet there, but that's the idea.

STUDENT: I was reminded of two obvious poems. One is the Bishop poem "The Sandpiper," which is the sandpiper running around looking, and the other, the Blake—"the world in a grain of sand."

SIMIC: I remember "The Sandpiper." I didn't remember, obviously, Blake. It wasn't developed like that, but I think it's probably going to be a version of that, inevitably. Except here, it's kind of a totalitarian context. I mean, some kind of a snoop who goes around for a secret government agency, checking out, making sure that all the grains of sand are behaving.

STUDENT: Yes. These are feeling images. But would you talk a little bit about what music you're feeling or striving for? For example, why did you break the line after "weed-choked" in the final version?

SIMIC: "In the rear of a weed-choked, / Rat-infested" . . . what happens is that if you break the line in free verse, the next line receives a kind of emphasis. If you had "In the rear of a weed-choked, rat-infested" you would not experience the "rat-infested" to the same degree. . . . One of the strange things about poetry is that if we have a longer line we tend to read it faster. If it's a very long line it becomes a rhetorical line, and the visual details get blurred. In one of those Creeley poems, or Williams poems: "So much depends / upon / a red"—if it was in one line, you would just run through. Because you're always in a rush to get to the end of the line. So I wanted to get "rat-infested" on a new line. There was a kind of rhythm there too, with "weed-choked / rat-infested." I don't have the music yet. I feel something probably going to emerge. How much more of your semester?

LONDON: Just until May 5.

SIMIC: If it happens before May 5, I'll fax it.

> [*Published version, "Official Inquiry Among the Grains of Sand"*]
>
> You're wholly anonymous.
> You believe yourself living incognito
> In the rear of a weed-choked,
> Rat-infested,
> Long-vacant seaside villa.

A gray gull,
Most likely the chief snoop
Secret government agency,
Is tiptoeing around importantly.

Aha! At the intersection of
The Visible-Invisible,
Past the lost dog hair,
Past the solitary sugar crumb:
There! With your pants down.
Clutching your mouth in horror.
Without a shadow of a doubt
The indistinguishable you.

LONDON: You said a poem is a moment of lucidity. I think that's probably very true about your writing. There is a certain kind of distillation that we feel in each of the poems. This goes way back. But my question is, at this point, all of these wonderful new books . . . I don't want to use the word "goal," I think that's too grandiose . . . but do you have a vision of the reality that you still feel you want to write?

SIMIC: [*Laughs*] I never had a vision. No. No, I don't have a vision. You see, Pearl, it doesn't really happen like that. For example, I have at least twenty poems in various stages like this, some more advanced than others. So, my whole life is simply how to fix these things. I don't care what happens in the end. If it turns out that there's only one stanza here, I'll be perfectly happy. If it works, it works. You have these things that are half-assed, and they need to be made good. So, you don't say to yourself, "Well, I would like to write this or that." And of course as you write, these things, they generate others. Others come out of them. This might split into two different poems.

STUDENT: I keep thinking of Joseph Cornell.

SIMIC: Yeah. Right. Joseph Cornell in the sense that he, too, worked simultaneously on dozens and dozens of different boxes. He would have two items in one, and then he would wait five, sometimes ten years to put another, totally inconsequential-seeming thing inside.

STUDENT: You said, "Even as I concentrate all my attention on the fly on the table, I glance fleetingly at myself." In "Official Inquiry Among the Grains of Sand," does that make you the sand, the gull . . . ?

SIMIC: I think the sand, sure. I always find seagulls to be very frightening.

LONDON: Very what?

SIMIC: They're out there in that snowy Atlantic—icebergs out there, it's mean, you know. Or Kittery or York—close by where I live—and it's a miserable day, just awful, snowing and some bitter wind from Labrador blowing down, and those gulls they're just . . . [*pantomimes gulls; laughter*] I mean they're frightening, they're frightening.

STUDENT: The stomach acid of a gull will melt a nail.

SIMIC: Melt a nail! I didn't know that. So I could not possibly, God, compare myself to a supreme creature like that.

LONDON: I think you're never content unless the meditation elicits, finally, the merely personal connection for you—and then, at the same time and in the same breath, you also say, "It doesn't seem necessary for one to equate the I with myself." Is that a contradiction?

SIMIC: No. Because if I can write a poem that works, and if in the process of writing this poem, everything I started to say—you know, quote unquote—became its opposite, and I *don't* sound like myself, I couldn't care less. My views are like anybody else's views. I think this about that, and I think this about something else. I'm not that smart or unusual. Expressing myself . . . it's not important to me. What is important is to have a poem that seems to work. If it works, that's what matters. Who made the famous comment about like a click of a box, a wooden box?

STUDENT: I think it was Auden.

SIMIC: It was Auden, right. One of those wonderful, well-made boxes, and when it closed it has that wonderful click. There's a sense of something well made in the arts. Given what I had here and how it turned out, it came together in a certain way; it works. I don't think, finally, if one has any sense, that most of one's poems truly work. If I look at most of my poems years after having written them, I can see they could have been a little better. Shoddy goods, you know? Sometimes awkwardness is inevitable and important. But there it is.

Eamon Grennan

"HERE'S A LITTLE packet of drafts I've assembled," Eamon Grennan wrote to Pearl London two weeks before his visit to her class. "Getting these pages together reminds me of the time & circumstances of each piece's composition. A little exercise in reminiscence." It is memory that serves in his own quietly breathtaking poems as well, a search for "something to hold onto in the face of disappearance," as he's said. "As far as I'm concerned, poetry is about elegy. Every poem is a memory of some kind, a celebratory elegy."

At the time of this conversation with London, in 1996, Grennan had published four books of poetry, from his first, *Wildly for Days* (1983), through *So It Goes* (1995). It's this last volume that contains "Ants," the poem he brought to London's class in draft form. As Grennan says that he is "extremely embarrassed by abstractions," so "Ants" exhibits much of the naturalist precision and sensuous (sometimes erotic) play on domestic themes for which he is so highly regarded. W. S. Merwin has said that "the kind of honesty that informs Eamon Grennan's poems carries with it a slight shock, part surprise, part burning." One clearly hears, too, that Irish mastery of language—free verse, but with an underlying, compelling rhythmic drive. His lines pulse. Amy Clampitt spoke of his "grace and precision such as come only with a perfect ear."

Eamon Grennan was born in Dublin in 1941 and educated at University College, Dublin. He received his doctorate in English at Harvard in 1974 and for more than thirty years taught at Vassar College, in Poughkeepsie, New York. Returning yearly to Ireland and often setting his poems there, Grennan regards himself, he says, "not as an exile, but as a migrant." His most recent books of poetry include *The Quick of It* (2005) and *Matter of Fact* (2008). His *Leopardi: Selected Poems* received the 1997 PEN Award for Poetry in Translation.

"Ants"

PEARL LONDON: When I took a first look at these wonderful work sheets of "Ants" I thought of Mary McCarthy, who said, when she first looked at Elizabeth Bishop's *North and South,* "Oh, the excitement of finding the mind that's hiding in her words." That's the way I felt. I think we already know all its secret niches, but we're going to look a little further.

EAMON GRENNAN: Please, God. I'll take off my shirt next.

LONDON: J. D. McClatchy, talking about your work, says, "He takes the ordinary and coaxes wonder from it." I think of your poem "Heirloom" and the glass salt cellar. I love that poem. What could be more ordinary than a salt cellar? And here it is the embodiment of all of the wonder you can imagine. It goes from Ireland and Mother's table to Poughkeepsie.

GRENNAN: Two things about that. Ireland to Poughkeepsie is a transition I want to try to maintain—as if I write in two worlds in a kind of amphibian way. And as for the object itself, I suppose Proust is the master of that—of attempting to enter into and expose the internal ramifications of the object. The emotional molecular structure, you might say, of an object. That's one way to think about it. The other is that when we were kids in school we were always asked to write these little essays like "An Old Shoe Tells Its Own Story" or "A Bicycle Tells Its Own Story." In an educational system not known, necessarily, for its liberalism, that imaginative exercise was probably a very good one. It has a touch of the epiphanal about it—at a very ordinary level. You can see the Joycean inside that. And I wonder if that kind of attention to that kind of object wasn't a source for the kind of thing I'm doing with the salt cellar.

LONDON: Exactly. It becomes luminous. It really does. There is a special dimension of reverence that we feel. Yet at the same time they are very earthbound images. I found this particularly in images about light. So I thought I would go through the last book and count the number of times that I found the word "light." How many—

GRENNAN: Ohhh. Too many.

LONDON: Thirty-one images of light. Just in the last book. What does this tell us about the mind that's hiding in the words?

GRENNAN: Well, it's not hiding for long, clearly. I don't know, except probably in another life I at least wanted to be a painter. The attempt to describe light, I suspect, is a painterly ambition.

LONDON: In the work sheets for "Clareville Road," you talk about Matisse and Bonnard, and then you took them out. I wonder why.

GRENNAN: I wanted to do my own impressionist sketch, and I didn't want it distracted by my betters, so to speak.

STUDENT: Instead of saying "a street of violence" you'll say "a snipered street"—that's poetry.

GRENNAN: I'm glad you picked that one out, because it's that kind of compression that incorporates a spectrum of response into a single noun or noun-verb that suggests, for me, anyway, that the language is alive. And unless the language is trying to get off the page in some way, then it becomes description. And I don't think poems are about things. I think they are coming out of things.

LONDON: You have been compared—although there are vast differences—to Elizabeth Bishop. Because of the use of the ordinary as a point of departure. Because of the attentiveness to detail and precision. And because in all of your work there is that, to use Bishop's phrase, "driving to the interior." I was thinking about this particularly when I read "The Porcupine." I couldn't help thinking of Elizabeth Bishop's "The Armadillo."

GRENNAN: Comparison with Bishop always covers one in shame because of the gap of achievement. When I compare what I do with what Bishop does very often I feel like a guy who has ended up at a cocktail party in Wellingtons [boots]. You feel so awkward and clumsy, and she *knows* and she's so *discreet* and she has a *focus* . . . and I'm all over the place.

LONDON: But she doesn't have the underlying religiosity. In literary terms your work has within it "a mysterious otherness" that hers doesn't.

GRENNAN: Well, she is so honest about that. "The Moose," of course, is the exception, because it is a little tabernacle of possibility at the edge of skepticism.

LONDON: And it's an incarnation of her mother.

GRENNAN: It's an incarnation of her mother, but first of all it's wonder, it's awe, it's something there, and we don't know what it is. I love her skepticism, and I love her ability to change her mind in the middle of things and move from one kind of description to another without pyrotechnics.

LONDON: There's almost a kind of Merwin-like ending to some of your poems. We don't have the clapping together of exact rhyme. We don't have Yeats's drop and up in the slant-rhyme. Yet we feel the closure.

GRENNAN: Everybody's got to feel it and hear it in their own way, obviously. For me, it has to have some sense of finality, but I also don't want it to be too visible or audible, so therefore there's a touch of the shrug about a lot of the endings. The content is sometimes a shrug, but the music is a closing of the gate in some way. The content itself is sort of "I don't know," but the music closes it off in some way. I mean, that's what I'd want to be the case.
     Like Bishop. Or again like Merwin. I think Merwin does it with music all the time.

LONDON: In *The Redress of Poetry*, Heaney says Bishop's supreme gift was her ability to ingest loss and transmute it. I was thinking that's what really pervades this last book of yours. So much of it deals so marvelously with loss.

GRENNAN: What Heaney says about Bishop is interesting because in some ways it's very like his own—I would describe Heaney as having a very powerful digestive tract. He's able to absorb, take in, and make things of what he takes in, as Bishop was ingesting loss. I don't find I ingest very well. I don't have a strong tract, I suspect, imaginatively. The act of wrestling is my method of digestion, if you like. We see the attempt to take it in and even the failure to take it in. It's more of a wrestling than a digesting.

LONDON: It's not a failure, though.

STUDENT: There's much more distance in your poems. You are both dealing with loss . . . but hers is so internal. In your work there seem to be—I almost hate to use the phrase—happier endings. Much more of a resolution or closure of the loss.

GRENNAN: I think Elizabeth Bishop has a tragic side that I don't have digestive capacity for.

LONDON: Wouldn't you say that's valid? Because underlying all of your work is a sense of profound affirmation. Whereas in Bishop the tentativeness is always there.

GRENNAN: She's brave enough not to have it. If I were to satirize it I would call it the Pollyanna side of myself. It is the wish to turn loss into some kind of gain.

LONDON: Absolutely. This goes back to the original transformation.

GRENNAN: There's an affirmative aspect, but it's perpetually tempered, I'd hope, by the recognition that it is in some ways whistling in the dark.

STUDENT: It's whistling in the mystery.

GRENNAN: The dark is the mystery. And whistling beyond consolation.

STUDENT: It's interesting because you both get to the same point using two completely different approaches. I can get the same feeling of affirmation from her work. From her willingness to show the loss for exactly what it is.

GRENNAN: Exactly. One of the great examples of that in Bishop is the birthday poem—"awful but cheerful." End of poem. What beautiful courage to be so simple in using those two words at the end of that poem.

Nor does she always reveal what the loss is. And mine, I suspect, have a more narrative drive. I always have a shadow narrative. A phantom narrative or a shadow narrative, for me it's a sort of grounding. Maybe the best deflection of a poem being abstractly about something is to locate a story, an action, which will carry the facts, and the facts will then offer you some abstractions. In more recent work I'm trying to get rid of narrative and just deal with what I would call lyric fragments. But there's a fractured aspect to any narrative I have.

STUDENT: Why is it important to fracture?

GRENNAN: Because I don't feel that the narrative itself is what I'm after. I'm not attempting to tell that story; I'm attempting to embody the procedures of that consciousness.

I suspect what I'm trying to do is work not linearly as narrative but radially. To work out of a center. To radiate out along spokes of implication and spokes of connection rather than proceeding on a line of narrative. That gives it another kind of spatial shadow. I think I'm moving toward thicker meditative procedures, put it like that. From the beginning to now there has been a gradual thickening of the meditative element.

LONDON: Poems from your first book are written in contained, spare couplets. They work very effectively. Now we come to what you call the thickened line, which I call the enjambed line. I think the enjambment is a very important psychological dimension to your writing.

GRENNAN: I'd agree with that absolutely. And what it might mean psychologically I'd be curious to speculate about. I would say, Pearl, that *Wildly for Days* was little highly arranged garden-plot poems—here's carrots, here's peas, you know the way you set out a wee garden—the poems are a bit like that. I was beginning. Then I started to flex my muscles, and I thought, I want to do larger things. And that simply accumulated until now.

What you say about enjambment interests me, because I've gotten more interested in a capaciousness of sentence structure, more interested in syntax, more interested in sentence. Poems tend to be built around line and sentence. But how do you make the line and the sentence cohere, play with one another, react to one another? The line is a retarding of thought, of onward motion. You have that sense of an ending in a line: it's a musical unit. And a sentence is a thought unit. So music and thought are dancing together.

Yeats made stanzas coincident with sentences. One of his main ambitions was to make the stanza and the sentence collaborate. And he gets that from John Donne and others of the Elizabethans, that great sense of stanzaic control making for capacious containers. And as I developed I was interested in getting more into sentences. The early stuff tended to be more remote of the self—little watercolors with the self way out. But the sentence was an attempt to incorporate the thinking self. Somebody like Ashbery or Jorie Graham does that in spades, and I do it in a very modest way. But that was the intention behind these more elaborate sentences and in the management of music, line, and sentence; music and sense. Enjambment seems to me to be a key instrument. It is the beater of time. Enjambment is your—not your metronome—but your pulse. It is the pulse of the writing. In the movement between music and sense, enjambment is the conductor.

LONDON: Would you say that one of the reasons that you do so many revisions, drafts, and work sheets is the struggle to hear it?

GRENNAN: Definitely. I don't think it's about meaning half the time. Most of the time it's not. This is why I love Elizabeth Bishop's work sheets—Bishop changes meanings. I do, too, some of the time. You just shift and say exactly the opposite thing. I love you; in fact, no, I don't love you. So the poem teaches you what you think some of the time.

STUDENT: You were saying as you're working through your poems that it's about how it sounds. But isn't it almost the same thing—the meaning and the sound?

GRENNAN: Fundamentally, but you can betray one in the interests of the other. I don't mean it's just sound. I mean rhythm; it's the rhythmic feel of the thing, it's the way the thing exists in the air and does a sort of series of beats—pulses.

LONDON: Over and over again in your writing I see you moving from the particular to the general but always with an attentiveness to detail. And at some point those particulars are overtaken by a much larger visionary understanding, by some kind of dimension that was not there initially. To what extent does this happen? Is it different with every poem?

GRENNAN: I think poems are journeys in that respect. That's why this shadow or phantom narrative is useful to me. Because the poem itself becomes a kind of journey. I think making the abstract particular—I certainly try to do that. I am extremely embarrassed by abstractions, by forms of thinking that move into abstract realms. So I back away by suggesting "this is all I know," and trying to allow the accumulated particulars to dramatize the abstract idea. I suppose that's an ambition. I wouldn't want a poem not to contain that in some way, even a short poem.

LONDON: Tell us about your thinking on page 1 of the work sheets of "Ants," where you say, "as if some seething gene of earthly rage / for order had been released." The use of "gene" here is so contemporary and so unexpected.

GRENNAN: I was after that collision of languages. I'm looking at an ant. But I'm looking at the ant with a microscope, really. The microscope in this case is the imagination. And the fury of the ant strikes me as so small and yet so powerful.

In the sandy soil & grit of the narrow Road outside ~~my window~~
an ant is dragging the faded body of a moth backwards
over ~~stones~~ pebbles, under blades of grass. Every step is a struggle:
the body lodges in a cleft between two curved uprights
of grass & won't budge; the ant dashes off a few ant-inches,
twirls like a dervish & dashes back for another go,
its movements the breathless fast forward of a silent movie
in which someone is trying to shift a ~~piano~~ sofa upstairs.
Everything is frantic, & beyond thought, but instinct with
invention, as if some seething gene of earthly rage
for order had been released, & all is a whirling
away & back, the code doesn't include surrender,
a solitary frenzy to do it, do it, do it,

I had a little Wallace Stevens in there—"a seething gene of earthly rage for order"—and then I thought, I better get rid of Stevens and try to deal with this on my own terms. I finally get rid of it and [in the final version] just have "a seething gene / of stubborn order, its code containing no surrender." A lot of the stuff is an attempt to compact things. To bring things into a single phrase that were scattered as a series of thoughts. What you discover in my stuff as you move through revisions is a linear thought compacted into a potentially explosive center of suggestion.

LONDON: So that's really the way your mind is working there.

```
nibbling at the filaments of lost hair, the white
specks of dandruff, the stuff of your own gradual
dismantling.  Soap, sugar, a ricepaper fleck of semen,
a drop of blood from the dead mouse the cat has carried in--
it is all one grist to this ancient and enduring mill
that makes out of our leftover and left-behind lives
their own digested poems of the world and, underground,
the occult network of their state, their lasting cities.
```

GRENNAN: As far as I can tell. It is moving from "get it all down in a language that seems kind of immediate" and on to "push, pull, and come back into the center of it."

LONDON: On another page you have: "it is all one grist to this ancient and enduring mill." Yet in the final version, "it is all one grist to this mill." What were you thinking there? I liked the earlier version.

GRENNAN: The "ancient and enduring." I just got fed up with adjectives at that point. I think it was as simple as that, Pearl. Also, I wanted to run "mill," "makes," and "minute" together [in the final version] and not get it bogged down. So I was interested in sound there. This grist mill—you can hear the assonance. You can hear "mill," "makes," "minute." I was more interested in performing an immediate music than in describing "ancient and enduring." The source of change there was my sense of the music, of the way the poem is moving. Changing the music shifts the sense, but how much of the sense can I retain if I want to shift the music a bit or get this music working as it does there?

[Published version, "Ants"]

A black one drags the faded remains of a moth
backwards over pebbles, under blades of grass.

Frantic with invention, it is a seething gene
of stubborn order, its code containing no surrender,
only this solitary working frenzy that's got you
on your knees with wonder, peering into the sheer
impedimentary soul in things and into
the gimlet will that dredges the dead moth
to where their dwelling is, the sleepy
queen's fat heart like a jellied engine
throbbing at the heart of it, her infants
simmering towards the light. On your table
a tiny red one picks at a speck of something
and hurries away: one of its ancestors
walked all over the eyes of Antinous, tickled
Isaac's throat, or scuttled across the pulse
of Alcibiades, turning up at the Cross
with a taste for blood. In a blink, one enters
your buried mother's left nostril, brings a message
down to your father's spine and shiny clavicle,
or spins as if dizzy between your lover's
salt breasts, running its quick indifferent body
ragged over the hot tract of her, scrupulous
and obsessive into every pore. And here's one
in your hairbrush, nibbling at filaments
of lost hair, dandruff flakes, the very stuff
of your gradual dismantling. Soap, sugar, a pale
fleck of semen or the blood-drop from a mouse
the cat has carried in, it's all one grist to this mill
that makes from our minute leftovers
a tenacious state of curious arrangements—the males
used up in copulation, females in work, life itself
a blind contract between honeydew and carrion,
the whole tribe surviving in that complex gap

where horror and the neighbourly virtues, as we'd say,
adjust to one another, and without question.

LONDON: Let's leave music for a minute and talk about an image on
another draft page. You have "On my table a tiny red one, antennae elbow-
stretched / like a croupier." And you absolutely leave that out.

GRENNAN: I know. I was sorry to see that go.

LONDON: I just thought that was stunning.

GRENNAN: But I couldn't deal with the French word in the poem, and I
thought the image finally looked a little overcalculated. It belonged to a
Muldoon or a Simic poem, it seemed to me, where image and startling
simile are the point. Whereas mine is much more biologically anchored.
And the reference to the croupier introduced a whole world of sophisti-
cated operations that I finally didn't want to contaminate the other more
biological stuff about decay and so on. It's interesting in itself, but this is a

```
We live in their midst. They fill the space we take
for our own.  They make highways and cities underground,
demolish buildings, lay great trees level with the dust.
On my table a tiny red one, antennae elbow-stretched
like a croupier hauling in his gains, picks a speck of
something, hurries away.  An ancestor carried off bits
of Hadrian's Antinous on the banks of the Nile, walking
all over his drowned, dazzling eyes of ambergris and gold.
And tickled the neck of Isaac and whispered into the palm
of the hand of Abraham where the knife nestled.  And turned
up at the cross with a thrist for blood.  A little later
one enters, underground, my mother's left nostril, leaves,
negotiates with a finger, bringing a message down to
my father's spine and shiny clavicle.  And here this minute,
like something in Ovid, one the colour of silver-speckled onyx
```

good example of "you have to smother your darlings" in revision, right? It would be nice to find the space to use that, but it wasn't that kind of poem.

STUDENT: I wanted to ask about the word "salt." In this poem we have "salt breast" and in other poems you have salt on the tip of the tongue, the salt cellar, the salt sea—you can read lots of poets and never run into the word.

GRENNAN: I'm glad you asked the question. On the one hand I'm using it to suggest an acuteness of perception, an acuteness of sense. On the other hand salt is a nice metaphor for the doubleness I'm after, the light and shade. Namely, salt as bitterness and salt as giving relish to things—and preserving things. Salt breast—obviously just sweat. But to use "salt" instead of saying "sweaty" suggests taste rather than tactility.

STUDENT: You talked about the dissolution of the local, going from local particularity to larger particularity.

GRENNAN: That's a good way to put it. Because the poem is about ants, they could be anywhere. It denies all those pieties that are so much part of the earlier poems—of home and locale, even the political locale in the northern fields. This ant could be in Greece or it could be in America or it could be in Ireland. It is just an ant.

STUDENT: Everyant.

GRENNAN: Everyant, exactly. There's an attempt in this poem to dissolve the local; not to transcend it but to take it up into an image that in some way is larger than it.

I will reveal to you a very shameful fact. How did Antinous get into this poem? You know who Antinous was? He was the lover of Alexander the Great, and he died in Egypt, and he was buried somewhere on the banks of the Nile. Where did I learn that? Well, I learned it from the encyclopedia.

Now, why did I look up Antinous in the encyclopedia? Because . . . a-n-t. Now you know. Talk about thinking!

LONDON: The mind hiding in the words!

GRENNAN: That's right. I must have seen Antinous when I was reading up about ants. And then I just sat and I sort of browsed. So, poem as a result of browsing. It's foraging.

LONDON: "Rummaging in the yellow splendor of the daylily"—I thought that that was absolutely beautiful. I loved "rummaging," I loved the image—and all of that was taken away. Why?

GRENNAN: Yeah, "rummaging" is a good word. Too bad to lose "rummage." But in another poem I talk about "the flagrant short-lived blaze of the daylily," I thought I'd keep it for that.

How little can you get away with? Deliberate explanation looks, I would say, like scaffolding. And by the time the poem is working it should be freestanding. You should have kicked away the scaffolding. The building has to stand on its own. But it may not get built without the scaffolding—remind yourself of that.

Postscript

Pearl London

WITH HER ELEGANT hawk face and courtly hummingbird flutter, Pearl London shaded a persuasive mix of intensity and distraction. Have I ever met anyone, especially someone not herself publicly a poet, so conversant, appreciative, besotted, obsessed, even so simply gaga about contemporary poetry? Pearl revered poetry and poets, yet there was nothing sentimental or sententious in her esteem. Poetry, for her, involved a ferocity of craft and the assiduous stresses of revision as much as any mystic inspiration and amounted to a full immersion in the understanding of our lives. Always when she talked about poetry—and inside and outside her classes at the New School Pearl only talked poetry—I was reminded of the ending of Elizabeth Bishop's great poem "At the Fishhouses." "It is like what we imagine knowledge to be," Bishop wrote, "dark, salt, clear, moving, utterly free, / drawn from the cold hard mouth / of the world. . . ." Pearl introduced herself to me a few days after I arrived at the New School in the fall of 1992, when she came to my office at 66 West Twelfth Street, ostensibly to seek my approval for the spring roster of poets in her course Works in Progress. As director of the writing program, I was technically her boss, improbable as it is to think of Pearl needing—or tolerating—supervision. Even after I started attending her classes and we were close friends, there would be a touching moment every semester when Pearl would "drop by" with "my list," a steadily transmogrifying and intricately plotted sequence of established and emerging poets stretching years into the future, as though I, or any other lucky director, could respond with anything other than awe and gratitude at the stylish ambition of her choices.

That ambition extended also into Pearl's classroom, particularly during her interviews with poets (Works in Progress tended to alternate interview sessions and intensive classes, when she primed students for the poets' visits through vivid close readings). Her preparation was part William Empson, part Vince Lombardi, and she greeted each poet with a vast folder of her accumulated notes and quotations, her questions neatly but expansively written out (did Pearl type?) on unlined yellow paper, the pages clipped together according to the topics she intended to pursue. Since she asked poets to send her poems about to be published and, if possible, drafts and work sheets, her seminar vaunted a whiff of discovery, even taboo, as she pored over with us and the authors their naked, primal evidence. Because of her months of study, Pearl knew the poems at least as well as the writers who had created them, and some of my favorite moments in the class found her graciously interrupting a wayward, wandering poet to fill in herself the specific answer she was certain that poet would eventually provide if only there were world and time and understanding enough.

Yet *did* Pearl write, was she secretly a poet? We know there were poems earlier in her life, along with translations and a graduate English literature degree. Over her last years Pearl kept saying she was about to show me a completed collection of new poems, whose subject, she said, the relationship of the dead to the living, possessed affinities with James Merrill's Ouija-board poems. No manuscript surfaced from her papers after her own death, though this brilliant selection of her conversations with other poets, inevitably now also conversations ghostly, haunted, otherworldly, is finally, you might say, that missing book.

ROBERT POLITO
Director, New School Writing Program

Acknowledgments

PEARL LONDON'S CLASS began nearly forty years ago now, so by rights my debt for this book is already many decades old. Pearl is, of course, sole provider, responsible for it in every way, sum and substance, though she didn't live to see it come to light. And all the hundred and more poets she invited over the years, and especially the twenty-three who were kind enough to help me guide their words into print after so long a time—they are responsible for it, too. To them I don't say thank you. I say, here is your book.

To others, a select few aiders and abettors, I can only send my gratitude: first, especially, to poet and gracious editor Deborah Garrison, who imagined how this collection of colleagues could and should see the light of day and whose insight never seems to falter, and to her hardworking assistant at Knopf, Caroline Zancan; to Timothy Seldes and Jesseca Salky, my agents at Russell & Volkening, who when they saw this project at their doorstep immediately wanted to do everything for it—and did just that; to Jonathan Binzen, writer and friend, who worked months with tape recorders, transcripts, and me but who is, mostly, just plain smart; to Sarah Funke, who seems to help people almost out of habit; to Anita Fore, director of legal services at The Authors Guild; to Alison Granucci of Blue Flower Arts; to Ryan Biracree and the Academy of American Poets; and to dear friends of this book, Alan M. Klein, Elizabeth England, Glenn Horowitz, Michael Pollan, Alphonse Fletcher, Jr., Dani Shapiro, Tamara Weiss, Elise Paschen, Rick Gekoski, and Brendan O'Connell.

Finally, there are three people in particular who knew long ago what crucial work Pearl London was doing: her son, Peter London; and at the New School, her close friends Robert Polito and Carla Stevens Bigelow. To them I owe a very great deal.

Index

Hill, Geoffrey, 106
Hirsch, Edward, xiv, xv, xvii, xviii, 216–32
   For the Sleepwalker, 216
   Night Parade, The, 216, 219
   Wild Gratitude, 216, 219
   "Wild Gratitude," 224–32
Homer, 129, 267, 296
Hopkins, Gerard Manly, 115
Howard, Richard, 46, 106, 191
Hughes, Langston, 71
Hughes, Ted, 271
   "Moortown," 271
Heaney, Seamus, xiii, 106, 121, 129, 257,
   315

I

iambic pentameter, 105, 155, 162, 189, 195
imagery, 297–8
imagination
   Simic, Charles, on, 297
   Williams, C. K., on, 182

J

Jacobs, Jane, 19
Jarrell, Randall, 106, 220
Jordan, June, xviii, 32, 66–82
   "Poem in Honor of South African
      Women," 67, 74 81
   Things That I Do in the Dark, 66, 70–1
Joyce, James, 270, 313

K

Kafka, Franz, 298
Kavanagh, Patrick, 267
   "Epic," 267
Keats, John
   "Belle Dame sans Merci, La," 21
   "Eve of St. Agnes, The," 144–6
Kinnell, Galway, xiii, 19, 108–19, 187
   "Another Night in the Ruins," 117

Book of Nightmares, The, 109, 113, 115,
   119
   "Little Sleep's-Head Sprouting Hair in
      the Moonlight," 118–19
   "Porcupine, The," 113
   Selected Poems, 109
Kizer, Carolyn, 106, 156, 192
Kumin, Maxine, xiii, xvii, 3–16
   "Cross-Country by Country Map," 6
   "For My Son on the Highways of His
      Mind," 4, 6–12
   Halfway, 4, 6
   House, Bridge, Fountain, Gate, 12, 16
   "Sperm," 4, 12–13
Kunitz, Stanley, xv, 163, 189

L

language
   Clampitt, Amy, on, 145
   Clifton, Lucille, on, 160–2
   Grennan, Eamon, 314
   Walcott, Derek, 122, 125–6
Larkin, Philip, 125
Lee, Li-Young, 277–90
   "Arise, Go Down," 283
   City in Which I Love You, The, 278, 279,
      288
   "Cleaving, The," 278, 285–9
   "Furious Versions," 282
   Rose, The, 278, 281
   Winged Seed, The, 277
Levertov, Denise, 55, 152
Levine, Philip, xvi, 36–47
   "Angel Butcher," 42, 44
   Name of the Lost, The, 36, 38–40
   1933, 36, 38 39, 46
   7 Years from Somewhere, 37, 39
   They Feed They Lion, 36, 38, 42, 45
   "You Can Have It," 43–4
Lifshin, Lyn, 198

line breaks
  Clifton, Lucille, on, 159
  Jordan, June, on, 73
  Kinnell, Galway, on, 116–17
  Merrill, James, on, 90
  Peacock, Molly, on, 194
  Simic, Charles, on, 306
  Williams, C. K., on, 183
line length, long
  Hass, Robert, on, 21, 24–5
  Williams, C. K., on, 177–8, 184–5,
    188
line length, short
  Hass, Robert, on, 20
  Peacock, Molly, on, 196
line vs. sentence
  Grennan, Eamon, on, 318
  Peacock, Molly, on, 197
  Simic, Charles, on, 186, 299
  Williams, C. K., on, 18
Lowell, Robert, vx, 65, 106, 121, 130, 207,
    236–7, 240, 245
  Life Studies, 237, 244
lyric poetry
  Glück, Louise, on, 63
  Hirsch, Edward, on, 218
  Lee, Li-Young, on, 283
  Plumly, Stanley, on, 175

M

MacBeth, George, 106
Mahon, Derek, 106
Major, Clarence, 7
Malraux, André, 189
Matthews, William, xviii, 246–56
  "My Father's Body," 246, 249–54
  Search Party, 247
  Time & Money, 246–7, 248–9
McCarthy, Mary, 312

McClatchy, J. D., 98, 262, 312
Melville, Herman, 110, 212
  Moby-Dick, 33, 111–12
memory
  Grennan, Eamon, on, 310
  Walcott, Derek, on, 128–30
  Williams, C. K., on, 182
Merrill, James, xiv, 83–96, 152
  "Lorelei," 87–8
  Mirabell: Books of Number (in The
    Changing Light at Sandover), 83–4, 86–7,
    88–9
  "Urban Convalescence, An," 96
Merwin, W. S., xiii, xv, 71–2, 311,
  315
metaphor, 223, 225
Michelet, Jules, 189
Millay, Edna St. Vincent, 156
Milosz, Czeslaw, 155
Milton, John, 129, 186
  Paridise Lost, 15, 116
  "Lycidas," 133, 144
Moore, Marianne, 106, 227
Morrison, Toni, 66–7, 71
Muldoon, Paul, 257–76, 323
  Annals of Chile, The, 258, 259
  "Cows," 263–76
  "Incantata," 262
  New Weather, 257
  Selected Poems, 264
  "Yarrow," 261

N

Nabokov, Vladimir, 254
narrative
  Grennan, Eamon, on, 317
  Kumin, Maxine, on, 7, 14
  Lee, Li-Young, on, 283
  Plumly, Stanley, on, 175

PERMISSIONS ACKNOWLEDGMENTS

Grateful acknowledgment is made to the following for permission to reprint previously published and unpublished material:

Alfred A. Knopf: Excerpt from "Black Buttercups" from *What the Light Was Like* by Amy Clampitt, copyright © 1985 by Amy Clampitt; "Wild Gratitude" from *Wild Gratitude* by Edward Hirsch, copyright © 1985 by Edward Hirsch; "You Can Have It" from *New Selected Poems* by Philip Levine, copyright © 1991 by Philip Levine; and excerpts from *The Changing Light at Sandover* by James Merrill, copyright © 1980, 1982 by James Merrill. Reprinted by permission of Alfred A. Knopf, a division of Random House, Inc.

The Anderson Literary Agency Inc.: "For My Son on the Highways of His Mind" by Maxine Kumin. Reprinted by permission of The Anderson Literary Agency Inc.

BOA Editions, Ltd.: "chemotherapy" from *Next: New Poems* by Lucille Clifton, copyright © 1987 by Lucille Clifton; and excerpts from "The Cleaving" from *The City in Which I Love You* by Li-Young Lee, copyright © 1990 by Li-Young Lee. Reprinted by permission of BOA Editions, Ltd., www.boaeditions.org.

Farrar, Straus and Giroux, LLC: Excerpts from "Confessional" from *In the Western Night: Collected Poems 1965–1990* by Frank Bidart, copyright © 1990 by Frank Bidart; "Cows" from *The Annals of Chile* by Paul Muldoon, copyright © 1994 by Paul Muldoon; and "Medusa" from *Flesh and Blood* by C. K. Williams, copyright © 1987 by C. K. Williams. Reprinted by permission of Farrar, Straus and Giroux, LLC.

Farrar, Straus and Giroux, LLC and Faber and Faber Ltd.: "Midsummer XLVIII" from *Midsummer* by Derek Walcott, copyright © 1984 by Derek Walcott. Reprinted by permission of Farrar, Straus and Giroux, LLC and Faber and Faber Ltd.

Graywolf Press, The Gallery Press, and Eamon Grennan: "Ants" from *So It Goes* by Eamon Grennan, copyright © 1995 by Eamon Grennan. Reprinted by permission of Graywolf Press, St. Paul, Minnesota, www.graywolfpress.org, The Gallery Press, and Eamon Grennan.

ILLUSTRATION CREDITS

Alexander Neubauer is the author of two previous works of non-fiction, *Conversations on Writing Fiction: Interviews with Thirteen Distinguished Teachers of Fiction Writing in America* and the acclaimed *Nature's Thumbprint: The New Genetics of Personality*. His book reviews and essays have appeared in *Time Out New York, Poets & Writers Magazine,* and other periodicals. For many years he taught fiction writing at the New School, in New York City. Born and raised in Manhattan, he now lives in Cornwall, Connecticut, with the writer April Stevens and their two children.

A NOTE ON THE TYPE

This book was set in Monotype Dante, a typeface designed by Giovanni Mardersteig (1892–1977). Conceived as a private type for the Officina Bodoni in Verona, Italy, Dante was originally cut only for hand composition by Charles Malin, the famous Parisian punch cutter, between 1946 and 1952. Its first use was in an edition of Boccaccio's *Trattatello in laude di Dante* that appeared in 1954. The Monotype Corporation's version of Dante followed in 1957. Although modeled on the Aldine type used for Pietro Cardinal Bembo's treatise De Aetna in 1495, Dante is a thoroughly modern interpretation of the venerable face.

Composed by North Market Street Graphics, Lancaster, Pennsylvania
Printed and bound by Berryville Graphics, Berryville, Virginia
Designed by Maggie Hinders